STUDENT SOLUTIONS MANUAL

A COURSE IN BUSINESS STATISTICS

STUDENT SOLUTIONS MANUAL

A COURSE IN BUSINESS STATISTICS

STATISTICS

Fourth Edition

David F. Groebner *Boise State University*
Patrick W. Shannon *Boise State University*
Phillip C. Fry *Boise State University*
Kent D. Smith *California Polytechnic State University*

PEARSON
Prentice
Hall

Upper Saddle River, New Jersey 07458

VP/Editorial Director: Jeff Shelstad
Acquisitions Editor: Mark Pfaltzgraff
Assistant Editor: Jane Avery
Manager, Print Production: Christy Mahon
Production Editor & Buyer: Carol O'Rourke
Printer/Binder: Technical Communication Services

10 9 8 7 6 5 4 3 2
ISBN 0-13-185191-8

Contents

CHAPTER 1

THE WHERE, WHY, AND HOW OF DATA COLLECTION

1.1.

A histogram is a graph showing the distribution of a quantitative variable. The horizontal axis contains the individual possible values for the variable or classes containing the possible values. The vertical bars have a height corresponding to the frequency of occurrence of each value or class. A bar chart is used to graphically describe a variable that has been broken down into distinct categories. The bars represent the value of the variable at each category level. The bars can be vertical or horizontal.

1.3.

Of the 18 patients shown in Figure 1-1, eleven are males and seven are females. The average total charges for each group individually can be found by averaging the eleven males' charges and the seven females' charges as follows:

$$\text{Average} = \frac{\sum\limits_{x=1}^{N} x_i}{N} = \frac{\text{sum of all data values}}{\text{number of data values}}$$

Males:

$$\text{Average} = \frac{\$12{,}031 + \$3{,}618 + \ldots + \$4{,}904}{11} = \frac{\$58{,}542}{11} = \$5{,}322.00$$

Females:

$$\text{Average} = \frac{\$5{,}419 + \$4{,}575 + \ldots + \$9{,}566}{7} = \frac{\$42{,}836}{7} = \$6{,}119.43$$

For these data, females tended to have higher total charges than males.

1.5.

Of the 18 patients listed in Figure 1-1, seven are younger than 75 and eleven are older than 75. The average age for each group is found using:

$$\text{Average} = \frac{\sum_{x=1}^{N} x_i}{N} = \frac{sum\ of\ all\ data\ values}{number\ of\ data\ values}$$

Under 75 years:

$$\text{Average} = \frac{\$4,575 + \$5,296 + \ldots + \$4,904}{7} = \frac{\$28,496}{7} = \$4,070.86$$

Over 75

$$\text{Average} = \frac{\$5,419 + \$12,031 + \ldots + \$9,566}{11} = \frac{\$72,882}{11} = \$6,625.64$$

Based on these results it seems that older patients have higher average total charges at the hospital than do younger patients.

1.7.

"Estimation is a technique by which we can know about all the data in a data set whenever the data set is so large that it is impractical for us to work with all the data. By looking at a subset of the larger data set estimates are formed which give us some insight into the larger data set."

1.9.

Hypothesis testing is used whenever one is interested in testing claims that concern a population. Using information taken from samples, hypothesis testing evaluates the claim and makes a conclusion about the population from which the sample was taken. Estimation is used when we are interested in knowing something about all the data, but the population is too large, or the data set is too big for us to work with all the data. In estimation, no claim is being made or tested.

1.11.

a. A commonly used measure of the center of the data is the mean or average.

b. To determine a value for the percentage of people in the market area that are senior citizens, the executives would rely on estimation--a set of statistical techniques which allow one to know something about a data set by using a subset of the data whenever the data set is too large to work with all the data.

c. The executives might want to test the hypothesis that the percentage of senior citizens in the market area is greater than the percentage of senior citizens nationwide. The executives could also test the hypothesis that the percentage of senior citizens is greater than or less than a specific value, say 27%.

1.13.

Some representative examples might include estimates of the number of CEO's who will vote for a particular candidate, estimates of the percentage increase in wages for factory workers, estimates of the average dollar advertising expenditures for pharmaceutical companies in a specific year, and the expected increase in R&D expenditures for the coming quarter.

1.15.

Both telephone surveys and mail questionnaires can use open-end questions.

1.17.

Telephone surveys are most frequently used for political polls. The reason is that the survey can be conducted in a shorter time span (usually over a 24 hour period.)

1-19.

Non-response bias is the most common type of bias when mail surveys are used. Most surveys end up with between a 5 and 10 percent return rate. Those that don't respond may have different opinions or provide different results than those that do respond.

1.21.

The bias that might be interjected in an experiment of this kind is measurement error. The times might be recorded incorrectly or different data collectors might use different start and end points resulting in measurement error.

1.23.

Measurement error is the most likely bias since it would be very possible to make a mistake in timing a customer. Selection bias is another possibility since the data collector may target certain customers who may not be representative of the general population.

1.25.

Among the advantages of using a mail questionnaire are the relatively low cost and the avoidance of any interviewer injected bias. However, mail questionnaires often suffer from low response rates (non response bias) and in some cases people who feel strongly one way or the other on an issue may heavily weight responses. Written surveys may also suffer from inaccurate responses when people refuse to tell the truth about sensitive matters such as age and income.

1.27.

a. Student answers will vary, but most likely a personal interview would be used.

b. The advantages are the interviewer can meet directly with the customer and get immediate feedback after the customer is in the store. The disadvantages include the high cost of conducting the personal interviews and the time required on the part of the customer who may be in a hurry to get home or to another store in the mall.

1.29.

a. Answers will vary but questions should be stated in such a way to allow for the respondents to provide a range of responses.

b. It would be necessary to read the open-end response and code the response into one of several general categories and assign a number or letter to the response based on judgment of the person reading the response.

1.31.

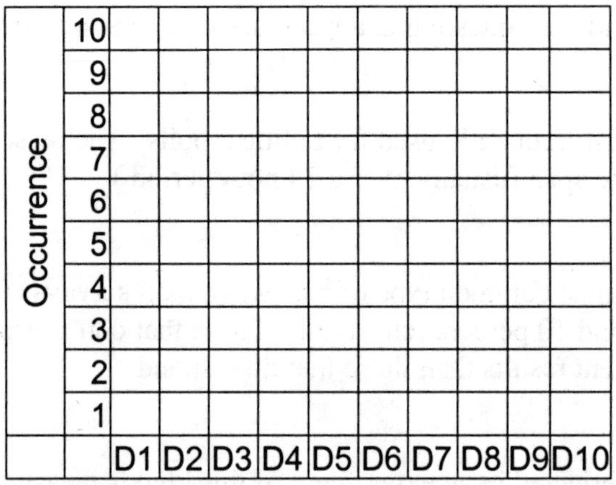

		D1	D2	D3	D4	D5	D6	D7	D8	D9	D10
	10										
	9										
	8										
	7										
	6										
	5										
	4										
	3										
	2										
	1										

(y-axis label: Occurrence)

1.33.

The basic requirement for a sample to be considered a statistical sample is the items selected must be selected randomly. Some system of randomness must be in place to assure that the possible samples have an equal chance of being selected at the onset. Different statistical sampling techniques exist including simple random sampling, stratified random sampling, cluster random sampling, and systematic random sampling.

1.35.

Even though the term systematic implies that some prior plan is being used to select the items, systematic (or sequential) random sampling is a still considered statistical sampling since the starting point is randomly determined. Thus, all possible samples have the same chance of being selected at the onset of the sampling.

1.37.

The starting point of row 20, column 18 gives the value 2. The five digit number associated with that stating point are the five digit from left to right beginning with the number 2. This is 24709. Going down we get the first three random numbers to be:

$$24709$$
$$47970$$
$$25640$$

Note that the highest number to be selected is 50000. Thus, even though the third number from the table came up 52629, this is skipped and we go to the next value less than or equal to 50000.

1.39.

Using Excel, we use the **Tools – Data Analysis – Random Number Generation** process shown as follows:

| 344.4182 |
| 91.51183 |
| 537.2394 |
| 809.2961 |
| 796.264 |

The next step is to complete the wizard as follows:

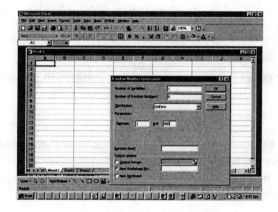

The resulting random numbers generated are:

| 344.4182 |
| 91.51183 |
| 537.2394 |
| 809.2961 |
| 796.264 |

Note, the students' answers will differ since Excel generates different streams of random numbers each time it is used. Also, if the application requires integer numbers, the **Decrease Decimal** option can be used.

1.41.

The November value is an estimate so it is not a parameter; it is a statistic. The value for October is a known value so it is a population parameter.

1.43.

    a. Stratified random sampling

    b. Simple random sampling or possibly cluster random sampling

    c. Systematic random sampling

    d. Stratified random sampling

1.45.

There may be cases where the sample size required to obtain a certain desired level of information from a simple random sample is greater than time or money will allow. In such cases, stratified random sampling has the potential to provide the desired information with a smaller sample size.

Student responses will vary but a possible example could involve a market research study looking at consumer expenditures for a product by family income. By dividing the population into the three income strata, low, medium, and high, the desired information can be obtained using a smaller sample size than would be the case with simple random sampling.

1.47.

Student answers will vary. In Excel, use either the method outlined in solution to problem 39 or the **RANDBETWEEN** function.

1.49.

    a. Since there are 4,000 customer files we could give each file a unique identification number consisting of 4 digits. The first file would be given the identification number "0001". The last file would be given the identification number of "4000". By assigning each employee a number and randomly selecting the number allows each possible sample an equal chance of being selected.

    b. Either use a random number table (randomly select the starting row and column), or use a computer program, such as Microsoft Excel or Minitab, which has a random number generator.

    c. Since each employee is assigned a 4-digit identification number, we would need a 4 digit random number for each random number selected.

1.51.

    a. Ease of use and timeliness.

    b. Assuming you want to use a nonstatistical method you could actually survey the first 100 people entering the store or you could wander around the store and just ask any 100 people that you happen to observe.

    c. Student answers will vary but they should consider bias of how people are selected and bias by evaluators.

1.53.

   a. Cross-sectional data

   b. Time series data

   c. Time series data

   d. Cross-sectional data

   e. Cross-sectional data

   f. Time series data

1.55.

   a. Question (1) would be ratio data
       Question (2) would be ordinal data

   b. Question (1) would be quantitative
       Question (2) is qualitative since it is divided into categories

   c. Question 1 would allow you to calculate it more accurately but Question 2 would also allow you to do this if you assume that all values would be at the midpoint of the interval.

1.57.

   a. Since the top category is greater than three this would have to be considered ordinal data.

   b. No, not as the survey is currently constructed. Since the last category > 3 does not allow us to identify the exact number of children that belong to customers checking this category we cannot calculate the average number of children. We could modify the survey so that the question is open-ended, such as "How many children do you have?" _____. By allowing for a specific numeric response, rather than the > 3 category, we can calculate the average number of children.

1.59.

   a. Ratio data.

   b. Ordinal data.

   c. Ratio data.

   d. Nominal data.

1.61.

If the data were collected and used by Anheuser-Busch they would be primary data. If the data were then used by competitors they would be considered secondary data.

         Distributor Name – nominal
         Brands Carried – nominal

1.63.

    a.   They would probably want to sample the cartons as they come off the assembly line at the Illinois plant for a specified time period. They would want to use a random sample. One method would be to take a systematic random sample. They could then calculate the percentage of the sample that had an unacceptable texture.

    b.   The product is going to be ruined after testing it. You would not want to ruin the entire product that comes off the assembly line.

1.65.

    a.   Student answers will vary but one method would be personal observation at grocery stores or another method would be to simply look at their sales. Are suppliers of the beer ordering bottles or cans?

    b.   If using personal observation just have people at grocery stores observe people over a specified period of time and note which are selecting cans and which are selecting bottles and look at the percentages of each.

    c.   You would be looking at ratio data because you could have a true 0 if, for example, no one purchased bottles.

    d.   The type of data depends on what data is being collected. Sales data would be quantitative.

CHAPTER 2

GRAPHS, CHARTS AND TABLES: DESCRIBING YOUR DATA

2.1.

The class width is determined using the following formula:

$$W = \frac{Maximum - Minumum}{\#ofclasses} = \frac{700 - 300}{10} = \frac{400}{10} = 40$$

Thus, 40 is the minimum width for each class.

a. The following classes could be developed:
   - 300 to < 340
   - 340 to < 380
   - 380 to < 420
   - etc.

b. The following classes could be developed:
   - 300 to 339.99
   - 340 to 379.99
   - etc.

2.3.

a. Sturges' rule for the number of classes is:
   $$Classes = 1 + 3.322(\log_{10}(n))$$
   where:
   $$n = \text{number of data values}$$
   In this case, there are n = 160 data values. Thus, the suggested number of classes is:
   $$Classes = 1 + 3.322(\log_{10}(160)) = 1 + 3.322(2.204) = 8.32$$
   Thus, the number of classes is rounded up to 9 classes.

b. Class width is:

$$W = \frac{Maximum - Minumum}{\#ofclasses} = \frac{3.25 - -2.80}{9} = \frac{6.05}{9} = .6722$$

Round this up to 0.68 or maybe even to 0.70 for clarity.

c. Using 0.70 as the class width we get:
   - -2.80 and under -2.10
   - -2.10 and under -1.40
   - etc

2.5.

a. The problem asks you to group the data. Using Sturges' rule we get:

Classes = $1 + 3.322(\log(60)) = 1 + 3.322(1.7782) = 6.907$ rounds to 7

Class width is:

$$W = \frac{Maximum - Minumum}{\#Classes} = \frac{10 - 2}{7} = 1.14$$

which we round up to 2.0

The relative frequency distribution is:

Class	Frequency	Relative Frequency
2.3	2	0.0333
4-5	25	0.4167
6-7	26	0.4333
8-9	6	0.1000
10-11	1	0.0167

b. The cumulative frequency distribution is:

Class	Frequency	Cumulative Frequency
2-3	2	2
4-5	25	27
6-7	26	53
8-9	6	59
10-11	1	60

c.

Class	Frequency	Relative Frequency	Cumu. Rel. Freq.
2-3	2	0.0333	0.0333
4-5	25	0.4167	0.4500
6-7	26	0.4333	0.8833
8-9	6	0.1000	0.9833
10-11	1	0.0167	1.000

The histogram is:

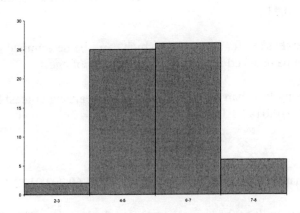

d. The ogive is a graph of the cumulative relative frequency distribution.

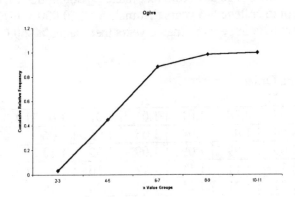

2.7.

	Years of College				
	None	1-2 years	3-4 years	5-6 years	>6 years
< $20,000	0.0458	0.0946	0.0860	0.0172	0.0115
$20,000 < $40,000	0.0630	0.0802	0.1146	0.0745	0.0143
$40,000 < $60,000	0.0258	0.0344	0.0602	0.1318	0.0258
≥ $60,000	0.0086	0.0143	0.0430	0.0372	0.0172

a. The proportion of those having at least 5 years of college that earn at least $40,000 = 0.1318 + 0.0258 + 0.0372 + 0.0172 = 0.2120

(Note, first printing of the text asked for less than 4 which can't be determined given the grouping of the data. Problem should have asked for less than 5 years of college.)

The proportion of those having less than 5 years of college and earning at least $40,000 = 0.0258 + 0.0344 + 0.0602 + 0.0086 + 0.0143 + 0.0430 = 0.1863.

b. 0.0372 + 0.0172 = 0.0544

c. Proportion that make less than $20,000 = 0.0458 + 0.0946 + 0.0860 + 0.0172 + 0.0115 = 0.2551

Of those that have not gone to college the proportion that make less than $20,000 = 16/50 = 0.32

d. The proportion that have not gone to college that make at least $60,000 = 3/50 = 0.06
The proportion that went to college 1-2 years that makes ≥ $60,000 = 5/78 = 0.0641
The proportion that went to college 3-4 years that makes ≥ $60,000 = 15/106 = 0.1415
The proportion that went to college 5-6 years that makes ≥ $60,000 = 13/91 = 0.1429
The proportion that went to college more than 6 years that makes ≥ $60,000 = 6/24 = 0.25

2.9.

a. Data Array in Ascending Order:

0.96	0.96	0.97	0.98	1.01	1.01	1.02	1.03	1.03	1.03
1.03	1.04	1.04	1.04	1.04	1.05	1.05	1.06	1.07	1.07
1.08	1.09	1.09	1.09	1.09	1.09	1.09	1.10	1.10	1.10
1.10	1.11	1.11	1.11	1.11	1.12	1.16	1.17	1.17	1.18
1.18	1.20	1.21	1.21	1.21	1.23	1.26	1.29	1.31	1.32
1.66									

b. Frequency Distribution and Histogram with 5 classes:

Class Width = (1.66 – 0.96)/5 = 0.14 round to 0.15

Classes	Frequency
0.95 < 1.10	27
1.10 < 1.25	19
1.25 < 1.40	4
1.40 < 1.55	0
1.55 < 1.70	1

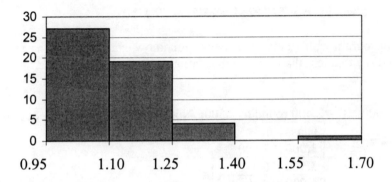

The estimate of at least $1.15 would be 12+4+1 = 17/51 = 33.33%; I assumed that 12 out of 19 of the class 1.10 < 1.25 would be 1.15 or above since this would be about 2/3 of the class width.

Frequency Distribution and Histogram with 15 classes:

Class Width = (1.66 – 0.96)/15 = 0.0467 round to 0.05

Classes	Frequency
0.95 < 1.00	4
1.00 < 1.05	11
1.05 < 1.10	12
1.10 < 1.15	9
1.15 < 1.20	5
1.20 < 1.25	5
1.25 < 1.30	2
1.30 < 1.35	2
1.35 < 1.40	0
1.40 < 1.45	0
1.45 < 1.50	0
1.50 < 1.55	0
1.55 < 1.60	0
1.60 < 1.65	0
1.65 < 1.70	1

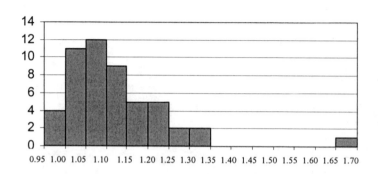

The estimate of at least $1.15 would be 5+5+2+2+1 = 15/51 = 29.41%;

c. Students might use the histogram with 15 classes because you know exactly where the $1.15 starts and then they could say that less than 30% of the stations charge $1.15 or more.

2.11.

a. class width = (25,000 – 1,000)/10 = 2,400 round to 2,500; Note, rounding up is not required.

Class
1,000 < 3,500
3,500 < 6,000
6,000 < 8,500
8,500 < 11,000
11,000 < 13,500
13,500 < 16,000
16,000 < 18,500
18,500 < 21,000
21,000 < 23,500
23,500 < 26,000

b. In order to compare it to other data sets she should prepare a relative frequency distribution. The reason for this is that if the number of observations differs between applications, proportions will be easier to compare.

2.13.

a.

	Knowledge Level			
	Savvy	Experienced	Novice	Total
Online Investors	32	220	148	400
Traditional Investors	8	58	134	200
	40	278	282	600

b.

	Knowledge Level		
	Savvy	**Experienced**	**Novice**
Online Investors	0.0533	0.3667	0.2467
Traditional Investors	0.0133	0.0967	0.2233

c. The proportion that were both on-line and experienced is 0.3667.

d. The proportion of on-line investors is 0.6667

2.15.

a.

Classes	**Frequency**
0 – 799.99	25
800 – 1599.99	3
1600 – 2399.99	7
2400 – 3199.99	0
3200 – 3999.99	3

b.

Classes	**Frequency**	**Relative Frequency**
0 – 199.99	23	23/38 = 0.6053
200 – 399.99	4	4/38 = 0.1053
400 – 599.99	3	3/38 = 0.0789
600 – 799.99	6	6/38 = 0.1579
800 – 999.99	0	0.0000
1000 – 1199.99	0	0.0000
1200 – 1399.99	1	1/38=0.0263
1400 – 1599.99	1	1/38 = 0.0263

c.

Classes	*Frequency*	**Relative Frequency**	**Cumulative Relative Frequency**
30-179.99	25	0.65789	0.65789
180 – 329.99	9	0.23684	0.89473
330 – 479.99	0	0.00000	0.89473
480 – 629.99	3	0.07895	0.97368
630 – 779.99	1	0.02632	1.00000

d.

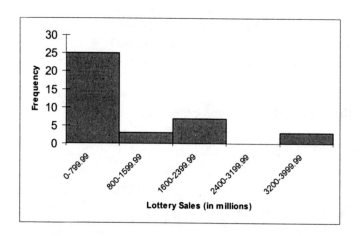

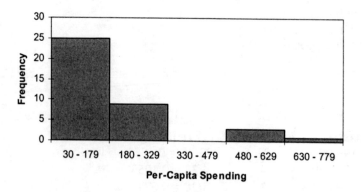

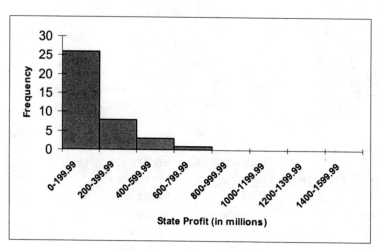

2.17.

a. & b.

Classes	Frequency	Relative Frequency
21 - 30	3	1.50%
31 - 40	5	2.50%
41 - 50	5	2.50%
51 - 60	125	62.50%
61 - 70	44	22.00%
71 - 80	5	2.50%
81 - 90	1	0.50%
91 - 100	12	6.00%

c.

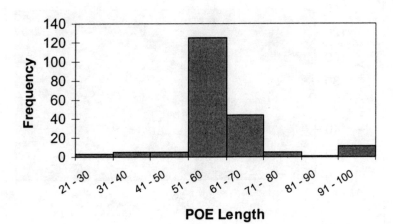

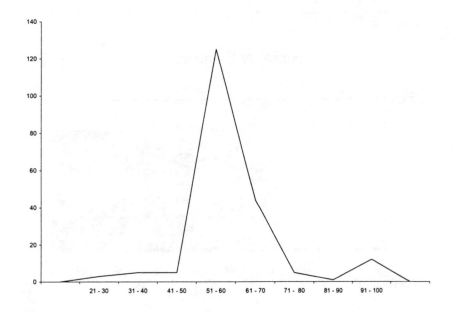

d.   WIM Length

Classes	Frequency	Relative Frequency
21 - 30	4	2.01%
31 - 40	4	2.01%
41 - 50	2	1.01%
51 - 60	133	66.83%
61 - 70	38	19.10%
71 - 80	3	1.51%
81 - 90	2	1.01%
91 - 100	13	6.53%

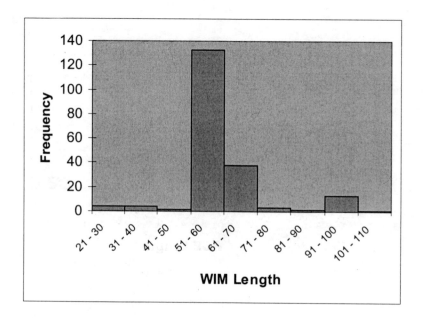

Cumulative Frequency

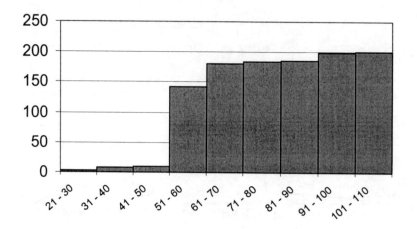

Students should indicate that the distribution shapes are very similar. Student answers will vary but students should comment on the similarities between the distributions and since they are very similar that whichever is the least costly and easiest to use should be used to gather the information.

e.

Sum of Month Code	WIM Tot ▾									
POE Total Length ▾	21-30	31-40	41-50	51-60	61-70	71-80	81-90	91-100	101-110	Grand Total
21-30	16									16
31-40	3	16						8		27
41-50		5	12	2	5					24
51-60				639	12			8		659
61-70				40	146	7		8		201
71-80					18	10				28
81-90							8			8
91-100							8	73	8	89
Grand Total	19	21	12	681	181	17	16	97	8	1052

Although most of the occurrences fall on the main diagonal where the POE and WIM lengths agree there are many exceptions. More study is needed before recommending the WIM.

2.19.

a.

Placebo Classes	Frequency
-14.99 thru -10.00	7
-9.99 thru -5.00	19
-4.99 thru 0.00	29
0.01 thru 5.00	23
5.01 thru 10.00	10
10.01 thru 15.00	1

Product 1 Classes	Frequency
-14.99 thru -10.00	1
-9.99 thru -5.00	5
-4.99 thru 0.00	20
0.01 thru 5.00	34
5.01 thru 10.00	28
10.01 thru 15.00	3

Product 2 Classes	Frequency
-9.99 thru -5.00	3
-4.99 thru 0.00	29
0.01 thru 5.00	23
5.01 thru 10.00	23
10.01 thru 15.00	3
15.01 thru 20.00	2

b.

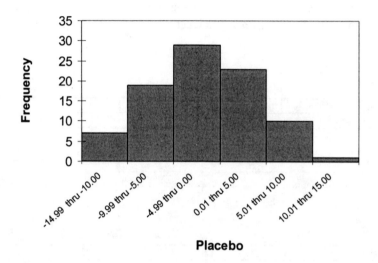

Placebo

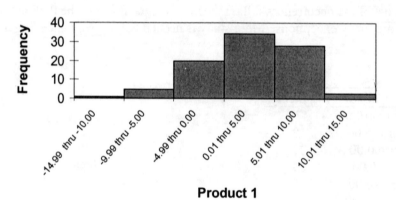

Product 1

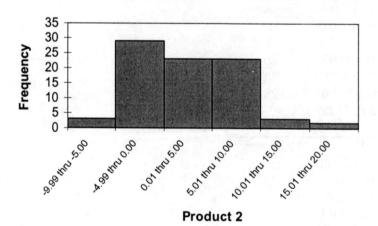

Product 2

c.

Placebo Classes	Frequency	Relative Frequency
-14.99 thru -10.00	7	0.0787
-9.99 thru -5.00	19	0.2135
-4.99 thru 0.00	29	0.3258
0.01 thru 5.00	23	0.2584
5.01 thru 10.00	10	0.1124
10.01 thru 15.00	1	0.0112

Product 1 Classes	Frequency	Relative Frequency
-14.99 thru -10.00	1	0.0110
-9.99 thru -5.00	5	0.0549
-4.99 thru 0.00	20	0.2198
0.01 thru 5.00	34	0.3736
5.01 thru 10.00	28	0.3077
10.01 thru 15.00	3	0.0330

Product 2 Classes	Frequency	Relative Frequency
-9.99 thru -5.00	3	0.0361
-4.99 thru 0.00	29	0.3494
0.01 thru 5.00	23	0.2771
5.01 thru 10.00	23	0.2771
10.01 thru 15.00	3	0.0361
15.01 thru 20.00	2	0.0241

d. Students should look at the percentage of people that lost weight on each plan versus the percentage that gained weight on each plan.

Plan	Lost Weight	Gained Weight
Placebo	61.8%	38.2%
Product 1	28.6%	71.4%
Product 2	38.6%	61.4%

Students should conclude that greater weight loss occurs on Placebo.
Students may also look at the largest amount of weight lost on each plan and the largest amount of weight gained.

2.21.

In this case, there are two variables that need to be graphed on the same bar chart. Categories will be the years. The following is a possible bar chart.

2.23.

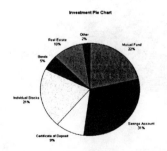

2.25.

Stem-and-Leaf Display		
Stem unit: 1		
0	7 8	
1	0 1 4 7 8	
2	0 0 1 4 8	
3	0 3 8	
4	3 4	
5	3 4 4	
6	3 4	

2.27.

   a.

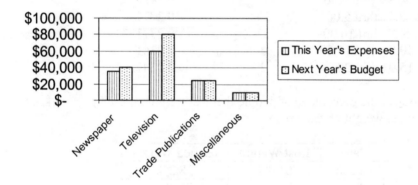

Advertising Budget

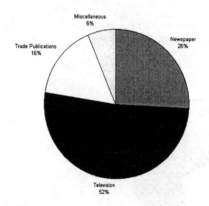

Next Year's Budget

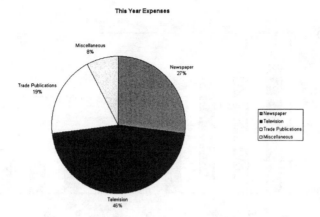

b. The bar charts allow the decision-maker to make a direct comparison between the current year and the budgeted expenses. Two individual pie charts are more difficult to compare.

2.29.

a.

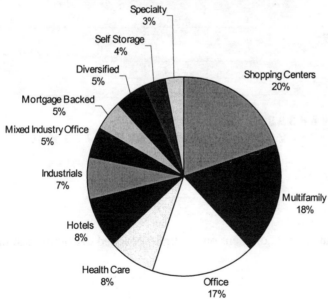

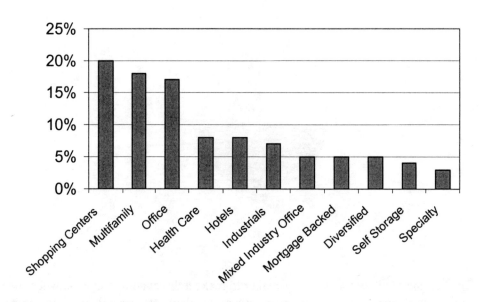

b. The pie chart may be more effective since we are looking at percentages. The slices of the pie give you a better comparison of percentages. However, the bar chart also shows where the most money has been invested in REITs.

2.31.

Stem-and-Leaf Display				
Stem unit: 10				
1	7			
2	5 6 6 7 7 7 8 8 8 9 9 9 9 9 9 10 10			
3	0 0 1 1 1 2 2 2 2 2 2 3 3 3 3 3 3 4 4 5 5 6 6 6 6 7 7 7 7 7 9 10 10			
4	1 3			

The student reports will vary but should comment on the tightly packed distribution in the upper $20 to upper $30 amounts.

2.33.

You could start out by graphing total appraisals. Looking at the graph below you can see that Heist Appraisal is higher than Allen & Associates and Appraisal International. However, the difference may not be significant.

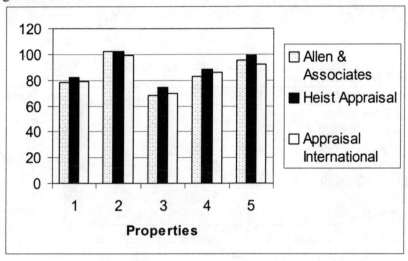

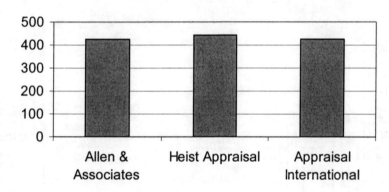

2.35.

Student answers will vary depending upon how they divide city into regions and also how they group the median prices. Below is an example of how students could approach the problem using Excel's pivot table feature. Based on this you can tell that the South has more low-priced homes and that the West has more high-priced homes.

Count of 1997 Median Price	Region				
1997 Median Price	East	North	South	West	Grand Total
70000-109999	10	15	18	4	47
110000-149999	9	6	11	9	35
150000-189999	4	2		5	11
190000-229999	2			1	3
230000-269999				2	2
270000-309999				1	1
310000-349999				1	1
Grand Total	25	23	29	23	100

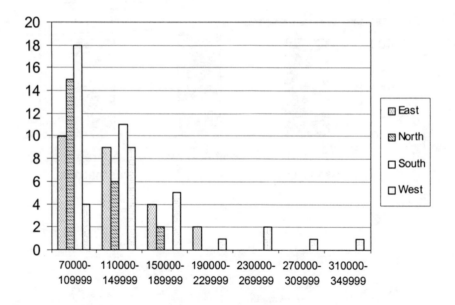

2.37.

a.

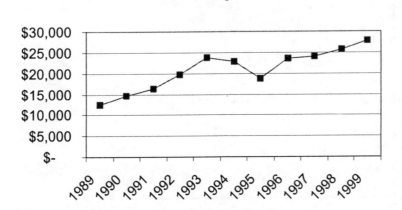

Advertising

Student reports will vary but should address the increasing trend that has occurred since 1989 with a slight down year in 1995.

2.39.

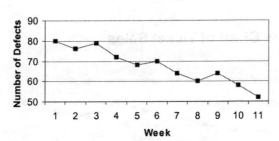

Line Chart of Defects

2.41.

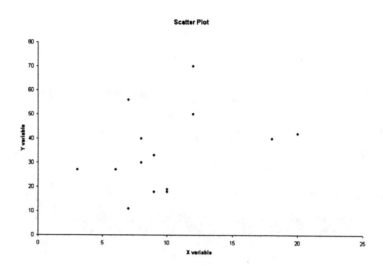

Based on the scatter plot, there appears to be a positive relationship between the x and y variables but not a strong linear relationship.

2.43.

a.

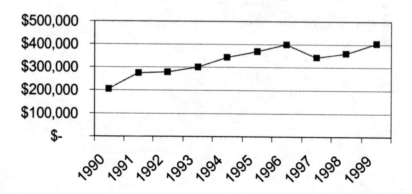

b. Based on the trend before 1997 he would have reached his goal in about 1999.

c. The director should reach his goal now in about 2002.

2.45.

Student answers will vary but some things that might be addressed is that there does seem to be a linear relationship between revenues and profits with revenues being the independent variable and profits being the dependent variable. It appears that profits increase by about $100,000 – $150,000 for every $1,000,000 increase in revenue. Because the trend line is approximately at a 45% angle there does not appear to be decreasing economies of scale in the relationship. Data in scatter plot are in thousands.

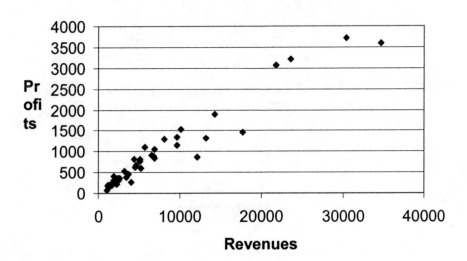

2.47.

a. The total miles for all taxis combined does not seem to be changing over time. It is neither increasing nor decreasing.

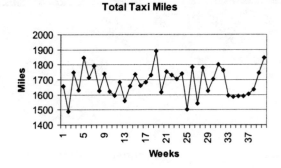

b.

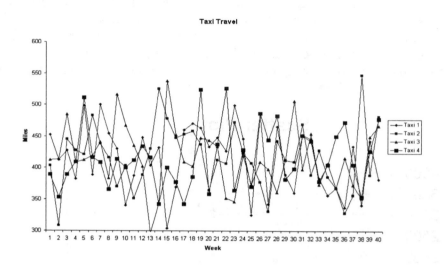

2.49.

a.

Histogram

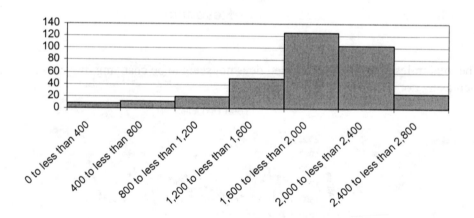

b.

Classes	Frequency	Relative Frequency
0 to less than 400	8	0.0234
400 to less than 800	12	0.0351
800 to less than 1,200	20	0.0585
1,200 to less than 1,600	50	0.1462
1,600 to less than 2,000	125	0.3655
2,000 to less than 2,400	103	0.3012
2,400 to less than 2,800	24	0.0702

The reason for converting from frequencies to relative frequencies is to make comparisons between distributions of different sizes easier to interpret.

c.

Classes	Frequency	Relative Frequency	Cumulative Rel. Freq.
0 to less than 400	8	0.0234	0.0234
400 to less than 800	12	0.0351	0.0585
800 to less than 1,200	20	0.0585	0.1170
1,200 to less than 1,600	50	0.1462	0.2632
1,600 to less than 2,000	125	0.3655	0.6287
2,000 to less than 2,400	103	0.3012	0.9299
2,400 to less than 2,800	24	0.0702	1.0000

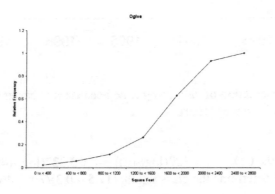

2.51.

a.

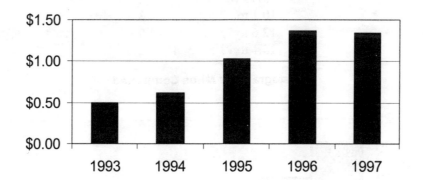

b.

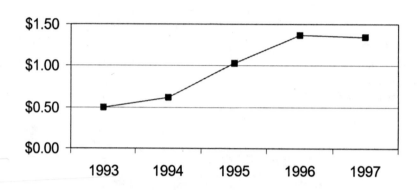

Kronos Net Income per Share

c. A line chart is a better presentation of data using time because it is easier to see the trend in the data with a line chart than with a bar chart.

2.53.

a. Using Sturge's rule from the CD: $1 + 3.322(\log_{10}(n)) = 1 + 3.322(\log_{10}(48)) = 1 + 3.322(1.6812)$ $= 6.5851$ or 7 classes. To determine the class width, $(17.5 - 0.3)/7 = 2.46$ so round up to 2.5 to make it easier

Classes	Frequency
0.1 to 2.5	21
2.6 to 5.0	15
5.1 to 7.5	3
7.6 to 10	4
10.1 to 12.5	3
12.6 to 15	0
15.1 to 17.5	2

Histogram for Miles Commuted

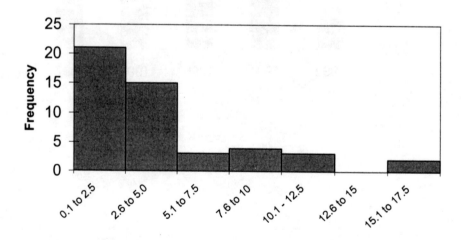

b.

Stem-and-Leaf Display		
Stem unit: 1		
0	3 4 5 7	
1	0 0 0 0 4 5 5 9	
2	0 0 0 0 0 4 5 5 5 7	
3	0 0 0 0 0 2 5 5 5 5 6	
4	0 0 0	
5		
6	4 5	
7	5	
8	3	
9	0 0 2	
10		
11	0	
12	0 0	
13		
14		
15		
16	0	
17	5	

c.

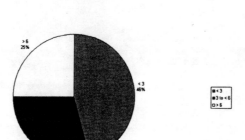

Pie Chart - Miles

d.

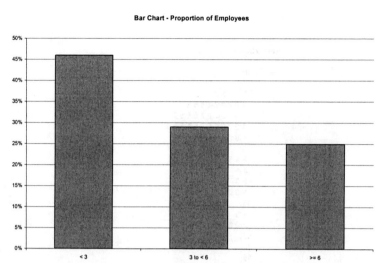

2.55.

a. Based upon the following table the percent of class that hold at least 120 seconds (2 minutes) is
$0.0311 + 0.0244 + 0.0171 + 0.0301 = 0.1029$

Classes (in seconds)	Number	Rel. Freq.
< 15	456	0.0899
15 < 30	718	0.1415
30 < 45	891	0.1756
45 < 60	823	0.1622
60 < 75	610	0.1202
75 < 90	449	0.0885
90 < 105	385	0.0759
105 < 120	221	0.0435
120 < 150	158	0.0311
150 < 180	124	0.0244
180 < 240	87	0.0171
≥ 240	153	0.0301

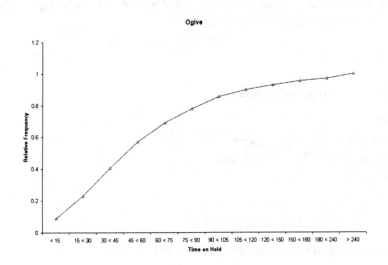

b. The number of people who have to wait more than 120 seconds (2 minutes is)
$158 + 124 + 87 + 153 = 522 * \$30 = \$15,660$ month.

2.57.

    a.   The independent variable is hours and the dependent variable is sales

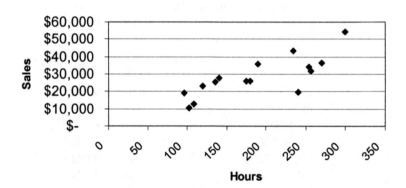

    b.   It appears that there is a linear relationship between hours worked and weekly sales. It appears that the more hours worked the greater sales. No stores seem to be substantially different in terms of the general relationship between hours and sales.

2.59.

    a.

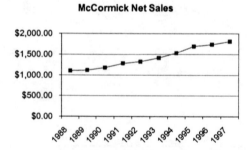

     There is an upward trend in sales over the years 1988 – 1997.

    b. It appears that capital expenditures increase as net sales increase in most instances.

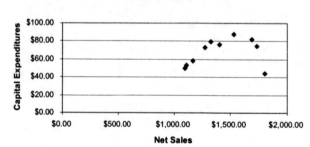

c.

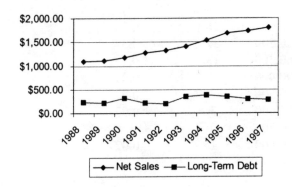

These graphs illustrate different things. The scatter plot is used to determine whether there is a linear relationship between two variables without regard to time. The line graph maintains the time relationship on the data and shows whether a trend exists over time. For time series data, line charts are generally preferred over scatter plots.

2.61.

a. Using Sturges' rule: $1 + 3.322(\log_{10}(n)) = 1 + 3.322(\log_{10}(100)) = 1 + 3.322(2.0) = 7.644$ or 8 classes. Determine the width $= (310495 - 70464)/8 = 30,004$ round to 30,100

Classes	Frequency
70,001 - 100,100	36
100,101 - 130,200	37
130,201 - 160,300	13
160,301 - 190,400	7
190,401 - 220,500	2
220,501 - 250,600	3
250,601 - 280,700	0
280,701 - 310,800	2

Histogram of 1997 Median Home Prices

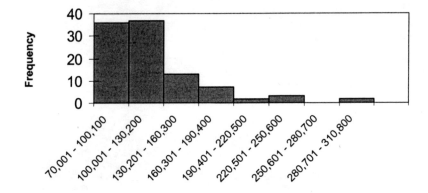

b.

Classes	Frequency	Rel. Freq.	Cumulative Rel Freq.
70,001 - 100,100	36	0.36	0.36
100,101 - 130,200	37	0.37	0.73
130,201 - 160,300	13	0.13	0.86
160,301 - 190,400	7	0.07	0.93
190,401 - 220,500	2	0.02	0.95
220,501 - 250,600	3	0.03	0.98
250,601 - 280,700	0	0	0.98
280,701 - 310,800	2	0.02	1.00

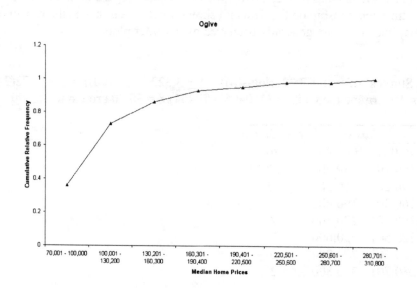

Ogive

c.

Classes	Frequency
70,001 - 120,000	65
120,001 - 170,000	23
170,001 - 220,000	8
220,001 - 270,000	3
270,001 - 320,000	2

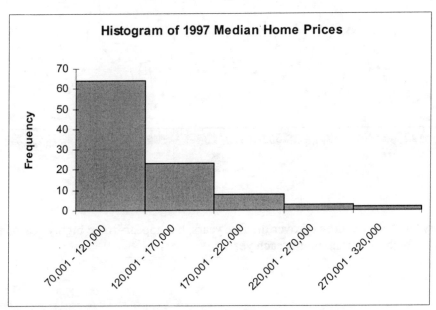

Distribution with 5 classes appears to be more skewed than when 9 classes are used. Less detail is available.

Cumulative Frequency Ogive

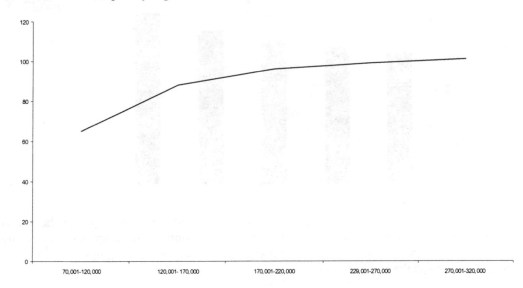

2.63.

    a.

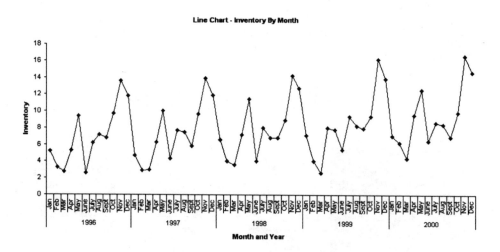

Inventory has been trending up over the five years, but appears to be highly seasonal with predictable highs at certain points each year.

    b.

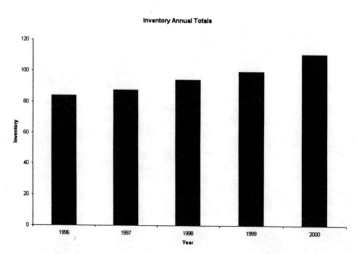

This bar chart is effective for showing the growth in total annual inventory over the five years. However, students should keep in mind that the sum of monthly inventory does not equate to how much inventory the store had on hand at the end of the year. Students might question why the store would graph the total inventory

CHAPTER 3

DESCRIBING DATA USING NUMERICAL MEASURES

3.1.

$$\mu = \frac{\sum_{i=1}^{N} x_i}{N} = 40/8 = 5$$

To compute the median, rank the observations. Because there are an even number of values, compute the average of the middle two to get the median.

$$1 \quad 3 \quad 4 \quad 5 \quad 6 \quad 6 \quad 6 \quad 9$$

Median = (5 + 6)/2 = 5.5

Mode is the value that appears most often. Mode = 6

3.3.

a.

$$\mu = \frac{\sum_{i=1}^{N} x_i}{N} = 234.19/11 = \$21.29$$

To compute the median, rank the observations and find the middle value.

15.67 15.67 18.95 18.95 20.79 20.79 23.45 23.45 25.49 25.49 25.49

Median = \$20.79
Mode = 25.49
Because the mean (21.29) is greater than the median (20.79) this data is right-skewed

b. The 1st quartile is equal to the 25th percentile

$$i = \frac{p}{100}(n+1) = (25/100)(12) = 3 \text{ or } 3^{rd} \text{ observation} = 18.95$$

The 3rd quartile is equal to the 75th percentile

$$i = \frac{p}{100}(n+1) = (75/100)(12) = 9 \text{ or 9th observation} = 25.49$$

3.5.

$$\mu = \frac{\sum_{i=1}^{N} x_i}{N} = 1194/12 = 99.5$$

To compute the median, rank the observations and find the middle value.

73	76	83	90	92	94	97	104	105	115	124	142

Median $= (94 + 97)/2 = 95.5$

$$Q1 = \frac{25}{100}(12+1) = 3.25th \text{ value}; \quad 83 + .25(90-83) = 84.74$$

$$Q3 = \frac{75}{100}(12+1) = 9.75th \text{ value}; \quad 105 + .75(115-105) = 112.50$$

No Mode

3.7.

a. $\bar{x}_W = \frac{\sum w_i x_i}{\sum w_i} = \frac{(19)(345)+(20.5)(560)+...+(27)(80)}{345+360+..+80} = 24{,}995/1{,}185 = 21.09$

b. Median is the center value. Since we have 1,185 values, the median will be the 593rd value from top or bottom. This will be in the class 21-22. Using the mid-point as an approximation for all values in the class, the median $= 21.5$

3.9.

a. Box and Whisker Plot done using PHStat

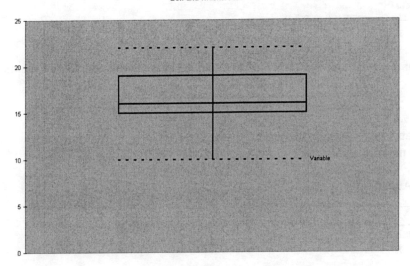

Box-and-whisker Plot

The lower limit is computed as Q1 – 1.5(Q3 – Q1) = 15 – 1.5 (19-15) = 9

The upper limit is Q3 + 1.5(Q3 – Q1) = 19 + 1.5(19-15) = 25.0

Since no value is less than 9 nor greater than 25, there are no outliers in these data.

b. The 60th percentile is found by using $i = \dfrac{p}{100}(n+1) = \dfrac{60}{100}(45+1) = 27.60$

Thus, the 60th percentile is somewhere between the 27th and 28th value from the top of the data sorted from low to high. This value is 17.

3.11.

a. Since the data are ordinal level, the median is a preferred measure of the center. The median is the center value when the data have been arranged in numerical order. The median is 8.

b. The interquartile range is: Q3 – Q1. Using Excel we get:

Q3 = 9 and Q1 = 7

IQR = 9 – 7 = 2

3.13.

a. Pre-Advertising Sample"

$$\bar{x} = \frac{\sum_{i=1}^{n} x_i}{n} = 378/10 = 37.8 \text{ years}$$

To compute the median, rank the observations and find the average of the middle two values.

25 29 30 33 34 36 40 44 52 55

Median = (34 + 36)/2 = 35 years
Since no values are repeated there is no mode.

Post-Advertising Sample:

$$\bar{x} = \frac{\sum_{i=1}^{n} x_i}{n} = 304/10 = 30.4 \text{ years}$$

To compute the median, rank the observations and find the average of the middle two values.

23 25 26 28 28 29 31 34 40 40

Median = (28 + 29)/2 = 28.5 years
This data are bi-modal since 28 occurs twice and 40 occurs twice.

b. The Pre-Advertising sample is right-skewed since the mean > median
    The Post-Advertising sample is right-skewed since the mean > median

c. Student answers will vary but they should indicate that the policyholders have gotten younger since the mean and median have both decreased.

3.15

a.

Box-and-whisker Plot	
Five-number Summary	
Minimum	0
First Quartile	2085
Median	2506
Third Quartile	3145.5
Maximum	8345

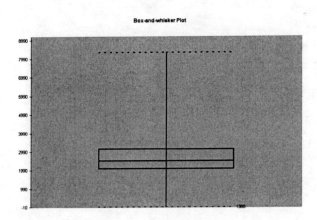

b. Based on the box and whiskers plot, it appears that the data are skewed. The box is not evenly centered within the range of the whiskers. The data appear to be right-skewed. Also, the mean is 2,847.8 which is higher than the median

3.17.

  a. Using Excel's Average and Median function you can calculate the following results:

Customer	Calendars
1	41,591
2	26,226
3	36,526
4	47,091
5	48,600
6	51,269
7	51,836
8	31,444
9	48,348
10	21,519
11	40,444
12	39,580
13	60,977
14	21,124
15	43,572
16	67,452
Mean	42,350
Median	42,582

  b.

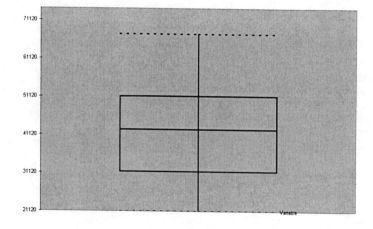

Box-and-whisker Plot

  c. Student answers will vary but students may say the data is slightly left-skewed since the mean is less than the median.

3.19.

a. Using Excel's filter features the following information can be calculated. Hint: Once you filter the data you will need to copy the results to a new page to calculate the mean and median

b.

Box-and-whisker Plot	
Five-number Summary	
Minimum	31476
First Quartile	39682
Median	42325.5
Third Quartile	44980
Maximum	52774

Category	Mean	Median
Commercial	61,780.70	65,000.00
Consumer	61,439.66	60,250.00
Real Estate	72,896.83	74,000.00

c. You can use the PHStat box and whiskers feature to produce these after sorting the data by loan type.

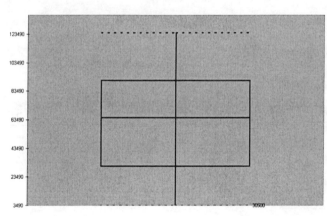

Commercial

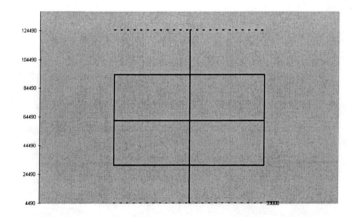

Consumer

The plots are similar and indicate that the data fairly symmetric.

3.21

The following statistics are computed assuming that the data represent a sample from a population.

Mean = 33.44
Median = 35
Range = High – Low = 42 – 17 = 25
Interquartile Range = Q3 – Q1 = 37.5 – 31.5 = 6

$$\text{Variance} = s^2 = \frac{\sum_{i=1}^{n}(x - \bar{x})^2}{n-1} = \frac{(33 - 33.4375)^2 + (42 - 33.4375)^2 + ...(35 - 33.4375)^2}{16 - 1}$$
$$= 52.13$$

$$\text{Standard Deviation} = s = \sqrt{s^2} = \sqrt{52.13} = 7.22$$

3.23

Range = 22.95 – 9.95 = 13

X	X - $\bar{x}$	$(X-\bar{x})^2$
17.87	0.989	0.978121
19.95	3.069	9.418761
22.95	6.069	36.83276
18.74	1.859	3.455881
9.95	-6.931	48.03876
11.22	-5.661	32.04692
21.98	5.099	25.9998
14.52	-2.361	5.574321
16.65	-0.231	0.053361
14.98	-1.901	3.613801
168.81		166.0125

$$\bar{x} = \frac{\sum_{i=1}^{n} x_i}{n} = 168.81/10 = 16.881$$

$$S^2 = \frac{\sum_{i=1}^{n}(x-\bar{x})^2}{n-1} = 166.0125/(10\text{-}1) = 18.4458$$

$$S = \sqrt{S^2} = \sqrt{18.4458} = 4.2949$$

The interquartile range is the differnce between the 3rd and 1st quartiles. These are found as follows:

$$i = \frac{p}{100}(n+1) = \frac{75}{100}(10+1) = 8.25$$

Thus the Q3 value is a value that is 25 percent of the distance between the 8th (19.95) and 9th (21.98) values after the data have been sorted from low to high. This is 19.95 + .25(21.98 – 19.95) = 20.46.

For Q1 we get $i = \frac{25}{100}(10+1) = 2.75$; Thus, Q1 is the value that is 75 percent of the distance between the 2nd (11.22) and the 3rd (14.52) data values after the data have been sorted. This is: 11.22+.75(14.52-11.22) = 13.70.

Then the interquartile range is Q3 – Q1 = 20.46 - 13.70 = 6.76

3.25.

The data are assumed to be a population since the six homes is every home built by the Price Corporation.

a. Range = 4,000 – 1,560 = 2,440

b.

X	X - μ	$(X - \mu)^2$
1,560	(747)	557,511.11
2,340	33	1,111.11
1,990	(317)	100,277.78
1,750	(557)	309,877.78
4,000	1,693	2,867,377.78
2,200	(107)	11,377.78
13,840		3,847,533

$$\sigma^2 = \frac{\sum_{i=1}^{N}(x - \mu)^2}{N} = 3,847,533/6 = 641,255.7$$

c.

$$\sigma = \sqrt{\sigma^2} = \sqrt{641,255.5} = 800.7843$$

d. Student answers will vary.

3.27.

X	$X - \bar{x}$	$(X - \bar{x})^2$
32	5.9	34.81
22	-4.1	16.81
24	-2.1	4.41
27	0.9	0.81
27	0.9	0.81
33	6.9	47.61
28	1.9	3.61
23	-3.1	9.61
24	-2.1	4.41
21	-5.1	26.01
261		148.9

a. range = 33 – 21 = 12

$$\bar{x} = \frac{\sum_{i=1}^{n} x_i}{n} = 261/10 = 26.1$$

$$S^2 = \frac{\sum_{i=1}^{n}(x - \bar{x})^2}{n-1} = 148.9/(10\text{-}1) = 16.5444$$

$$S = \sqrt{S^2} = \sqrt{16.5444} = 4.0675$$

the 1st quartile is equal to the 25th percentile

$$i = \frac{p}{100}(n+1) = (25/100)(10+1) = 2.75 \text{ or roughly the 3}^{rd}\text{ observation} = 23$$

the 3rd quartile is equal to the 75th percentile

$$i = \frac{p}{100}(n+1) = (75/100)(10+1) = 8.25 \text{ or roughly the 8th observation} = 28$$

Interquartile Range = 28 – 23 = 5

b. Student answers will vary but they should look at the number of standard deviations the new mean is from the old mean. Old Mean (37.8) – New Mean (26.1) = 11.7 which is 11.7/4.0657 = 2.8 or almost 3 standard deviations from the old mean. Given this, although we are working with a small sample, there appears to be evidence to suggest that the ages are lower than before the campaign.

3.29.

Assume that the data is a sample

X	$X - \bar{x}$	$(X - \bar{x})^2$
488	-6.5625	43.06640625
449	-45.5625	2075.941406
510	15.4375	238.3164063
551	56.4375	3185.191406
548	53.4375	2855.566406
569	74.4375	5540.941406
413	-81.5625	6652.441406
491	-3.5625	12.69140625
544	49.4375	2444.066406
457	-37.5625	1410.941406
472	-22.5625	509.0664063
432	-62.5625	3914.066406
426	-68.5625	4700.816406
461	-33.5625	1126.441406
469	-25.5625	653.4414063
415	-79.5625	6330.191406
477	-17.5625	308.4414063
484	-10.5625	111.5664063
505	10.4375	108.9414063
485	-9.5625	91.44140625
487	-7.5625	57.19140625
485	-9.5625	91.44140625
554	59.4375	3532.816406
497	2.4375	5.94140625
493	-1.5625	2.44140625
479	-15.5625	242.1914063
579	84.4375	7129.691406
535	40.4375	1635.191406
595	100.4375	10087.69141
474	-20.5625	422.8164063
566	71.4375	5103.316406
436	-58.5625	3429.566406
15,826		74,053.8750

a. $\bar{x} = \dfrac{\sum\limits_{i=1}^{n} x_i}{n} = 15{,}826/32 = 494.5625$

To compute the median, rank the observations and compute the average of the middle two.
Median = (485 + 487)/2 = 486
Mode = 485
Range = 595 – 413 = 182
The 1st quartile is equal to the 25th percentile

$i = \dfrac{p}{100}(n+1) = (25/100)(32+1) = 8.25$ so the Q1 is one-fourth the way between the 8th

(461)and 9th (469) data values after the data have been sorted. Thus Q1 = 461 +.25(469-461) = 463

The 3rd quartile is equal to the 75th percentile

$i = \dfrac{p}{100}(n+1) = (75/100)(32+1) = 24.75$ so the Q3 is three-fourths of the way between the 24th

(535) and the 25th (544) data values after the data have been sorted. Thus Q3 = 535 + .75(544-535) = 541.75

Interquartile Range = 541.75 – 463 = 78.75

$S^2 = \dfrac{\sum\limits_{i=1}^{n}(x - \bar{x})^2}{n-1} = 74{,}053.8750/(32\text{-}1) = 2{,}388.8347$

$S = \sqrt{S^2} = \sqrt{2{,}388.8347} = 48.8757$

b.

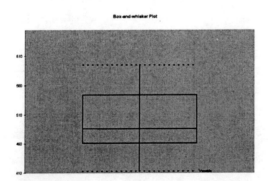

Box-and-whisker Plot

c. Report should included a discussion of measures of the center and spread and a discussion of characteristics oif the bex and whisker daigram.

3.31

a. Excel's Average function can be used to find the population mean: Mean = $3,304
    Excel's Median function can be used: Median = $3,125
    There is no mode
    The Max and Min functions in Excel can be used to find the Range = $1,660
    The VARP function can be used to find the population variance = 187,801.9
    The STDEVP function can be used to find the population standard deviation = 433.36

b. PHStat's Box and Whisker's tool can be used to develop the graph:

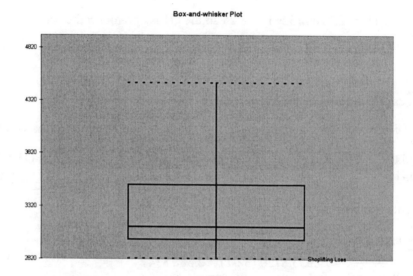

c. Excel's Graph tool can be used to develop a line chart:

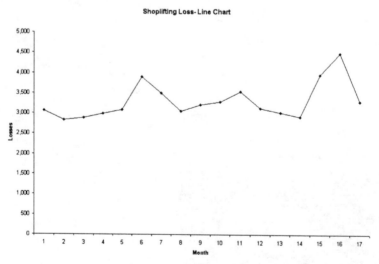

d. Student reports will vary but should effectively integrate graphs and descriptive measures.

3.33.

Excel's descriptive statistics tool can be used to determine the answers to this problem. You can use the descriptive statistics tool to determine the interquartile range by inputting the positions but the answer may be slightly different than doing it by hand using the equations shown in the text.

a.

Credit Card Account Balance	
Mean	753.68
Standard Error	17.00202273
Median	737
Mode	600
Standard Deviation	294.4836719
Sample Variance	86720.63304
Kurtosis	-0.517456441
Skewness	0.113822027
Range	1394
Minimum	99
Maximum	1493
Sum	226104
Count	300
Largest(75)	974
Smallest(75)	544

The interquartile range is the Largest (75) from the table above minus the Smallest (75) from the table above. $974 - 544 = 430$ Note the largest 75 corresponds to Q3 (3rd Quartile) and the smallest 75 corresponds to Q1 (1st quartile).

b. For Males:

Credit Card Balances - Male	
Mean	746.512931
Standard Error	19.33632279
Median	738.5
Mode	1018
Standard Deviation	294.5220941
Sample Variance	86743.2639
Kurtosis	-0.605714694
Skewness	0.085179909
Range	1344
Minimum	99
Maximum	1443
Sum	173191
Count	232
Largest(58)	960
Smallest(58)	538

The interquartile range is the Largest (58) from the table above minus the Smallest (58) from the table above. 960 – 538 = 422

For Females:

Credit Card Account Balance - Female	
Mean	778.1323529
Standard Error	35.80014705
Median	737
Mode	600
Standard Deviation	295.2155754
Sample Variance	87152.23595
Kurtosis	-0.199115911
Skewness	0.219080607
Range	1358
Minimum	135
Maximum	1493
Sum	52913
Count	68
Largest(17)	990
Smallest(17)	587

The interquartile range is the Largest (17) from the table above minus the Smallest (17) from the table above. 990 – 587 = 403

c.   Student answers will vary.

3.35.

The coefficient of variation is used to measure the relative variability of two or more distributions. It is computed using:

$$CV = \frac{\sigma}{\mu}(100)$$

For Distribution A we get: $CV = \frac{\sigma}{\mu}(100) = \frac{100}{500}(100) = 20\%$

For Distribution B we get: $CV = \frac{\sigma}{\mu}(100) = \frac{4.0}{10.0}(100) = 40\%$

Thus, even though distribution B has a standard deviation that is only 4 percent the size of A's standard deviation, distribution is relatively more variable because the mean of A is so much greater than the mean of B.

3.37

The standardized value is computed using:

$$z = \frac{x - \mu}{\sigma}$$

Distribution A: $z = \frac{50,000 - 45,600}{6,333} = 0.695$

Distribution B: $z = \frac{40 - 33.40}{4.05} = 1.63$

The smaller the z value, the relatively closer the x value is to the mean. Thus, the 50,000 value is .6948 standard deviations from the mean of distribution A while the value 40 is 1.6296 standard deviations from the mean of distribution B. The value from distribution A is relatively closer to its mean.

3.39.

a. The population standard deviation is computed using

$$\sigma = \sqrt{\sigma^2} = \sqrt{\frac{\sum_{i=1}^{N}(x - \mu)^2}{N}}$$

For Population A: Mean = 201.63   Standard Deviation = 37.75
For Population B: Mean = 1,013.63   Standard Deviation = 98.65
Population B has the greatest spread based on the standard deviation.

b. The coefficient of variation is computed using: $CV = \frac{\sigma}{\mu}(100)$

For Population A: $CV = \frac{37.75}{201.63}(100) = 18.72\%$

For Population B: $CV = \frac{98.65}{1,013.63}(100) = 9.73\%$

Since Population A has the higher coefficient of variation, it is relatively more variable than Population B.

3.41.

a. $z = \dfrac{x - \mu}{\sigma} = \dfrac{455 - 400}{30} = 1.833$

b. $z = \dfrac{x - \mu}{\sigma} = \dfrac{400 - 400}{30} = 0.00$

c. According to the empirical rule, approximately 95% of the data fall within ± 2 standard deviations of the mean if the population is bell shaped. Thus 95 percent of the z-scores would fall within the range -2 to $+2$. If the distribution is skewed then Tchebysheff's theorem must be used and we know that at least 75 percent of the data values will fall within ± 2 standard deviations of the mean. Thus at least 75 percent of z values for a skewed distribution will fall within the range -2 to $+2$.

3.43.

Type A				Type B		
298	1.7	2.89		297	-1.4	1.96
291	-5.3	28.09		315	16.6	275.56
290	-6.3	39.69		291	-7.4	54.76
310	13.7	187.69		292	-6.4	40.96
296	-0.3	0.09		301	2.6	6.76
299	2.7	7.29		286	-12.4	153.76
300	3.7	13.69		287	-11.4	129.96
305	8.7	75.69		290	-8.4	70.56
289	-7.3	53.29		302	3.6	12.96
285	-11.3	127.69		323	24.6	605.16
2963		536.1		2984		1352.4

a. Type A:

$$\bar{x} = \frac{\sum_{i=1}^{n} x_i}{n} = 2963/10 = 296.3$$

$$s^2 = \frac{\sum_{i=1}^{n}(x-\bar{x})^2}{n-1} = 536.1/(10-1) = 59.567$$

$$s = \sqrt{s^2} = \sqrt{59.567} = 7.718$$

Type B:

$$\bar{x} = \frac{\sum_{i=1}^{n} x_i}{n} = 2984/10 = 298.4$$

$$s^2 = \frac{\sum_{i=1}^{n}(x-\bar{x})^2}{n-1} = 1352.4/(10-1) = 150.267$$

$$s = \sqrt{s^2} = \sqrt{150.267} = 12.258$$

Using the Tchebysheff's Rule since you do not know the shape of the distribution you can calculate 3 standard deviation ranges for each type so that 89% of the observations should lie within this range.

Type A:
  296.3 ± 3(7.718)
  273.146 – 319.454
Type B:
  298.4 ± 3(12.258)
  261.626 – 335.174

The technician is probably correct because for Type A at 3 standard deviations 274 would barely be in the range.

b. To be more conservative you should probably look at 2 standard deviations.
Type A:

$$296.3 \pm 2(7.718)$$
$$280.864 - 311.736$$

Type B:

$$298.4 \pm 2(12.258)$$
$$273.884.1 - 322.916$$

Students will probably estimate that this was a Type B ball.

c. Based upon the calculations in a and b above there is a small chance that a Type B ball could go this far.

3.45.

Student answers will vary but one approach would be to standardize the results for each manager
Plant 1: $(810 - 700)/200 = .55$ standard deviations
Plant 2: $(2600 - 2300)/350 = .86$ standard deviations
Plant 3: $(1320 - 1200)/30 = 4$ standard deviations
Based upon this the manager of Plant 3 performed far better than the other plants on a relative basis.

3.47

a. Use Excel's Descriptive Statistics tool to determine the sample mean and sample standard deviation for the two data sets. The results are shown below:

mileage, highway		mileage, city	
Mean	24.8333	**Mean**	18.4
Standard Error	0.76276	Standard Error	0.539476119
Median	24	Median	18.5
Mode	21	Mode	19
Standard Deviation	**4.1778**	**Standard Deviation**	2.954832395
Sample Variance	17.454	Sample Variance	8.731034483
Kurtosis	-1.2915	Kurtosis	0.496563717
Skewness	0.01937	Skewness	-0.25743034
Range	14	Range	13
Minimum	18	Minimum	11
Maximum	32	Maximum	24
Sum	745	Sum	552

Yes the data supports the premise that cars will get better mileage on the highway than around town. The mean for highway (24.8) is higher than the mean for city (18.4) but there is not a lot of difference between the standard deviations.

b. To answer this question, calculate the coefficient of variation for each variable.
Highway CV = 4.1778/24.8333 = 16.8%
City CV = 2.9548/18.4 = 16.1%
City driving has slightly less variability than highway driving.

c. Calculate how many standard deviations the mean of city driving is from the highway driving mean (24.8). The calculation is shown below:

$(24.8333 - 18.4)/2.9548 = 2.17$.

This is approximately 2 standard deviations away from the mean. Using the empirical rule this means that 95% of the values would be within 2 standard deviations. That means ½ of the remaining 5% would be at least 24.8333, which means 2.5%.

3.49.

The median would be preferred to the mean in data sets that have extremely high or low values that affect the mean. An example is home prices. The median is also preferred as a measure of the center if a quantitative variable is measured on an ordinal scale such as in the case where customers are asked to provide their view of a product using a 1 to 5 scale where 1 = Excellent down to 5 being Very Poor.

3.51.

By definition a sample is a subset of a population. The most different sample selected from a population will have a different mean because it includes different values on which the mean is calculated. The sample mean will rarely equal the population mean exactly.

3.53.

Some problems are that it does not look at total hours taken. One student could have taken one class on campus and got an A so would have a 4.0 grade point average. Another student could have taken many hours and got all A's except one or two B's and would have lower than a 4.0 grade point average and people might conclude that the first student is a better student than the second based only upon grade point average. It also does not look at the difficulty of the classes taken. Comparing across two universities has the same problems as mentioned previously along with the fact that all universities are different and the type of classes and difficulty level of classes will be completely different. None of this is accounted for in calculating a grade point average.

3.55.

The standard deviation is an average measure of the differences from the mean. The mean is considered to be the center of the data so this measures how spread out the data are from the mean. Student examples will vary.

3.57.

a.

$$\bar{x} = \frac{\sum_{i=1}^{n} x_i}{n} = 127/8 = 15.875$$

b. To compute the median, rank the observations and compute the average of the middle two.

9 12 12 13 16 16 17 32

Median = $(13 + 16)/2 = 14.5$

c. The mode is 12 and 16

d.

X	$X - \bar{x}$	$(X - \bar{x})^2$
13	-2.875	8.265625
32	16.125	260.0156
12	-3.875	15.01563
9	-6.875	47.26563
16	0.125	0.015625
17	1.125	1.265625
16	0.125	0.015625
12	-3.875	15.01563
127		346.875

$$s^2 = \frac{\sum_{i=1}^{n}(x - \bar{x})^2}{n-1} = 346.875/(8\text{-}1) = 49.5536$$

$$s = \sqrt{s^2} = \sqrt{49.5536} = 7.0394$$

e.   The extreme value does not effect the median or the mode. It does, however, cause the mean to increase because it gives a higher number to the sum of the numbers which causes the mean to be higher.

f.   In this case the median might be a better measure since you have an extreme outlier. This would give you a better representation of future lines of bowling.

g.   The top quartile would be above 75% so you would need to calculate the 75th percentile to determine the minimum number of games.
The 3rd quartile is equal to the 75th percentile

$i = \dfrac{p}{100}(n+1) = (75/100)(8+1) = 6.75$; Thus, the Q3 value is 75 percent of the distance

between the 6th (16)and 7th (17) values after the data have been arranged in numerical order.
Thus, Q3 = 16 + .75(17-16) = 16.75.

3.59.

Note, even though the company surveyed 30 families, only 15 surveys were returned.

X	X - $\bar{x}$	$(X-\bar{x})^2$
38	13.26667	176.004444
44	19.26667	371.204444
11	-13.7333	188.604444
26	1.266667	1.60444444
19	-5.73333	32.8711111
13	-11.7333	137.671111
45	20.26667	410.737778
27	2.266667	5.13777778
11	-13.7333	188.604444
19	-5.73333	32.8711111
19	-5.73333	32.8711111
26	1.266667	1.60444444
20	-4.73333	22.4044444
19	-5.73333	32.8711111
34	9.266667	85.8711111
371		1,720.9333

a. The mean measures the numerical center of the data by summing the values and dividing by the number of observations.

$$\bar{x} = \frac{\sum_{i=1}^{n} x_i}{n} = 371/15 = 24.7333$$

b. To compute the median, rank the observations and select the middle value since the number of observations is odd.

$$11\ \ 11\ \ 13\ \ 19\ \ 19\ \ 19\ \ 19\ \ 20\ \ 26\ \ 26\ \ 27\ \ 34\ \ 38\ \ 44\ \ 45$$

Median = 20
The median < mean which means the data is skewed right.

c. The mode is 19

d. The standard deviation is essentially an average of how the data is spread around the mean.

$$s^2 = \frac{\sum_{i=1}^{n}(x-\bar{x})^2}{n-1} = 1720.9333/(15\text{-}1) = 122.9238$$

$$s = \sqrt{s^2} = \sqrt{122.9238} = 11.0871$$

e.   The 1st quartile is equal to the 25th percentile

$$i = \frac{p}{100}(n+1) = (25/100)(15+1) = 4 \text{ or } 4^{th} \text{ observation} = 19$$

The 3rd quartile is equal to the 75th percentile

$$i = \frac{p}{100}(n+1) = (75/100)(15+1) = 12 \text{ or } 12^{th} \text{ observation} = 34$$

Interquartile Range = 34 - 19 = 15

The interquartile range is often preferred to the range because if you have outliers it will likely minimize the effect of the outliers because you do not use the extreme outside values since you are only looking at the middle 50% of the values.

f.

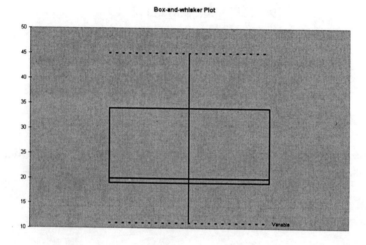

Box-and-whisker Plot

The box plot shows that the distribution is not symmetrical since the median line is not centered in the box but instead is located very close to the Q1 value.

3.61.

X	X - μ	$(X - \mu)^2$
800	269.75	72,765.0625
100	-430.25	185,115.0625
230	-300.25	90,150.0625
700	169.75	28,815.0625
1900	1369.75	1,876,215.0625
300	-230.25	53,015.0625
400	-130.25	16,965.0625
700	169.75	28,815.0625
250	-280.25	78,540.0625
500	-30.25	915.0625
340	-190.25	36,195.0625
670	139.75	19,530.0625
340	-190.25	36,195.0625
250	-280.25	78,540.0625
450	-80.25	6,440.0625
700	169.75	28,815.0625
500	-30.25	915.0625
200	-330.25	109,065.0625
75	-455.25	207,252.5625
1200	669.75	448,565.0625
10605		3,402,823.75

a. $\mu = \dfrac{\sum\limits_{i=1}^{N} x_i}{N} = 10{,}605/20 = 530.25$

b. To compute the median, rank the observations and find the average of the middle value two values.

   75 100 200 230 250 250 300 340 340 400 450 500 500 670 700 700 700 800 1200 1900

   Median = (400+450)/2 = 425

c. the 33rd percentile is:

   $i = \dfrac{p}{100}(n+1) = (33/100)(20+1) = 7$ or 7th observation = 300

   The first 6 oil wells will be closed which are those producing at 75, 100, 200, 230, 250, 250

3.63.

X	X - $\bar{x}$	(X - $\bar{x}$)^2
229	-135.417	18,337.6736
345	-19.4167	377.0069
599	234.5833	55,029.3403
229	-135.417	18,337.6736
429	64.58333	4,171.0069
605	240.5833	57,880.3403
339	-25.4167	646.0069
339	-25.4167	646.0069
229	-135.417	18,337.6736
279	-85.4167	7,296.0069
344	-20.4167	416.8403
407	42.58333	1,813.3403
4373		183,288.9167

a. $\bar{x} = \dfrac{\sum\limits_{i=1}^{n} x_i}{n} = 4373/12 = 364.4167$

b. $s^2 = \dfrac{\sum\limits_{i=1}^{n}(x - \bar{x})^2}{n-1} = 183{,}288.9167/(12\text{-}1) = 16{,}662.6288$

$s = \sqrt{s^2} = \sqrt{16{,}662.6288} = 129.0838$

3-65.

Compute the coefficient of variation for height and weight using: $CV = \dfrac{s}{\bar{x}}(100)$

Height = $CV = \dfrac{2.5}{69.5}(100) = 3.60\%$

Weight = $CV = \dfrac{12}{177}(100) = 6.78\%$

The distribution of weights is more variable based on the higher coefficient of variation.

3.67.

a.

	Net Sales	Cap. Exp.	Curr. Debt	LT Debt	Equity
Average	1,413.06	67.90	112.72	279.75	415.12
Median	1,362.40	73.85	96.80	283.85	415.50
St. Dev.	262.77	15.08	85.51	65.05	69.88

b.

Year	z-value Net Sales	z-value Cap. Exp.	z-value Curr. Debt	z-value LT Debt	z-value Equity
1988	-1.19	-1.16	-0.74	-0.77	-1.73
1989	-1.15	-0.96	-1.08	-1.06	-0.99
1990	-0.94	-0.63	-0.96	0.49	-0.73
1991	-0.52	0.34	-0.40	-1.11	-0.37
1992	-0.34	0.76	0.12	-1.21	0.33
1993	-0.05	0.54	-0.33	1.02	0.74
1994	0.44	1.31	1.18	1.45	1.07
1995	1.06	0.94	2.16	1.06	1.49
1996	1.22	0.45	-0.04	0.18	0..50
1997	1.48	-1.60	0.10	-0.05	-0.32

1988 & 1989 are somewhat unique in that all the variables were below their means since all z-values are negative. In the same way 1994 & 1995 are unique in that all the variables were above their means.

3.69.

x	$x - \bar{x}$	$(x - \bar{x})^2$
34	-5.05556	25.55864
24	-15.0556	226.6698
43	3.944444	15.55864
56	16.94444	287.1142
74	34.94444	1221.114
20	-19.0556	363.1142
19	-20.0556	402.2253
33	-6.05556	36.66975
55	15.94444	254.2253
43	3.944444	15.55864
54	14.94444	223.3364
34	-5.05556	25.55864
27	-12.0556	145.3364
34	-5.05556	25.55864
36	-3.05556	9.33642
24	-15.0556	226.6698
54	14.94444	223.3364
39	-0.05556	0.003086
703		3726.944

a. $\bar{x} = \dfrac{\sum\limits_{i=1}^{n} x_i}{n} = 703/18 = 39.0556$

b.   To compute the median, rank the observations and average the middle two values.

19 20 24 24 27 33 34 34 34 36 39 43 43 54 54 55 56 74

Median = (34+36)/2 = 35

c. $$s^2 = \frac{\sum_{i=1}^{n}(x-\bar{x})^2}{n-1} = 3726.944/(18\text{-}1) = 219.232$$

$$s = \sqrt{s^2} = \sqrt{219.232} = 14.8065$$

d.   Use Excel's histogram feature to create the frequency distribution.

Classes	Frequency
15 - 24	4
25 - 34	5
35 - 44	4
45 - 54	2
55 - 64	2
65 - 74	1

e.   Use Excel's histogram feature to create the histogram.

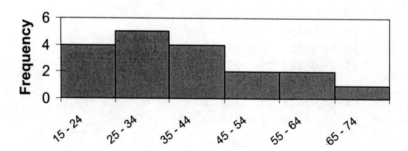

Waiting Time Histogram

f.

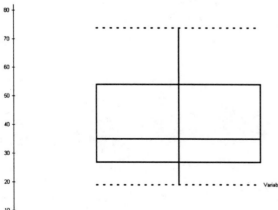

Box-and-whisker Plot

g. The 3rd quartile is equal to the 75th percentile

$i = \dfrac{p}{100}(n+1) = (75/100)(18+1) = 14.25;$ Thus, the Q3 value is 25 percent of the distance

between the 14th (54) and the 15th (54) values. This is 54.
The minimum number of minutes the customer would have to wait is 54 minutes

3.71.

a. Comparing only the mean bushels/acre you would say that Seed Type C produces the greatest average yield per acre. Student answers will vary but may include things such as making sure soil type is the same, make sure watering and fertilizing is the same, etc.

b. Students need to calculate the coefficient of variation for each Seed Type.

CV of Seed Type A = 25/88 = 0.2841 or 28.41%
CV of Seed Type B = 15/56 = 0.2679 or 26.79%
CV of Seed Type C = 16/100 = 0.1600 or 16%

Seed Type C shows the least relative variability.

c. Seed Type A

Approximately 68% will be within 1 standard deviation
$88 \pm 25 =$ 63 to 113

Approximately 95% will be within 2 standard deviations
$88 \pm 2(25) =$ 38 to 138

Approximately 100% will be within 3 standard deviations
$88 \pm 3(25) =$ 13 to 163

Seed Type B
Approximately 68% will be within 1 standard deviation
$56 \pm 15 =$ 41 to 71

Approximately 95% will be within 2 standard deviations
$56 \pm 2(15) =$ 26 to 86

Approximately 100% will be within 3 standard deviations
$56 \pm 3(15) =$ 11 to 101

Seed Type C
Approximately 68% will be within 1 standard deviation
$100 \pm 16 =$ 84 to 116

Approximately 95% will be within 2 standard deviations
$100 \pm 2(16) =$ 68 to 132

Approximately 100% will be within 3 standard deviations
$100 \pm 3(16) =$ 52 to 148

d.   Student answers will vary but students should say Seed Type A because the 135 is within 2 standard deviations. Since it has higher variability there is a greater chance that it will produce135.

e.   Student answers will vary but they will probably select Seed Type C since it has a higher mean to begin with and now the 115 would be within 1 standard deviation.

3.73.

Students can use Excel to answer questions a-c.

a.

CPA Firm	Taxes Owed	Difference	CPA Firm	Taxes Owed	Difference
1	$16,637	-$5,077	26	$6,087	$5,473
2	$11,804	-$244	27	$8,711	$2,849
3	$8,915	$2,645	28	$9,753	$1,807
4	$9,915	$1,645	29	$10,282	$1,278
5	$14,787	-$3,227	30	$13,385	-$1,825
6	$11,058	$502	31	$11,326	$234
7	$15,662	-$4,102	32	$16,183	-$4,623
8	$13,293	-$1,733	33	$14,232	-$2,672
9	$15,970	-$4,410	34	$8,482	$3,078
10	$9,103	$2,457	35	$16,274	-$4,714
11	$13,223	-$1,663	36	$12,758	-$1,198
12	$7,852	$3,708	37	$9,411	$2,149
13	$9,200	$2,360	38	$14,632	-$3,072
14	$13,607	-$2,047	39	$12,655	-$1,095
15	$13,793	-$2,233	40	$6,403	$5,157
16	$9,048	$2,512	41	$11,260	$300
17	$14,487	-$2,927	42	$8,478	$3,082
18	$9,409	$2,151	43	$11,586	-$26
19	$13,342	-$1,782	44	$10,299	$1,261
20	$14,093	-$2,533	45	$7,805	$3,755
21	$12,836	-$1,276	46	$13,422	-$1,862
22	$9,376	$2,184	47	$10,628	$932
23	$10,819	$741	48	$9,300	$2,260
24	$10,473	$1,087	49	$5,429	$6,131
25	$3,677	$7,883	50	$6,064	$5,496

b.

Classes	Frequency
-6928.42 to -5077.00	1
-5076.99 to -3225.57	5
-3225.56 to -1374.14	11
-1374.13 to 477.29	7
477.30 to 2328.72	12
2328.73 to 4180.15	9
4180.16 to 6031.58	3
6031.59 to 7883.01	2

c.

Difference	
Mean	**415.52**
Standard Error	436.0660531
Median	**621.5**
Mode	#N/A
Standard Deviation	**3083.452632**
Sample Variance	**9507680.132**
Kurtosis	-0.501771097
Skewness	0.177525892
Range	12960
Minimum	-5077
Maximum	7883
Sum	20776
Count	50

d. The value of $11,560 would be between the 28th ($11,326) and 29th ($11,586)observation. This is found by sorting the values for the "tax owed" variable. Since $11,500 is closer to the 29th value than it is the to the 28th value, we will use i = 29 and solve for the percentile as follows:

$$i = \frac{p}{100}(n+1) \quad \text{so } 29 = p/100(50+1) \quad p = 56.86 \text{ or approximately the 57th percentile.}$$

This shows that about 57 percent of the tax consultants in this study showed less tax owed than did the IRS.

3.75.

Students can use Excel or Minitab to solve this problem.

a.

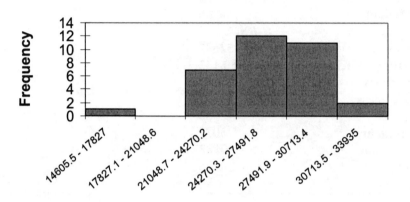

b.

	Manufacturing	White Collar
Mean	26398.18	24117.06
Median	27204	24139
Mode	none	none

c.

1998 Average manufacturing Income	z-score Manufacturing	1998 Average White Color Income	z-score White Collar
23340	-0.915876589	19016	-1.856687805
29823	1.025678321	25449	0.484800284
25795	-0.180643316	27242	1.137417747
25513	-0.26509781	23867	-0.091017244
25884	-0.153989239	20585	-1.285602026
27509	0.332672296	21454	-0.969302765
27450	0.315002739	26237	0.771617105
26475	0.023005818	24403	0.104076432
22083	-1.292328003	24647	0.192887732
28008	0.482114823	21142	-1.082864755
25219	-0.353146113	21284	-1.031179491
27369	0.290744533	25381	0.460049594
21719	-1.401340187	22437	-0.611509699
28176	0.532428138	28589	1.627699801
26814	0.124530901	23209	-0.33051657
21177	-1.563660527	24673	0.202351231
27204	0.241329669	30229	2.224628212
29857	1.035860778	22122	-0.726163632
28641	0.671688208	22923	-0.434615061
29022	0.78579162	20020	-1.491251143
29660	0.976862426	27112	1.090100251
33935	2.257156617	24066	-0.018585077
21293	-1.52892038	20203	-1.424642668
28719	0.695047962	25552	0.5222903
30795	1.31677679	28870	1.729978389
28757	0.706428354	22940	-0.428427388
26766	0.110155668	25210	0.397808887
26445	0.014021297	27968	1.401667763
27519	0.335667136	21519	-0.945644017
21766	-1.387264438	25966	0.672978325
17827	-2.566931998	24278	0.058578839
27390	0.297033697	24139	0.007985517
23190	-0.960799192	23131	-0.358907067

d. Students should number the cities and then calculate the mean and standard deviation for both groups combined.

   Mean = $25,257.6212

   Standard Deviation = $3,244.3609

   $25,257.6212 + 2($3,244.3609) = $31,746.343

City 22 is the only city that meets this criteria.

3.77

Students will need to delete all data points that have missing values (-99)

a.

Classes	Frequency
-62.4 - 2	1
2.1 - 66.5	36
66.6 - 131	27
131.1 - 195.5	1
195.6 - 260	2
260.1 - 324.5	1
324.6 - 389	0
389.1 - 453.5	0
453.6 - 518.0	1

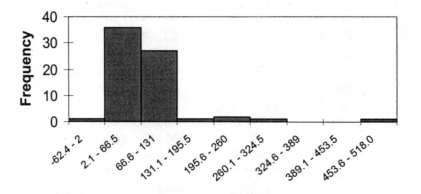

EPS Histogram

b.

EPS	
Mean	**78.50724638**
Standard Error	8.886962375
Median	**62**
Mode	18
Standard Deviation	**73.82065373**
Sample Variance	5449.488917
Kurtosis	18.55933579
Skewness	3.617340494
Range	516
Minimum	2
Maximum	518
Sum	5417
Count	69

c. The 1st quartile is equal to the 25th percentile

$$i = \frac{p}{100}n = (25/100)(69) = 17.25 \text{ or 18th observation} = 41$$

The 3rd quartile is equal to the 75th percentile

$$i = \frac{p}{100}n = (75/100)(69) = 51.75 \text{ or } 52^{nd} = 97$$

Interquartile Range = 97 – 41 = 56

d.

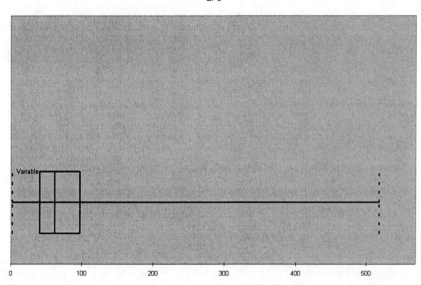

EPS

e.

1st quartile = 41

2nd quartile = median = 62

3rd quartile = 97

There are no negative earnings per share so you do not see large gains and large losses.

CHAPTER 1–3

SPECIAL REVIEW

SR.1.

a-c. Student answers will vary but class limits should be set so that classes are mutually exclusive and all-inclusive. Class intervals should be of equal size and chosen so that observations are approximately equally distributed over the interval.

SR.3.

a. Using Sturges' rule: $1 + 3.322(\log_{10}(n)) = 1 + 3.322(\log_{10}(51)) = 1 + 3.322(1.7076) = 7.67$ or 7 classes.

Determine the width for 1996 = $(65.33 - 22.5)/7 = 6.12$ round to 6.15
Determine the width for 1997 = $(65.06 - 24.41)/7 = 5.81$ round to 5.85

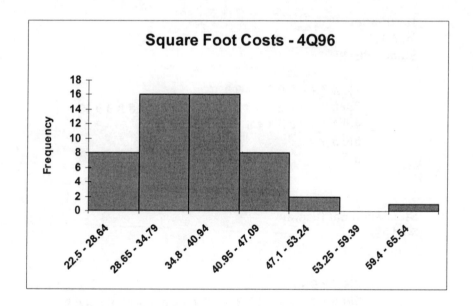

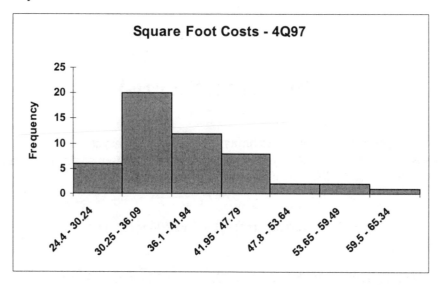

b.

4th Quarter -1996				
for 4Q96				
Stem unit:	10			
2	3 4 7 7 8 8 8 8 9 9 9 9 10			
3	0 0 0 1 1 2 2 2 3 3 3 5 5 5 5 6 6 7 7 7 8 8 9 9 10			
4	0 1 1 1 2 2 3 3 4 6			
5	0 3			
6	5			

Stem-and-Leaf Display				
for 4Q97				
Stem unit:	10			
2	4 7 9 9 10 10			
3	0 1 1 1 1 1 1 1 2 2 3 3 3 3 3 4 4 4 5 6 7 7 8 8 8 8 8 9 9			
4	0 1 1 1 2 3 3 4 5 5 5 6 10			
5	1 5 7			
6	5			

Distributions are very similar between years. Histograms and stem & leaf diagrams illustrate essentially the same information. Some detail is lost with the histograms.

SR.5.

a.

	Revenues	Profits	Employees
Mean	6354.71	803.43	21530.3
Median	3428	401	11000
Std Deviation	7457.66	881.812	21269.35

b. Mellon Bank Corporation is slightly below the average for profits and revenues and slightly above the average for number of employees.

c. You need to calculate the coefficient of variance for each variable.

	Revenues	**Profits**	**Employees**
Coefficient of variation	1.173564	1.097558	0.9878812

Revenues has the largest relative variation.

d.

Classes	Frequency
0.000 - 0.014	1
0.015 - 0.029	16
0.030 - 0.044	25
0.045 - 0.059	5
0.060 - 0.074	2
0.075 - 0.089	2

Profit per Employee

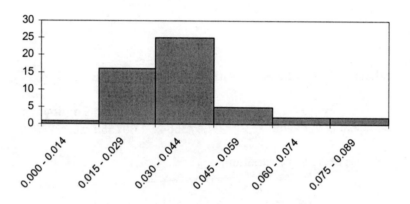

	Profits per Employee
Mean	0.0365
Median	0.0353
Standard Deviation	0.0140

Student reports will vary but should mention most of the profits per employee are between .03 and .044. The data is positively skewed.

e.   two standard deviations above the mean is

$0.0365 + 2(0.0140) = 0.0645$

three banks have a profit per employee ratio above 0.0645

CHAPTER 4

USING PROBABILITY
AND PROBABILITY DISTRIBUTIONS

4.1.

   a. P(Male) = # males / Total = 678/1,336 = 0.5075

   b. P(20-40) = # 20-40/Total = 630/1,336 = 0.4716

   c. P(20-40 and Male) = 340/1,336 = 0.2545

   d. $P(<20|Males) = \dfrac{\#<20}{\# Males} = \dfrac{168}{678} = 0.2478$

$$P(<20|Females) = \dfrac{\#<20}{\# Females} = \dfrac{208}{658} = 0.3161$$

Gender and age are not independent.

4.3.

Probability of selecting a red chair is equal to the number of ways a red chair can be selected (1) over the total number of chairs available (4). P (Red) = ¼ = 0.25.

4.5.

If we take the relative frequency of days when it has rained (25) and divide by the total number of days, or opportunities for rain, (200), then we find the historical probability of rain of any day equal to P(Rain) = 25/200 = 0.125. The probability that it will not rain is therefore 1-P(Rain) = 1-0.125 = 0.875.

4.7.

P(smoke) = # smoke/Total = 600/2000 = 0.30

4.9.

Origination	Early	On-Time	Late	Total
San Francisco	25	50	100	175
Los Angeles	50	100	75	225
Total	**75**	**150**	**175**	**400**

   a. P(Early) = 75/400 = 0.1875.

   b. P(Los Angeles) = 225/400 = 0.5625.

   c. P(Early Given Los Angeles) = 50/225 = 0.2222. P(Early) = 50/400 = 0.125

d.   Let E = Early, O= On-Time, and L = Late. The events are as follows:

Elementary Event	Flight 1	Flight 2	Flight 3
Event 1	E	E	E
Event 2	E	E	O
Event 3	E	E	L
Event 4	E	O	E
Event 5	E	O	O
Event 6	E	O	L
Event 7	E	L	E
Event 8	E	L	O
Event 9	E	L	L
Event 10	O	E	E
Event 11	O	E	O
Event 12	O	E	L
Event 13	O	O	E
Event 14	O	O	O
Event 15	O	O	L
Event 16	O	L	E
Event 17	O	L	O
Event 18	O	L	L
Event 19	L	E	E
Event 20	L	E	O
Event 21	L	E	L
Event 22	L	O	E
Event 23	L	O	O
Event 24	L	O	L
Event 25	L	L	E
Event 26	L	L	O
Event 27	L	L	L

The sample space consists of the 27 elementary events listed in the table. Sample Space = {Event 1, Event 2, Event 3, ..., Event 27}

4.11.

Male	150
Female	130
Total	280

a.   P(Female) = 130/280 = 0.4643

b.   Relative frequency approach since it is based on actual observations.

c.   No. Once the first customer is selected, the probabilities for both a male and a female customer being selected as the second winner change. Therefore the events are not independent.

4.13.

a. Yes. The value (outcome) of the first digit does not change the probability of the value (outcome) of the second or third digit.

b. No. The outcome of the first digit does not preclude the second and third digit from having the same outcome.

c. Events cannot be both mutually exclusive and independent.

4.15.

Students can use Excel's pivot table feature to answer these questions.

a. P(Atlanta) = 24/110 = 0.2182

Manufacturing Plant	Total
Boise	78
Atlanta	24
Reno	8
Grand Total	110

b. P(Wiring) = 23/110 = 0.2091

Complaint Code	Total
Corrosion	35
Cracked Lens	45
Wiring	23
Sound	7
Grand Total	110

c. P(Atlanta and Wiring) = 8/110 = 0.0727

Complaint Code	Manufacturing Plant			
	Boise	Atlanta	Reno	Grand Total
Corrosion	30	3	2	35
Cracked Lens	31	11	3	45
Wiring	13	8	2	23
Sound	4	2	1	7
Grand Total	78	24	8	110

d.   P(Day Shift and Atlanta and Cracked Lens) = 8/110 = 0.0727

	Manufacturing Plant	Shift	
	Atlanta		
Complaint Code	Day	Swing	Graveyard
Corrosion	1	1	1
Cracked Lens	8	2	1
Wiring	5	2	1
Sound	2		
Grand Total	16	5	3

e.   The most likely profile would be the largest number which would be the Boise day shift for cracked lens

	Manufacturing Plant							
	Boise			Atlanta			Reno	
Complaint Code	Day	Swing	Grave-yard	Day	Swing	Grave-yard	Day	Swing
Corrosion	20	10		1	1	1	2	
Cracked Lens	21	10		8	2	1	3	
Wiring	10	1	2	5	2	1	1	1
Sound	2	2		2				1
Grand Total	53	23	2	16	5	3	6	2

4.17.

a.   P(Dry) = P(Clear and Dry) + P(Cloudy and Dry)
   $$= 0.20 + 0.30$$
   $$= 0.50$$

b.   P(Rainy or Cloudy & Dry) = P(Rainy) + P(Cloudy & Dry) − P(Rainy and Cloudy &Dry)
   $$= 0.40 + 0.30 - 0.0 = .70$$

c. $P(Cloudy|Dry) = \dfrac{P(Cloudy \text{ and } Dry)}{P(Dry)} = \dfrac{0.30}{0.50} = 0.60$

4.19.

This method will not work since the roulette wheel (if it is fair) has no memory and thus the outcomes are independent. Thus regardless of how many times the wheel has come up a certain color, the chances of the next spin giving a specific color is no different that it is on the first spin or any other spin.

4.21.

a.   P(matched) = 2/3

b.   P(both wrong) = (1/3)*(1/3) = 1/9

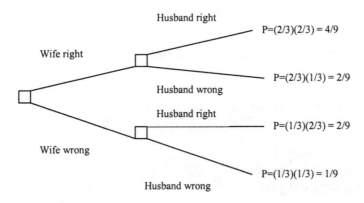

4.23.

P(Michigan1 and Maryland2) + P(Maryland1 + Michigan2) = (15/500)(6/499) + (6/500)(15/499) = 0.00072

4.25.

a.   List the number of ways four German instructors and one American instructor could be assigned and then determine the probabilities of each of these ways.

A-G-G-G-G = (1/3)(1/3)(1/3)(1/3)(1/3) = 0.00412
G-A-G-G-G = (1/3)(1/3)(1/3)(1/3)(1/3) = 0.00412
G-G-A-G-G = (1/3)(1/3)(1/3)(1/3)(1/3) = 0.00412
G-G-G-A-G = (1/3)(1/3)(1/3)(1/3)(1/3) = 0.00412
G-G-G-G-A = (1/3)(1/3)(1/3)(1/3)(1/3) = 0.00412

The sum of these probabilities is 0.02060

b.   P(G-G-G) = 1/3(1/3)(1/3) = 0.03704

c.   (0.0206)(0.03704) = 0.00076; because this probability is so low that if it really did happen then the assignments are probably not made randomly.

4.27.

If they purchase 4 black-and-white copiers, their probability of being able to provide a color copy is 0.0. Their probability of being able to provide a black-and-white copy on demand is 1 – [(0.1)(0.1)(0.1)(0.1)] = 0.9999. If they buy all color copiers the probability of providing a black-and-white copy is the same as providing a color copy since color copiers can make black-and-white copies. This probability is 1 – [(0.2)(0.2)(0.2)(0.2)] = 0.9984. They cannot get to 99.9% on color copies regardless of the configuration.

4.29.

  P(Line 1) = 0.4
  P(Line 2) = 0.35
  P(Line 3) = 0.25

  P(Defective|Line 1) = 0.05
  P(Defective|Line 2) = 0.10
  P(Defective|Line 3) = 0.07

  You need to calculate the probability of each line given you know the cases are defective. Use Bayes' Rule to calculate this.

  P(Defective) = P(Defective|Line1)P(Line1) + P(Defective|Line2)P(Line2) + P(Defective|Line3)P(Line3) = (0.05)(0.4) + (0.1)(0.35)+(0.07)(0.25) = 0.0725

  P(Line1|Defective) = (0.05)(0.4)/0.0725 = 0.2759
  P(Line2|Defective) = (0.10)(0.35)/0.0725 = 0.4828
  P(Line3|Defecitve) = (0.07)(0.25)/0.0725 = 0.2413

  The unsealed cans probably came from Line 2

4.31.

  P(Clerk 1) = 0.4
  P(Clerk 2) = 0.3
  P(Clerk 3) = 0.3
  P(Defective|Clerk 1) = 0.02
  P(Defective|Clerk 2) = 0.025
  P(Defective|Clerk 3) = 0.015

  You need to calculate the probability of each clerk given you know the chocolates are defective. Use Bayes' Rule to calculate this

  P(Defective) = P(Defective|Clerk 1)P(Clerk 1) + P(Defective|Clerk 2)P(Clerk 2) + P(Defective|Clerk 3)P(Clerk 3) = (0.02)(0.4) + (0.025)(0.3) + (0.015)(0.3) = 0.02

  P(Clerk 1|Defective) = (0.02)(0.4)/0.02 = 0.4
  P(Clerk 2|Defective) = (0.025)(0.3)/0.02 = 0.375
  P(Clerk 3|Defective) = (0.015)(0.3)/0.02 = 0.225

  Clerk 1 is most likely responsible for the boxes that raised the complaints.

4.33.

List all possible ways that three doctors can be assigned such that no set of three doctors will be in the office together more than once.

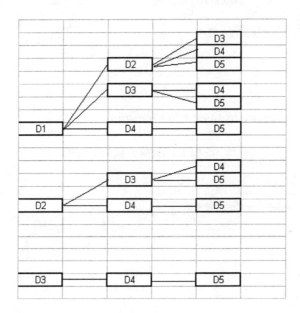

D1-D2-D3
D1-D2-D4
D1-D2-D5
D1-D3-D4
D1-D3-D5
D1-D4-D5
D2-D3-D4
D2-D3-D5
D2-D4-D5
D3-D4-D5

10 weeks can be covered by this schedule

4.35.

There are a total of 6 companies.

a. P(Ace) = 1/6 = 0.1667

b. P(Win1 and Win2) = (1/6)(1/6) = 0.0278

c. P(Lose1 and Lose2) = (5/6)(5/6) = 0.6944

d. P(Win1 and Lose2) + P(Lose1 and Win2) = (1/6)(5/6) + (5/6)(1/6) = 0.2778

e. P(Win1 and Lose2) + P(Lose1 and Win2) + P(Win1 and Win2) = 0.1389 + 0.1389 + 0.0278 = 0.3056 or 1 − P(Lose 1 and Lose 2) = 1 − 0.6944 = 0.3056

4.37.

From problem 4.36 the probability of $9.99 = 0.0003
P(11.11) & P(12.22) etc = (1/10)(1/10)(1/10)(1/10) = .0001
(0.0001)(9)(0.65) = 0.00059
The remaining 5% customers = (1/100)(0.05) = 0.0005

P(free gas) = 0.0003 + 0.00059 + 0.0005 = 0.00139

4.39.

Students can use Excel's pivot table feature to answer this question.

a. P(Wiring/Atlanta) = P(Wiring and Atlanta)/P(Atlanta) = (8/110)/(24/110) = 0.3333

	Manufacturing Plant			
Complaint Code	Boise	Atlanta	Reno	Grand Total
Corrosion	30	3	2	35
Cracked Lens	31	11	3	45
Wiring	13	8	2	23
Sound	4	2	1	7
Grand Total	78	24	8	110

b. Using the table from above and the information in the problem you know:
P(Boise/return) = 78/110 = 0.7091
P(Atlanta/return) = 24/110 = 0.2182
P(Reno/return) = 8/110 = 0.0727

Assuming the sample represents the population of returned products, the cost assignment should
be based on the conditional probability of a city given that the product was returned. Thus, Boise
will get 70.91% of the cost, Atlanta will get 21.82% and Reno will get 7.27% regardless of
production volume.

4.41.

x	P(x)	xP(x)	x-E(x)	$[x-E(x)]^2$	$[x-E(x)]^2P(x)$
100	0.3	30	-38	1444	433.2
150	0.4	60	12	144	57.6
160	0.3	48	22	484	145.2
		138			636

a. E(x) = 138
b. Var(x) = 636
c. Std Dev(x) = 25.2190

4.43.

Keep in mind that you are betting $5.00. A total of 12 on two dice occurs if both die come up six. Assuming independent events, the probability of this happening is $(1/6)(1/6) = 1/36 = .0278$

$$E(x) = \sum xP(x)$$

x	P(x)	xp(x)
+$45	.0278	$1.25
-$5	.9722	-4.86

Expected value = $1.25 + -$4.86 = -$3.61

4.45.

The following is used:

$$E(x + y) = E(x) + E(y)$$

For variable x: $E(x) = 225$

x	P(x)	xP(x)
100	0.25	25
200	0.4	80
300	0.2	60
400	0.15	60
		225

For variable y: $E(y) = 415$

y	P(y)	yP(y)
500	0.25	125
300	0.4	120
400	0.2	80
600	0.15	90
		415

Then $E(x + y) = 225 + 415 = 640$

4.47.

To find the correlation, use equation 4-18:

$$\rho = \frac{\sigma_{xy}}{\sigma_x \sigma_y}$$

The covariance is found by equation 4-17:

x	P(x)	xP(x)	x - E(x)	y	P(y)	yP(y)	y - E(y)	[x - E(x)][y - E(y)]	P(xy)	[x - E(x)][y - E(y)]P(xy)
100	0.25	25	-125	500	0.25	125	85	(10,625.00)	0.10	(1,062.50)
200	0.40	80	-25	300	0.40	120	-115	2,875.00	0.50	1,437.50
300	0.20	60	75	400	0.20	80	-15	(1,125.00)	0.30	(337.50)
400	0.15	60	175	600	0.15	90	185	32,375.00	0.10	3,237.50
		225				415				3,275.00

The covariance is 3,275   The relationship between the two variables is positive

The standard deviation for variable x is found as follows:

x	P(x)	xP(x)	x-E(x)	$[x-E(x)]^2$	$[x-E(x)]^2 P(x)$
100	0.25	25	-125	15625	3906.25
200	0.4	80	-25	625	250
300	0.2	60	75	5625	1125
400	0.15	60	175	30625	4593.75
		225			9875

$$\sigma_x = \sqrt{9,875} = 99.37$$

The standard deviation for y is found using:

y	P(y)	yP(y)	y - E(y)	$[y-E(y)]^2$	$[y-E(y)]^2 P(y)$
500	0.25	125	85	7,225	1,806.25
300	0.40	120	-115	13,225	5,290.00
400	0.20	80	-15	225	45.00
600	0.15	90	185	34,225	5,133.75
		415			12,275.00

$$\sigma_y = \sqrt{12,2751} = 110.79$$

The correlation is: $\rho = \dfrac{\sigma_{xy}}{\sigma_x \sigma_y}$ = (3,275)/[(99.37)(110.79)] = 0.2975

The correlation measures the strength of the linear relationship between the two variables. In this case, there is a weak positive linear relationship.

4-49.

a. To determine the probability you need to divide the number of days by the total of 200.

x	P(x)	xP(x)	x-E(x)	$[x-E(x)]^2$	$[x-E(x)]^2 P(x)$
0	0.110	0.000	-2.885	8.3232	0.9156
1	0.100	0.100	-1.885	3.5532	0.3553
2	0.200	0.400	-0.885	0.7832	0.1566
3	0.275	0.825	0.115	0.0132	0.0036
4	0.140	0.560	1.115	1.2432	0.1741
5	0.100	0.500	2.115	4.4732	0.4473
6	0.025	0.150	3.115	9.7032	0.2426
7	0.050	0.350	4.115	16.9332	0.8467
		2.885			3.1418

a. E(x) = 2.885

b. 1.7725

d. The coefficient of variation is:

$$CV = \frac{\sigma}{\mu}(100) = \frac{\sigma_x}{E(x)}(100) = \frac{1.7725}{2.885}(100) = 61.44\%$$

e. Students need to look at the 3rd quartile. This is accomplished by determining the cumulative P(x). The 75th percentile would be between 3 and 4. Since you want at least 75% you should choose x=4 which means you would need 4(3) = 12 employees.

x	P(x)	Cum P(x)
0	0.110	0.110
1	0.100	0.210
2	0.200	0.410
3	0.275	0.685
4	0.140	0.825
5	0.100	0.925
6	0.025	0.950
7	0.050	1.000

4.51.

To determine the expected salaries and standard deviation of salaries for the current pay plan, students can create a new variable which is the cars per day based upon the midpoint times $2/car The mean of the current plan is $53.40 with a standard deviation of $23.67

Salary (x)	P(x)	x P(x)	x-E(x)	$[x-E(x)]^2$	$[x-E(x)]^2 P(x)$
$ 10.000	0.10	1.00	-43.40	1883.560	188.3560
$ 30.000	0.17	5.10	-23.40	547.560	93.0852
$ 50.000	0.35	17.50	-3.40	11.560	4.0460
$ 70.000	0.22	15.40	16.60	275.560	60.6232
$ 90.000	0.16	14.40	36.60	1339.560	214.3296
		53.40			560.4400

To determine the salary for $6 per hour you would need to assume 8 hours in a day which would be a constant wage of $48. Since this is a constant $48 this would be the expected value of this pay plan. Employees would be better off staying with the $2 per car because it has an expected value of $53.40.

4.53.

The relative frequency of occurrence approach takes the number of times the item of interest occurred and divides it by the total number of times the event or activity was done. An example of this might be that a health insurance company is interested in the number of errors that occur in claims. They could look at a sample of claims and count the number of times errors occurred divided by the sample size that they reviewed.

4.55.

Classical probability assessment, sometimes referred to as *a priori* probability, is the method of determining probability based on the ratio of the number of ways the event of interest can occur to the total number of ways any event can occur when the individual elementary events are equally likely. In most business situations, it is often not possible for the decision-maker to enumerate all the possible ways an event can occur. Furthermore, it is unlikely that the individual elementary events are equally likely. Therefore, classical probability assessment is rarely applied to business situations. In most business applications the decision-maker is more likely to rely on the relative frequency of occurrence, and/or the subjective probability assessment methods.

4.57.

a. Whenever events are such that the occurrence of one event precludes any of the others from occurring, the events are said to be mutually exclusive. Some examples of mutually exclusive events are:1) the Federal Reserve Board can either raise interest rates or not, 2) at the end of the trading day the Dow Jones Industrial Average will have either gone up, gone down, or remained unchanged, 3) a company can either increase their number of employees, reduce their number of employees, or leave their workforce levels unchanged, 4) a company can either choose to advertise during the Super Bowl or not, and 5) a worker on the night shift either shows up for work early, on-time, late, or not at all.

b. Two events are said to be independent if the occurrence of one event in no way influences the probability of the occurrence of the other event. Some examples of independent events are: 1) who wins the world series is independent of whether a company searches for oil in the Gulf; 2) introducing a new product is independent of which holidays a company recognizes; 3) a company's corporate debt rating is independent of the computer time required to process employee paychecks; 4) a company's selection of a financial institution is independent of next year's employee raises; and 5) the location of a new store is independent of the debt/equity ratio.

4.59.
If the selection is made without replacement, the events for the two selections are dependent.

a. Sample Space is:

      D and G

      G and D

The probability is: $P(D \text{ and } G) + P(G \text{ and } D)$

      $(4/10 \times 6/9) + (6/10 \times 4/9) = 0.5333$

b. The probability is: $P(G \text{ and } G) = 6/10 \times 5/9 = 0.3333$

4.61.

a. e_1 = bid awarded

   e_2 = bid not awarded

b. $SS = (e_1, e_2)$

c. $SS = (e_1, e_2, e_3, e_4, e_5, e_6, e_7, e_8)$

Event	Contract 1	Contract 2	Contract 3
e_1	Awarded	Awarded	Awarded
e_2	Awarded	Awarded	Not awarded
e_3	Awarded	Not awarded	Awarded
e_4	Awarded	Not awarded	Not awarded
e_5	Not awarded	Awarded	Awarded
e_6	Not awarded	Awarded	Not awarded
e_7	Not awarded	Not awarded	Awarded
e_8	Not awarded	Not awarded	Not awarded

4.63.

a. $P(\text{win}) = 1/500 = 0.002$

b. $P(\text{win}) = 3/500 = 0.006$

c. The probability assessment method used in a and b is the classical probability approach.

4.65.

a. $P(\text{on time}) = 4900/10000 = 0.49$

b. $P(\text{late}) = 4000/10000 = 0.40$

c. $P(\text{early}) = (10000-4900-4000)/10000 = 0.11$

d. Student answers will vary, but they should comment that this is based on a sample and that the probability on any given flight may be significantly different. Relative frequency of occurrence assumes that the conditions will be the same for all flights which might not be the case. However, if the sampling that resulted in 10,000 flights was done statistically, then relative frequency of occurrence might be acceptable as a probability assessment method.

4.67.

The probability of correctly guessing on any one question is .25. The questions are independent.

a. P(C and C and C) = .25 x .25 x .25 = 0.0156

b. Sample space is:

$$P(C \text{ and } C \text{ and } C) = .25 \text{ x } .25 \text{ x } .25 = 0.0156$$

Or

$$P(C \text{ and } C \text{ and } W) = .25 \text{ x } .25 \text{ x } .75 = 0.0469$$

Or

$$P(C \text{ and } W \text{ and } C) = .25 \text{ x } .75 \text{ x } .25 = 0.0469$$

Or

$$P(W \text{ and } C \text{ and } C) = .75 \text{ x } .25 \text{ x } .25 = 0.0469$$

The probability of interest is found by summing these probabilities:

P(Passing) = .0156 + .0469 + .0469 + .0469 = 0.1563

Thus, the chances of passing a three question multiple choice exam if two or more correct answers are required is only 0.1563. Moral of the story is that you had better plan on studying.

c. Sample space is:

$$P(C \text{ and } C \text{ and } C) = .50 \text{ x } .50 \text{ x } .50 = 01250$$

Or

$$P(C \text{ and } C \text{ and } W) = .50 \text{ x } .50 \text{ x } .50 = 01250$$

Or

$$P(C \text{ and } W \text{ and } C) = .50 \text{ x } .50 \text{ x } .50 = 01250$$

Or

$$P(W \text{ and } C \text{ and } C) = .50 \text{ x } .50 \text{ x } .50 = 01250$$

The probability of interest is found by summing these probabilities:

P(Passing) = .1250 + .1250 + .1250 + .1250 = 0.5000

4.69.

x	P(x)	xP(x)	x-E(x)	$[x-E(x)]^2$	$[x-E(x)]^2P(x)$
-1000	0.1	-100	(1,750)	3,062,500	306,250
0	0.1	0	(750)	562,500	56,250
500	0.3	150	(250)	62,500	18,750
1000	0.3	300	250	62,500	18,750
2000	0.2	400	1,250	1,562,500	312,500
		750			712,500

y	P(y)	yP(y)	y-E(y)	$[y-E(y)]^2$	$[y-E(y)]^2P(y)$
-1000	0.2	-200	(1,100)	1,210,000	242,000
0	0.4	0	(100)	10,000	4,000
500	0.3	150	400	160,000	48,000
1000	0.05	50	900	810,000	40,500
2000	0.05	100	1,900	3,610,000	180,500
		100			515,000

a. E(x) = 750;   E(y) = 100

b. StDev(x) = 844.0972;   StDev(y) = 717.635

c. CV(x) = 844.0972/750 = 1.1255
    CV(y) = 717.635/100 = 7.1764

d. Student answers will vary but they should comment on the fact that you cannot compare standard deviations of datasets with different means. They should be standardized by calculating the coefficient of variation. In this case it shows that the 2nd stock is actually more risky than the 1st stock.

4.71.

If two events are independent then the probability of both events occurring should be equal to the product of the two individual events, so if the two stocks are independent then 0.6(0.7) = 0.42 which does not equal 0.15. Therefore, the two events are not independent.

4.73.

P(Sales) = P(Sale on 1st) + P(Sale on 2nd/no sale on 1st) + P(Sale on 3rd/no sale 1st & 2nd) + P(Sale on 4th/No sale on 1st, 2nd, 3rd) = 0.7 + (0.6)(0.3) + (0.5)(0.3)(0.4) + (0.4)(0.3)(0.4)(0.5) = 0.7 + 0.18 + 0.06 + 0.024 = 0.964

4.75.

Develop a table of the workers. This is what could initially be filled in. Students could then finish the table and convert it to probabilities

	Favor	Against	
Office Worker			
Production Worker	370		750
	715		1200

	Favor	Against	
Office Worker	345	105	450
Production Worker	370	380	750
	715	485	1200

	Favor	Against	
Office Worker	0.2875	0.0875	0.3750
Production Worker	0.3083	0.3167	0.6250
	0.5958	0.4042	1.0000

a.   P(favor) = 0.5958

b.   P(office worker and against) = 0.0875

c.   If it is independent then P(favor)P(Office Worker) should equal (Office Worker and Favor)

(0.5958)(0.3750) = 0.2234; If they were independent it should equal 0.2875, since this is not true they are not independent

4.77.

P(AE|MC) = P(AE and MC)/P(MC) = 0.2/(0.4+0.2) = 0.3333

4.79.

P(Profit) = .90

$P(Governor|\Pr ofit) = .80$ $P(Governor|loss) = .60$

$P(NoGovernor|\Pr ofit) = .20$ $P(NoGovernor|Loss) = .40$

Find:

$$P(\Pr ofit|NoGovernor) = \frac{P(\Pr ofit \ and \ NoGovernor)}{P(NoGovernor)} =$$

$$\frac{P(\Pr ofit)P(NoGovernor|\Pr ofit)}{P(\Pr ofit)P(NoGovernor|\Pr ofit) + P(Loss)P(NoGovernor|Loss)} =$$

$$\frac{(.90)(.20)}{(.90)(.20) + (.10)(.40)} = \frac{0.18}{0.22} = 0.82$$

Thus, if the Governor can't attend, the chances of a profitable conference drops from 0.90 to 0.82.

CHAPTER 5

DISCRETE AND CONTINUOUS PROBABILITIY
DISTRIBUTIONS

5.1.

n = 4; p = .2; binomial

$$P(x) = \frac{n!}{x!(n-x)!} p^x q^{n-x}$$

let x = 0,1,2,3, and 4 when p = 0.2 and q = 0.8

For example: x = 0

$$P(0) = \frac{4!}{0!(4-0)!} (.2^0)(.8^{4-0}) = 0.4096$$

x	P(x)
0	.4096
1	.4096
2	.1536
3	.0256
4	.0016

5.3.

a. n = 20; p = .40; binomial

Use binomial table; P(x = 10) = .1171

b. P(7 < x < 12) = P(x = 8) + P(x = 9) + P(x = 10) + P(x = 11)

= .1797 + .1597 + .1171 + .0710

= .5275

c. P(x ≥ 12) = P(x = 12) + P(x = 13) + ... P(x = 20)

= .0355 + .0146 + .0049 + .0013 + .0003

= .0566

5.5.

a. $C_x^n = \frac{n!}{x!(n-x)!} = \frac{8!}{4!(8-4)!} = 70$ ways

b. $C_6^{10} = \frac{10!}{6!(10-6)!} = 210$ ways

c. $C_3^{10} = \dfrac{10!}{3!(10-3)!} = 120$ ways

d. $C_7^{10} = \dfrac{10!}{7!(10-7)!} = 120$ ways

5.7.

Use binomial table for n = 5; p = .40

a. $P(x = 4) = .0768$

b. $P(x \geq 4) = .0768 + .0102 = .0870$

c. $E[x] = np = 5(.40) = 2$

$SD[x] = \sqrt{npq} = \sqrt{5(.40)(.60)} = 1.0954$

5.9.

Use binomial table for n = 20

a. $P(x = 5) = .0746$

b. $P(x \geq 7) = .1124 + .0609 + .0271 + .0099 + .0030 + .0008 + .0002$
$= .2143$

c.   No specific probability of a success was given. Students could select either p=.40 or p= .25 from parts a. and b. or a value in between. The following uses p = .30
$E[x] = np = 20(.30) = 6$

d.   No specific probability of a success was given. Students could select either p=.40 or p= .25 from parts a. and b. or a value in between. The following uses p = .30

$SD[x] = \sqrt{npq} = \sqrt{20(.30)(.70)} = 2.0494$

5.11.

a. $E(x) = \sum xP(x) = 0(.4096) + 1(.4096) + 2(.1536) + 3(.0256) + 4(.0016) = .80$

b. $E(x) = np = 4(.20) = .80$

5.13.

a.   n = 5; p = .70; binomial
$P(x = 5 \text{ males}) = .1681$

b.   n = 5; p = .70; binomial
$P(x = 0 \text{ males}) = .0024$

5.15.

   a. p = .10; n = 10 chairs; binomial

      $P(x \geq 2) = 1 - P(x \leq 1) = 1 - (.3874 + .3487) = 1 - .7361 = .2639$

   b. p = .15; n = 10 chairs; binomial

      $P(x \geq 2) = 1 - P(x \leq 1) = 1 - (.3474 + .1969) = 1 - .5443 = .4557$

   c. The fact that 2 of the Stevens company chairs need to be replaced when ten are tested does not by itself prove that the Steven's chairs are superior. The chance of 2 or more needing to replaced is .2639. In fact if the Stevens's claim is correct, the expected number that would need to be replaced is 10(.10) = 1.0. Finding more than one does not help Stevens in any way to prove their claim.

5.17.

  n=8, p=0.37

   a. P(x=5) = 0.0971

   b. $P(x<4) = P(x \leq 3) = 0.6626$

   c. $P(x>2) = P(x \geq 3) = 1 - P(x \leq 2) = 1 - 0.3811 = 0.6189$

5.19.

  n = 6; p = .67; binomial

  $E[x] = np = 6(.67) = 4.02$ Thus, about 4 adults in a random sample of 6 are expected to say that the pennies should be continued.

5.21.

  n=5, p = 0.21

   a. Expected number = 5(0.21) = 1.05

   b. Variance = 5(0.21)(0.79) = 0.8295, standard deviation = 0.9108

5.23.

  n = 10 parts; p = .05 (defect rate) ; binomial

  If x $\leq$ 2 defects, keep the shipment.

   a. $P(x \leq 2) = .0746 + .3151 + .5987 = .9884$

   b. Suppose p = .10

      $P(x \leq 2) = .1937 + .3874 + .3487 = .9298$

   c. While the sampling plan is very good (prob = .9884) at keeping shipments that actually contain .05 defects, the sampling plan also keeps most (prob = .9298) of the shipments which contain twice (p = .10) as many defects as allowed. Thus the plan is one-sided. It favors the supplier.

5.25.

a. It is a binomial distribution with n=3, p= probability of defective module

b. p = .05; P(x≥1) = 1 – P(x=0) = 1 – 0.8574 = 0.1426; yes it is larger

c. For n = 3 the highest the p level can be such that the P(x ≥ 1) < .025 is less than .01 (0.0084). At p = .01, P(x ≥ 1) = 1 - 0.9703 = 0.0297 which is still slightly larger than the required .025 level. At p = 0.0084, P(x ≥ 1) = 0.02499.

5.27.

a. P(x=5) = 0.1755

b. P(x≤5) = 0.6160

c. P(x≥3) = 1 – P(x≤2) = 1 – 0.12465 = 0.87535

5.29.

a. Mean = E[x] = λt = 5(2) = 10
    Standard Deviation = SD[x] = $\sqrt{\lambda t}$ = 3.1623

b. P(x ≤ 3) = .0076 + .0023 + .0005 + .0000 = .0104

5.31.

The appropriate probability distribution is the Hypergeometric distribution

x	P(x)
0	0.375645
1	0.462332
2	0.148607
3	0.013209
4	0.000206

5.33.

Use the Hypergeometric distribution and the formula:

$$P(x_1, x_2, x_3, \ldots x_k) = \frac{C_{x_1}^{X_1} \bullet C_{x_2}^{X_2} \bullet C_{x_3}^{X_3} \bullet \cdots \bullet C_{x_k}^{X_k}}{C_n^N}$$

$$P(2,2,6) = \frac{C_2^{10} \bullet C_2^{15} \bullet C_6^{15}}{C_{10}^{40}} = \frac{45 \bullet 105 \bullet 5,005}{847,660,528} = .0279$$

5.35.

$\lambda = 3/400 = 0.0075$; $t = 1200$; $\lambda t = 9$

a. $P(x=0) = 0.000123$

b. $P(x>14) = P(x \geq 15) = 1 - P(x \leq 14) = 1 - 0.9585 = 0.0415$

c. $P(x<9) = P(x \leq 8) = 0.4557$

d. There is only a 4.15% chance of finding 15 or more errors if the claim is actually true. Students will probably conclude that the error rate is probably higher than 3 per 400.

5.37.

Use the Hypergeometric distribution with: $P(x) = \dfrac{C_{n-x}^{N-X} \bullet C_x^X}{C_n^N}$

Then with $N = 20$; $n = 4$; $X = 4$; $x = 0$

$P(x \geq 1) = 1 - P(x = 0).$ $P(0) = \dfrac{C_{4-0}^{20-4} \bullet C_0^4}{C_4^{20}} = \dfrac{1,820 \bullet 1}{4,845} = .3756.$

$1 - 0.3756 = 0.6244.$

5.39.

a. The desired event can occur is they all select fruit trees or pine trees or maple trees. The probabilities of these outcomes are:

$P(4,0,0) = \dfrac{C_4^{10} \bullet C_0^8 \bullet C_0^{14}}{C_4^{32}} = \dfrac{210 \bullet 1 \bullet 1}{35,960} = .0058$

$P(0,4,0) = \dfrac{C_0^{10} \bullet C_4^8 \bullet C_0^{14}}{C_4^{32}} = \dfrac{1 \bullet 70 \bullet 1}{35,960} = .0019$

$p(0,0,4) = \dfrac{C_0^{10} \bullet C_0^8 \bullet C_4^{14}}{C_4^{32}} = \dfrac{1 \bullet 1 \bullet 1,001}{35,960} = .0278$

The overall probability is found by summing these: $.0058 + .0019 + .0278 = .0355$

b. $P(0,3,1) = \dfrac{C_0^{10} \bullet C_3^8 \bullet C_1^{14}}{C_4^{32}} = \dfrac{1 \bullet 56 \bullet 14}{35,960} = .0218$

c. $P(0,2,2) = \dfrac{C_0^{10} \bullet C_2^8 \bullet C_2^{14}}{C_4^{32}} = \dfrac{1 \bullet 28 \bullet 91}{35,960} = .0709$

5.41.

a. $P(x>18.7) = P(z > (18.7 – 15)/2.5) = P(z > 1.48) = 0.5 – 0.4306 = 0.0694$

b. $P(z > \text{some value}) = (100 – 90^{th} \text{ percentile}) = 0.1; z = 1.28; 1.28 = (x – 15)/2.5; x = 18.2$ is the 90th percentile

c. $P(-2 < z < 2) = 0.4772 + 0.4772 = 0.9544$

5.43.

a.   Use the normal distribution table
$$P(0.00 < z \le 2.33) = .4901$$

b. $P(-1.00 < z \le 1.00) = .3413 + .3413 = .6826$

c. $P(1.78 < z < 2.34) = (.4904) - (.4625) = .0279$

5.45.

a. $\begin{aligned} \mu &= 7.5 \\ \sigma &= 3 \end{aligned}$ $z = \dfrac{x-\mu}{\sigma} = \dfrac{8.5-7.5}{3} = 0.33$; therefore $P(x \ge 8.5) = .50 - .1293 = .3707$

b. $\begin{aligned} \mu &= 7.5 \\ \sigma &= 3 \end{aligned}$ $z = \dfrac{x-\mu}{\sigma} = \dfrac{6.5-7.5}{3} = -0.33$; therefore $P(x \ge 6.5) = .50 + .1293 = .6293$

c. $\begin{aligned} \mu &= 7.5 \\ \sigma &= 3 \end{aligned}$ $z = \dfrac{x-\mu}{\sigma} = \dfrac{9.5-7.5}{3} = 0.67$; therefore $P(x \ge 9.5) = .50 - .2486 = .2514$

d. $\begin{aligned} \mu &= 7.5 \\ \sigma &= 3 \end{aligned}$ $z = \dfrac{x-\mu}{\sigma} = \dfrac{3.0-7.5}{3} = -1.50$ and $\dfrac{5.5-7.5}{3} = -.67$
$$P(3.0 \le x \le 5.5) = .4332 - .2486 = .1846$$

5.47.

$$\mu = 10.5$$
$$\sigma = \sqrt{16.7} = 4.087$$

a. $z = 3.00 ;\quad z = \dfrac{x-\mu}{\sigma} ;\quad 3.0o = \dfrac{x-10.5}{4.087} ; x = 22.76$

b. $-1.96 = \dfrac{x-10.5}{4.087} ; x = 2.49$

5.49.

a. $z_{.37} = -1.13;\ z = \dfrac{x-\mu}{\sigma}\ ;\ -1.13 = \dfrac{23-\mu}{9.3}\ ;\ \mu = 33.51$

b. P(at least four out of five are 1 standard deviation below the mean) =
$\qquad\qquad$ 1 – P(0 of four > 1 st. deviation below the mean)

$\qquad\qquad$ P(z < -1.00) = .50 - .3413 = .1587
$\qquad\qquad$ P(z ≥ -1.00) = 1 - .1587 = .8413 = P(≥ 1 st. deviation below mean)

$\qquad\qquad$ P(0 of four 1 st. dev or more below mean) =
$\qquad\qquad$ P(all 4 are at or above 1 st. dev below the mean) =
$\qquad\qquad\qquad\qquad$ .8413 x .8413 x .8413 x .8413 = .5010
$\qquad\qquad$ P(at least 1 out of four 1 st. deviation or more below the mean) = 1 - .5010 = .4990

5.51.

$z_{.25} = -.675\ ;\ -.675 = \dfrac{17-22}{\sigma};\ \sigma = 7.407$

5.53.

Students can use Excel's NORMDIST function to calculate the probabilities of each of the ranges of acres using a mean of 4300 and a standard deviation of 750. Students can then use the discrete probability functions from chapter 4 to calculate the average cost and average number of firefighters.

Acres (x)	P(x)	Cost (Millions)	Firefighters	Average Cost	Average Firefighters
0 < 2050	0.0013	0.05	25	0.000065	0.0325
2050 < 2800	0.0214	0.15	50	0.00321	1.07
2800 < 3550	0.1359	0.25	100	0.033975	13.59
3550 < 4300	0.3413	0.35	130	0.119455	44.369
4300 < 5050	0.3413	0.4	150	0.13652	51.195
5050 < 5600	0.1171	0.75	160	0.087825	18.736
5600 < 6550	0.0402	1	175	0.0402	7.035
≥ 6550	0.0013	1.5	200	0.00195	0.26
	0.9998 *			0.4232	136.2875

* less than 1.00 due to rounding

a. The average cost is 0.4232 million or $423,200

b. The average number of firefighters is 136.29 or 137

c. Since you know the average number of firefighters is 137 you can then calculate the standard deviation of fire fighters and then treat it as a normal distribution to calculate the answer.

P(x)	Firefighters (x)	Average Firefighters	x-E(x)	[x-E(x)]²	[x-E(x)]²P(x)
0.0013	25	0.0325	-111.288	12384.91	16.10038
0.0214	50	1.07	-86.2875	7445.533	159.3344
0.1359	100	13.59	-36.2875	1316.783	178.9508
0.3413	130	44.369	-6.2875	39.53266	13.4925
0.3413	150	51.195	13.7125	188.0327	64.17555
0.1171	160	18.736	23.7125	562.2827	65.8433
0.0402	175	7.035	38.7125	1498.658	60.24604
0.0013	200	0.26	63.7125	4059.283	5.277067
0.9998	*	136.2875			563.42

The standard deviation is the square root of 563.42 = 23.74

The z value for 75% is 0.675; 0.675 = (firefighters – 137)/23.74 = 153.02 or 154 firefighters

d. $P(x < 160) = P(z < (160 – 137)/23.74) = P(z < 0.97) = .5 + 0.3340 = 0.8340$

5.55.

a. $P(x>85) = P(z > (85 – 72)/4) = P(z > 3.25) = $ essentially 0 percent

b. $P(x>82) = P(z > (82 – 72)/4) = P(z > 2.5) = 0.5 – 0.4938 = 0.0062$

c. The number of fliers is actually a discrete variable. The normal distribution assumes that the value can take on an infinite number of possible outcomes.

5.57.

a. $P(x>16.7) = P(z > (16.7 – 16)/0.35) = P(z > 2.00) = 0.5 – 0.4772 = 0.0228$

b. If the probability of being greater than some value is 0.005 then $z = 2.575$

   $2.575 = (16.7 – mean)/0.35 = 15.8$ so the mean would need to be 15.8

c. $2.575 = (16.7 – 16)/$standard deviation $= 0.2718$

d. Because you want 16 ounce drinks it would probably be better to have your mean ounces be 16 and adjust the standard deviation.

5.59.

$15.62 + 2(0.35) = 16.32$

a. $P(x>16.32) = P(z > (16.32 - 15.62)/0.35) = P(z > 2.00) = 0.5 - 0.4772 = 0.0228$

b. $P(x>16.32) = P(z > (16.32 - 16)/0.35) = P(z > 0.91) = 0.5 - 0.3186 = 0.1814$

$P(x>2|n=3, p=0.1814) = P(z > \dfrac{2-(3)(0.1814)}{\sqrt{3(0.1814)(1-0.1814)}} = 2.18)$ which is $0.5000 - 0.4854 =$

0.0146.

5.61.

a. $z = \dfrac{x-\mu}{\sigma} = \dfrac{7.50-4.11}{1.37} = 2.48$; $P(x > \$7.50) = .50 - .4934 = .0066$

b. $-1.645 = \dfrac{3.50-\mu}{1.37}$; $\mu = \$5.75$

5.63.

With a probability of no more than 5%, $z = -1.645$
$-1.645 = (3.5 - \text{mean})/0.5$; the mean would have to be 4.32 inches

5.65.

a.

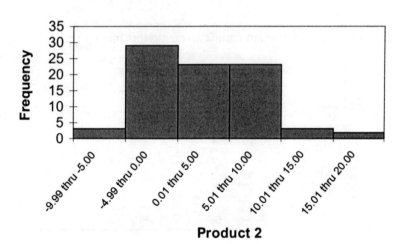

It does not appear that Product 2 is as close to normal distribution as Plan 1 was.

b.   Students can use Excel's descriptive statistics to determine the mean and standard deviation

Product # 2	
Mean	2.584337349
Standard Error	0.539795898
Median	2.4
Mode	-1.9
Standard Deviation	4.917774678
Sample Variance	24.18450779
Kurtosis	-0.045617579
Skewness	0.480907671
Range	23.7
Minimum	-6.6
Maximum	17.1
Sum	214.5
Count	83

c.   Remember that positive values indicate weight gain so students need to determine the Probability that the weight loss is more negative than 12.

$$P(x<-12) = P(z < (-12 - 2.5843)/4.9178) = P(z < -2.97) = 0.5 - 0.4985 = 0.0015$$

d.   No, this would not be an appropriate claim. The probability of losing 12 or more pounds is only 0.15%. In fact the average for this plan is a weight gain of 2.58 pounds.

5.67.

a.   Students can use Excel's histogram feature to create this histogram.

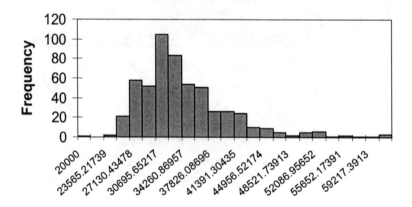

Histogram

It could be considered approximately normally distributed.

b. Students can use Excel's descriptive statistics feature to make these calculations.

Household Annual Income	
Mean	**32801.09489**
Standard Error	266.1365661
Median	31000
Mode	30000
Standard Deviation	**6230.097282**
Sample Variance	38814112.14
Kurtosis	3.044243192
Skewness	1.481126946
Range	41000
Minimum	20000
Maximum	61000
Sum	17975000
Count	548

c. $P(x > 40000) = P(z > 40000 - 32801.0949)/6230.0973 = P(z > 1.16) = 0.5 - 0.3770 = 0.1230$

d. To grant discounts to less than 7% the z value would be -1.48

$-1.48 = (x - 32801.0949)/6230.0973$; the income cutoff would be $23,581.36

5.69.

a. $P(x>50) = (60-50)/(60-20) = 0.25$

b. $P(x = 45) = 0$; you cannot find the probability of a specific value in a continuous distribution.

c. $P(25<x<35) = (35.25)/(60-20) = 0.25$

d. $P(x<34) = (34-20)/(60-20) = 0.35$

5.71.

a. $P(x > 200) = (400-200)/(400-100) = 200/300 = 0.67$

b. $P(150 < x < 300) = (300 - 150)/(400 - 100) = 150/300 = 0.50$

c. $P(180 < x < 260) = (260 - 180)/(400 - 100) = 80/300 = 0.2667$

5.73.

a.

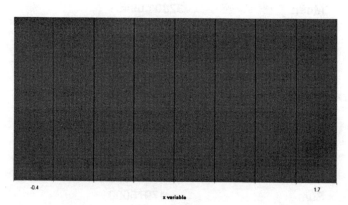

Uniform Distribution

b. $P(x > 0) = (1.7 - 0.0)/(1.7 - -.40) = 1.7/2.10 = 0.8095$

5.75.

Exponential distribution with $1/\lambda = .25$ seconds.

a. $P(.20 \le x \le .60) = P(x \le .60) - P(x < .20)$

Use Appendix E and equation 5-17

$P(x \le .60) = 1 - .8607 = .1393$

$P(x < .20) = 1 - .9512 = .0488$

$P(.20 \le x \le .60) = .1393 - .0488 = .0905$

b. $P(x > 4) = 1 - P(x \le 4) = 1 - (1 - .3679) = 0.3679$

c. $P(x > 0.30) = 0.9277$

5.77.

a. $P(x<7) = (7-5)/(8.5-5) = 2/3.5 = 0.5714$

Because the growth rate is thought to be uniformly distributed using a constant growth factor may lead to invalid results. The probability of the growth being less than 7 inches is more than 50%

so the model would probably overstate the actual pine tree growth.

b. $P(x>6) = (8.5-6)/(8.5-5) = 0.7143$; if they use this as the constant growth rate they will probably understate the actual pine tree growth.

5.79.

$\lambda = 12/\text{hour} = 0.2 \text{ per minutes}; P(x<4) = 1 - e^{-(.2)(4)} = 1 - 0.4493 = 0.5507$

5.81.

Students can use Excel's EXPONDIST function to solve this problem.

a. $\lambda = 1/4000 = .00025$; $P(x<2100) = \text{EXPONDIST}(2100,0.00025,\text{true}) = 0.4084$; Yes because this is a pretty high probability of a failure at less than 2100.

b. $100,000(0.4084) = 40,840$

5.83.

If sampling is done without replacement then the probability of an outcome changes because the total outcomes decrease by 1 each time an item is removed. However, if the total outcomes are large the change in the probability will be so small it would still be acceptable to use the binomial distribution.

5.85.

As the sample size is increased for a given level of the probability of success, p, the probability distribution becomes more symmetric, or bell-shaped.

5.87.

Examples will be different for each student. The students should discuss that the mean and the variance of the Poisson distribution is the same so if you reduce one you will also be reducing the spread which is the variance.

5.89.

To calculate the probability of a continuous distribution you must calculate the area under the curve. A single point has no area so the probability of a specific value must be zero.

5.91.

a. $f(x) = 1/(0.80-0.40) = 2.5$

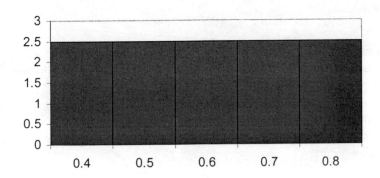

b. $P(x<0.65) = (0.65 - 0.4)/(0.8 - 0.4) = 0.625$

c. $P(x>0.7) = (0.8 - 0.7)/(0.8 - 0.4) = 0.25$

d. $P(0.6<x<0.75) = (0.75 - 0.6)/(0.8 - 0.4) = 0.375$

e. $(0.8 - 0.4)(.9) = .36$ so $0.4 + 0.36 = 0.76$ which is the 90th percentile

5.93.

    a. $P(x>8) = 1 - P(x\leq 8) = 1 - 0.9319 = 0.0681$

    b. $P(3\leq x\leq 6) = P(x=3) + P(x=4) + P(x=5) + P(x=6) = 0.1404 + 0.1755 + 0.1755 + 0.1402 = 0.6376$

    c. $P(x<3/\text{mean} = 2.5) = P(x\leq 2) = 0.5438$

5.95.

    a. $P(x=0) = 0.6065$

    b. $P(x<3) = P(x=0) + P(x=1) + P(x=2) = 0.6065+0.3033+0.0758 = 0.9856$

    c. Mean $= 0.5(3) = 1.5$
        $P(x=0) = 0.2231$

    d. $P(x\geq 5) = 1 - P(x\leq 4) = 1 - 0.9998 = 0.0002$. Since the probability of this occurring is so small if the mean errors is actually 0.5 then you would conclude that the mean errors is actually higher than 0.5.

5.97.

    a. $P(x\geq 5) = 0.0250 + 0.0036 + 0.0002 = 0.0288$

    b. Expected number of patients who will require admittance $= np = 7(0.3) = 2.1$

5.99.

    $n = 15, p = 0.10$

    a. $P(x<7) = P(x\leq 6) = 0.9997$

    b. $P(x=0) = 0.2059$

5.101.

    a. If a distribution is truly a normal distribution the mean and the median will be exactly the same. Since the mean and median are different this cannot be a normal distribution.

    b. It would be possible for the mean to be \$700 and the standard deviation to be \$600. However, since an account balance cannot likely be negative, a distribution with mean = \$700 and standard deviation equal to \$600 is most likely not a normal distribution since we would expect data within $\pm$ 3 standard deviations.

5.103.

    a. A rebate to the 20% using the least water would be a z value of -0.84

        $-0.84 = (x - 18)/6$; minimum level should be 12.96 or 13 gallons

    b. $P(x<13) = P(z < (13 - 14)/6) = P(z < -0.17) = 0.5 - 0.0675 = 0.4325$

5.105.

a. $P(x>4.90) = P(z > (4.9 - 4.5)/1.1) = P(z > 0.36) = 0.5 - 0.1406 = 0.3594$

b. $P(x<6.25) = P(z < (6.25 - 4.5)/1.1) = P(z < 1.59) = 0.5 + 0.4441 = 0.9441$

c. $P(3.25<x<5.75) = P[(3.25 - 4.5)/1.1 < z < (5.75 - 4.5)/1.1] = P(-1.14 < z < 1.14) = 2(0.3729) = 0.7458$

5.107.

a. $E[x] = np = 10(.10) = 1.0$ This is the expected number of watches that will fail in a random sample of 10 watches

b. $SD[x] = \sqrt{npq} = \sqrt{10(.10)(.90)} = \sqrt{.9} = .9487$; The standard deviation measures the variation in the number of failed watches from sample to sample when the sample size is ten.

5.109.

a. A probability of 0.05 in the right-tail area corresponds to a z value of 1.645

$1.645 = (x - 3)/1.5$ so $x = 5.4675$ inches so the trim saw length should be set to 10 ft 5.4675 in.

b. $1.645 = (4.4675 - 3)/\text{st. dev.}$; so the standard deviation should be 0.892 inches

5.111.

$P(x>74) = P(z > (74 - 58)/14) = P(z > 1.14) = 0.5 - 0.3729 = 0.1271$
$P(x>90) = P(z > (90 - 58)/14) = P(z > 2.29) = 0.5 - 0.489 = 0.011$

Only 1.1 percent of the employees could be expected to take more sick leave than the second employee. That employee has taken excessive sick leave. The first employee took more sick leave than 87.29 percent of the employees. The office manager would have to decide whether this is to be considered excessive.

5.113.

a. $P(5.85 < x < 6.15) = P[(5.85 - 6)/0.1 < z < (6.15 - 6)/0.1] = P(-1.5 < z < 1.5) = 2(0.4332) = 0.8664$; since this is less than 99% Bryce Brothers should not purchase this machine.

b. for 99% chance z would be ± 2.575
$2.575 = (6.15 - 6)/\text{standard deviation}$; standard deviation $= 0.058$ inch

5.115.

a. $P(x \geq 4) = 1 - P(x \leq 3) = 1 - 0.9130 = 0.0870$; students will probably say that the percentage is actually higher than 40%

b. The expected number $= 5(0.4) = 2.0$

5.117.

a. the number of arrivals per second is $45/(15*60) = .05$ customers per second
$P(x<20) = 1 - e^{-(20)(.05)} = 1 - 0.3679 = 0.6321$

b. $P(x>30) = e^{-(30)(.05)} = 0.2231$

c. $P(30 < x < 60) = P(x < 60) - P(x < 30) = (1 - e^{-(60)(.05)}) - (1 - e^{-(30)(.05)}) = 0.9502 - 0.7769 = 0.1733$

5.119.

The probability calculated in Exercise 5.118 part a. certainly suggests that there is a problem with the disks or the operator. One way to determine if you think the problem is with the disks is to observe the results from other operators. If similar results occur you could conclude it is the disk. If other operators are not having this problem then you could probably conclude that it is the operator.

5.121.

a.   p=0.5, n=10

x	P(x)
0	0.000977
1	0.009766
2	0.043945
3	0.117188
4	0.205078
5	0.246094
6	0.205078
7	0.117188
8	0.043945
9	0.009766
10	0.000977

Dade County Emergency Services

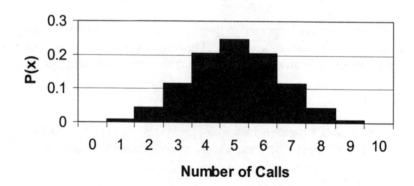

The distribution does appear to be symmetrical because the probability is equal to 0.5.

b.

x	P(x)
0	5.9049E-06
1	0.00013778
2	0.0014467
3	0.00900169
4	0.03675691
5	0.10291935
6	0.20012095
7	0.26682793
8	0.23347444
9	0.12106082
10	0.02824752

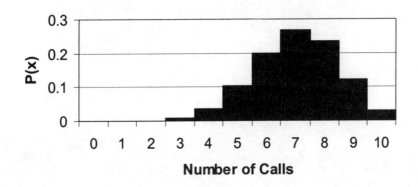

As the probability moves away from 0.5 in either direction the distribution will become skewed which is the case in this problem.

5.123.

a. n=100, p=0.9
   $P(x<90) = P(x\leq89) = 0.4168$

b. p(dissatisfied) = 1 – 0.9 = 0.1, n=100
   $P(x>10) = 1 – P(x\leq10) = 1 – 0.5832 = 0.4168$
   Notice that this is the same answer from part a

c. n=100, p=0.9
   $P(x=78) = 0.0002$

5.125.

    a. $P(x < 10) = P(z < (10 - 14.25)/2.92) = P(z < -1.46) = 0.5 - 0.4279 = 0.0721$

    b.   Since the core is 3" you need to make sure that this is not more than 32% of the diameter of the log. To determine this 3/0.32 = 9.375. This allows you to have a log with a diameter of 9.375

        $P(x < 9.375) = P(z < (9.375 - 14.25)/2.92) = P(z < -1.67) = 0.5 - 0.4525 = 0.0475$

CHAPTER 6

INTRODUCTION TO SAMPLING DISTRIBUTIONS

6.1.

a. Population mean = (5+3+2+6+6+7+3+3+6+7+7+9+7+5+3+12+6+10+7+2)/20 = 5.8

b. Sample mean = (6+12+10+3+2+2)/6 = 5.8333

The sampling error = sample mean − population mean = 5.8333-5.8 = 0.0333.

c. Highest possible sample mean for n = 6 is (7+7+7+9+10+12)/6 = 8.6667
Lowest possible sample mean for n = 6 is (2+2+3+3+3+3+)/6 = 2.6667
Range of extreme sampling error =(2.6667-5.8) ----- (8.6667-5.8)
= -3.1333 to 2.8667

6.3.

a. $\mu = \dfrac{\sum x}{N} = \dfrac{1,954}{11} = 177.64$

$\bar{x} = \dfrac{\sum x}{n} = \dfrac{650}{3} = 216.67$

Sampling error = 216.67 - 177.64 = 39.03

b. The smallest 3 values that could be in a sample from the population are:

100 100 105 $\bar{x} = \dfrac{\sum x}{n} = \dfrac{305}{3} = 101.67$

Sampling error = 101.67 - 177.64 = -75.97

The largest 3 values that could be in a sample from the population are:

400 330 200 $\bar{x} = \dfrac{\sum x}{n} = \dfrac{930}{3} = 310.0$

Sampling error = 310.0 − 177.64 = 132.36

The range in potential sampling error is −75.97 to 132.36

c.   The smallest 5 values are:

100 100 105 120 129 $\bar{x} = \dfrac{\sum x}{n} = \dfrac{554}{5} = 110.8$

Sampling error = $110.8 - 177.64 = -66.84$

The largest 5 values are:

400 330 200 190 150 $\bar{x} = \dfrac{\sum x}{n} = \dfrac{1.270}{5} = 254.0$

Sampling error = $254.0 - 177.64 = 76.36$

It is seen that the range of potential sampling error is greater when the sample is size five compared with a sample of size 3. In general, increasing the sample size will reduce the range for potential sampling error.

6.5.

a. $\mu = \dfrac{\sum x}{N} = \dfrac{864}{20} = 43.20$ days

b. $\bar{x} = \dfrac{\sum x}{n} = \dfrac{206}{5} = 41.20$ days

Sampling error = $41.20 - 43.20 = -2$ days

c. The smallest 5 values that could be in a sample are:

7 15 16 17 19 $\bar{x} = \dfrac{\sum x}{n} = \dfrac{74}{5} = 14.8$

The sampling error = $14.8 - 43.20 = -28.4$ days

The largest 5 values that could be in a sample are:

107 88 80 77 66 $\bar{x} = \dfrac{\sum x}{n} = \dfrac{418}{5} = 83.6$

The sampling error = $83.6 - 43.2 = 40.4$ days

The range in sampling error is from -28.4 days to 40.4 days.

6.7.

$\bar{x} = \dfrac{\sum x}{n} = \dfrac{170.6}{10} = 17.06$

Sampling error = $17.06 - 16.9 = 0.16$ gallon

6.9.
The sample mean = 40.9 In this case the sample mean is very close to the population mean which is 40.89.

6.11.
$\mu = 1,000 \quad \sigma = 200$

a. $z = \dfrac{\bar{x} - \mu}{\dfrac{\sigma}{\sqrt{n}}} = \dfrac{970 - 1,000}{\dfrac{200}{\sqrt{5}}} = -.34;$ $P(z < -.34) = .50 - .1331 = .3669$

b. $z = \dfrac{\bar{x} - \mu}{\dfrac{\sigma}{\sqrt{n}}} = \dfrac{970 - 1,000}{\dfrac{200}{\sqrt{10}}} = -.47;$ $P(z < -.47) = .50 - .1808 = .3192$

c. The probability of extreme sampling error is reduced when the sample size is increased since the sampling distribution is less variable.

6.13.

a. $P(x > 450) = P(z > (450 - 400)/50) = P(z > 1) = 0.5 - 0.3413 = 0.1587$

b. $P(\bar{x} > 450) = P(z > (450 - 400)/(50/\sqrt{3}) = P(z > 1.73) = 0.5 - 0.4582 = 0.0418$

c. As the sample size increases the standard deviation of the sampling distribution is reduced. This means the spread of the sampling distribution is reduced.

6.15.

a. $\bar{x} = \dfrac{\sum x}{n} = \dfrac{987.5}{40} = 24.69;$ Sampling error $= 24.69 - 24.90 = -0.21$

b. $z = \dfrac{\bar{x} - \mu}{\dfrac{\sigma}{\sqrt{n}}} = \dfrac{24.69 - 24.9}{\dfrac{1.30}{\sqrt{40}}} = -1.02;$ $P(z \le -1.02) = 0.50 - 0.3461 = 0.1539$

6.17.
$P(\bar{x} > 200) = P(z > (200 - 195)/[(20/\sqrt{100})\sqrt{(350 - 100)/(350 - 1)}] = P(z > 2.95) = 0.5 - 0.4984 = 0.0016$

6.19.

a. $P(\bar{x} < 31) = P(z < (31 - 31)/(0.86) = P(z < 0) = 0.5$
b. standard error $= \sigma/\sqrt{n} = 4.3/\sqrt{25} = 0.86$
c. To reduce the standard error the company could increase the sample size.

6.21.

a. $P(\bar{x} > 15) = P(z > (15 - 14.6)/(4.3/\sqrt{100}\,)) = P(z > 0.93) = 0.5 - 0.3238 = 0.1762$

The probability of getting a sample mean of 15 or greater is only 17.62% so although the probability is not high, it is also not that small. There is not sufficient evidence to conclude that the population values are untrue.

b.   If the population mean is 14.6 with a standard deviation of 4.3, it is not very likely that we would see 3 sample of 100 each having a sample mean greater than 15. The probability of 1 sample having a mean greater than 15 is 0.1762 (part a). Assuming the sample are independent the probability of 3 samples each of size 100 would be $(0.1762)(0.1762)(0.1762) = 0.00547$. Now, we can quite safely say that the original assumptions are false.

6.23.

a. $P(\bar{x} > 0.392) = P(z > (0.392 - 0.375)/(0.050/\sqrt{50}\,)) = P(z > 2.4) = 0.5 - 0.4918 = 0.0082$

b.   You should conclude that the sample is not representative of the population if the true population thickness is 0.375. On the other-hand you might conclude that since the probability of this observed result is so low, the standards are not being satisfied.

6.25.

a.   Students can use Excel to calculate the mean and standard deviation of the population. Remember to use STDEVP to calculate the standard deviation of the population.

Mean = 468.89; standard deviation = 804.12

b.   Student answers will vary depending on the specific class limits used. A possible histogram is:

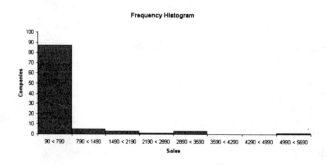

Based upon the histogram with 8 classes, the data do not appear to be normally distributed. The data are right skewed.

c.   Student answers will vary depending upon the sample selected. Report should address the issue of sampling error.

6.27.

$$z = \frac{\bar{x} - \mu}{\frac{\sigma}{\sqrt{n}}}; \quad z = \frac{450 - 0}{\frac{2000}{\sqrt{200}}} = 3.18; \quad P(z > 3.18) = .50 - .50 \cong 0.0$$

Thus, there is virtually no chance that a sample of 200 would give a mean difference of 450 pounds if the population difference is 0 with a 2000 pound standard deviation.

6.29.

a. Number of items in the population with the attribute = 40. Population size = 50. Population proportion = 40/50 = 0.8000.

b. Number of items in the sample with the attribute = 7. Sample size = 15. Sample proportion = 7/15 = 0.4667. Sampling error = sample proportion – population proportion = 0.4667 – 0.8000 = -0.3333.

c. Highest possible sample proportion = 1.0000 when the sample selects 15 items all having the attribute of interest. Lowest possible sample proportion = 0.3333 when the sample selects all 10 of the items without the attribute of interest and 5 with the attribute of interest. Range of sampling error = (0.3333 – 0.8000) ----- (1.0000 – 0.8000) = -0.4667 to 0.2000.

d. For a sample size of 30 the highest possible sample proportion remains 1.0000 when 30 items having the attribute of interest are selected. The lowest possible sample proportion becomes 0.6667 when the 10 items without the attribute of interest are all selected and the remaining 20 items in the sample have the attribute of interest. The range of extreme sampling error becomes (0.6667 – 0.8000) ----- (1.000 – 0.8000)
   = -0.1333 to 0.2000.

Note that the range of extreme sampling error has narrowed from the case where the sample size was 15. When everything else is held constant, increasing the sample size will reduce the potential for extreme sampling error.

6.31.

a. $\sigma = \sqrt{\frac{p(1-p)}{n}} = \sqrt{\frac{.65(1-.65)}{100}} = .0477$

$$z = \frac{\bar{p} - p}{\sqrt{\frac{p(1-p)}{n}}}; \quad z = \frac{.63 - .65}{\sqrt{\frac{.65(1-.65)}{100}}} = -.42; \quad P(z < -.42) = .50 - .1628 = .3372$$

b. $z = \dfrac{.63 - .65}{\sqrt{\dfrac{.65(1 - .65)}{200}}} = -.59$; $P(z < -.59) = .50 - .2224 = .2776$

When the sample size is increased, the spread in the sampling distribution is reduced making the probability of a value between any two point less than it would have been for a smaller sample size. Less chance of extreme sampling error.

6.33. $z = \dfrac{.33 - .30}{\sqrt{\dfrac{.30(1 - .30)}{60}}} = .51$; $P(z > .51) = .50 - .1950 = .3050$

6.35.

a. $z = \dfrac{.42 - .40}{\sqrt{\dfrac{.40(1 - .40)}{1000}}} = 1.29$; $P(z < 1.29) = .50 + .4015 = .9015$

b. $z = \dfrac{.44 - .40}{\sqrt{\dfrac{.40(1 - .40)}{1000}}} = 2.58$; $P(z > 2.58) = .50 - .4951 = .0049$

6.37.

$\bar{p} = 35/300 = 0.1167$

a. $P(\bar{p} \geq 0.1167) = P(z \geq (0.1167 - .08)/\sqrt{[0.08(1 - 0.08)]/300}) = P(z \geq 2.34) = 0.5 - 0.4904 = 0.0096$

The probability of getting a sample proportion as high as the new style coupon if the redemption rate is actually 0.08 is less than 1%. Therefore, the redemption rate is probably not the same.

b.   Yes because it seems like this coupon is more effective than some of the other coupons.

6.39.

a. $P(\bar{p} < 0.68) = P(z < (0.68 - 0.70)/\sqrt{[0.70(1 - 0.70)]/500}) = P(z < -0.98) = 0.5 - 0.3365 = 0.1635$

b.   The probability of having 68% or fewer customers return the movie before the 3rd night is only 16% if the population proportion is actually 70%. While this probability is not extremely small, it is small enough to cast doubt about the 70% claim. Students might suggest increasing the sample size and analyzing the larger data set before reaching a final conclusion.

6.41.

Students can use Excel's pivot table feature to group by Medicare.

a.   P(Medicare) = 116/138 = 0.8406

BC	5
CAID	7
CARE	116
HMO	1
INS	3
OGVT	1
OTHR	4
SELF	1
Grand Total	138

b. $P(\bar{p} > 0.8406) = P(z > (0.8406 - 0.80)/ \sqrt{[0.80(1 - 0.80)]/138}) = P(z > 1.19) = 0.5 - 0.383 =$ 0.117

c.   Since the probability of finding a sample with a proportion of .8406 or greater if the true proportion is .80 is only 11.7% then you may reasonably assume that the proportion of people on Medicare is actually greater than 80%.

6.43.

a.   Students can use the Excel Pivot Table feature to determine the proportion of trucks exceeding the 55 MPH speed limit. On the group and outline feature they should accept the starting and ending values and tell it to group by 28.

Count of Speed at WIM Scale	
Speed at WIM Scale	Total
28-55	153
56-83	47
Grand Total	200

The P(>55) = 47/200 = 0.235

b. $P(\bar{p} \leq 0.235) = P(z < (0.235 - 0.30)/ \sqrt{[0.30(1 - 0.30)]/200}) = P(z \leq -2.01) = .50 - .4778 =$ .0222

Thus, there is about a 2 percent chance that the sample proportion will be less than or equal to .235 if the population proportion is .30. Given this small probability, it is unlikely that the true population proportion is as high as .30

6.45.

A sampling distribution is made up of all possible values that a particular estimator can take for a population. For a particular population, the sampling distribution of the mean is all possible values that the sample mean can take when samples are of an identical size.

6.47.

Sampling error is the difference between the population mean and a particular sample mean. Since the distribution of sample means centers on the population mean, the estimate of the spread of the sampling distribution also estimates the average amount by which the sample mean differs from the population.

6.49.

The sampling distribution of the sample mean will have less dispersion than the population because the means cannot take on values as extreme as those in the population. Even if extreme values are selected in the sample, the mean will take on a more central value.

6.51.

a. The true population mean is 405.55. The mean of the sample means should be the same as the population mean.

b. $12.25 = [(\text{sigma}/\sqrt{150}\,)\sqrt{(1250-150)/(1250-1)}\,] =$

sigma = 159.83

6.53.

The population mean = 56.78

The population standard deviation: $9.6 = \text{sigma}/\sqrt{400}$; sigma = 192

The mean of the sampling distribution is equal to the mean of the population. The standard deviation of the sampling distribution is equal to the population standard deviation divided by the square root of the sample size.

6.55.

If the population is normally distributed, the distribution of all possible sample means will also be normally distributed. Since the normal distribution is symmetrical, half of the sample means are greater than the true population mean. Therefore, the probability of finding a sample mean that is greater than the population mean is 0.5.

6.57

a. The mean of the sampling distribution will be 68; it is the same as the population mean. The standard deviation for the sampling distribution of the mean is $12/\sqrt{100} = 1.2$. The spread of the distribution of sample means is less than the spread of the population because the sample mean, as an average of the sample values, dos not exhibit as many extreme values as the population does.

b. The relationship between the sampling distributions of the two means will be the standard deviations of the two distributions. For n = 100, the standard deviation is 1.2 and for n = 500, the standard deviation is 0.537.

6.59.

a. The standard error of the sampling distribution will be reduced by approximately 29 percent. The reduction is a factor of $1 - 1/\sqrt{2}$.

b. $P(z > 2.5) = 0.5 - 0.4938 = 0.0062$

6.61.

a. Because this is a large sample the sampling distribution will be approximately normally distributed regardless of the distribution of the parent population. The mean of the sampling distribution will be $21,500 and the standard error will be $1700/\sqrt{200} = \$120.21$

b. The sampling distribution would still be approximately normally distributed but the spread would be wider. The mean would be $21,500 and the standard error would be $1700/\sqrt{60} = \$219.47$

c. $P(\bar{x} > 21300) = P(z > (21300 - 21500)/(1700/\sqrt{60})) = P(z > -0.91) = 0.5 + 0.3186 = 0.8186$

6.63.

a. $P(\bar{x} < 26) = P(z < (26 - 30)/(5/\sqrt{5})) = P(z < -1.79) = 0.5 - 0.4633 = 0.0367$; Since the probability of a sample mean being less than 26 hours is only 0.0367, the company has only a small risk by making this offer and might be advised to go ahead with it.

b. $P(\bar{x} < 28) = P(z < (28 - 30)/(5/\sqrt{5})) = P(z < -0.89) = 0.5 - 0.3133 = 0.1867$; This time the risk is higher to the company since there is almost a 19 percent chance that the sample mean will exceed 28 hours.

6.65

a. $P(\bar{x} \le 24.25) = P(z \le (24.25 - 25)/(3/\sqrt{64})) = P(z \le -2.0) = 0.5 - 0.4772 = 0.0228$. There is only slightly more than a 2% chance of getting a sample average of 24.25 or less if the true population average is 25. This would indicate that the EPA mileage rating may be high for city driving.

b. $P(\bar{x} \ge 34) = P(z \ge (34 - 32)/(2/\sqrt{64})) = P(z \ge 8) = 0$; This would imply that the average highway miles is greater than 32 or that the standard deviation is greater than 2 or both.

6.67.

a. $P(19500 < x < 22000) = P[(19500-20000)/3000 < z < (22000-20000)/3000] = P(-0.17 < z < 0.67)$
$= 0.2486 + 0.0675 = 0.3161$

b. $P(19500 < \bar{x} < 22000) = P[(19500-20000)/(3000/\sqrt{36}) < z < (22000-20000)/(3000/\sqrt{36})] =$
$P(-1.0 < z < 4) = 0.5 + 0.3413 = 0.8413$

The differences in probabilities result from the smaller spread of the sampling distribution.

6.69.

$P(\bar{x} \geq 31.14) = P(z \geq (31.14 - 30)/ (8/\sqrt{150}) = P(z \geq 1.75) = .50 - .4599 = .0401$; Based on this rather small probability , students might conclude that either the mean or the standard deviation are wrong.

6.71.

a. $P(\bar{x} > 120.2) = P(z > (120.2 - 120)/ (0.8/\sqrt{36}) = P(z > 1.5) = 0.5 - 0.4332 = 0.0668$

b. $P(\bar{x} < 119.73) = P(z < (119.73 - 120)/ (0.8/\sqrt{36}) = P(z < -2.03) = 0.5 - 0.4788 = 0.0212$

c. $P(\bar{x} > 120.3) = P(z > (120.3 - 120)/ (0.8/\sqrt{36}) = P(z > 2.25) = 0.5 - 0.4878 = 0.0122$
    The probability of an average length greater than 120.3 is only 0.0122. If the sample average is 120.3 the operator should conclude that the saw is not cutting average lengths of 120.

d. Need to calculate the probability that a board would be more than 1.5 different than 120.
    $P(z>1.5/0.8) = P(z > 1.88) = 0.5 - 0.4699 = 0.0301$. Since you are looking for either 1.5 larger or smaller than the mean the probability would be the same. The probability that any one board would be more than 1.5 different is then $(.0301)(2) = 0.0602$. Since they are ordering 1000 boards, the expected number of boards that would be different would be $(0.0602)(1000) = 60.2$. Therefore it is not a good proposition for the company.

6.73.

a. Sampling error

b. $P(\bar{p} \leq 0.28) = P(z \leq (0.28 - 0.34)/ \sqrt{[0.34(1 - 0.34)]/300}) = P(z \leq -2.19) = 0.5 - 0.4857 = 0.0143$
    Thus, it does not seem that the 34% figure is correct based upon these sample results.

6.75.

a. $\bar{p} = 18/49 = 0.367$

    $P(\bar{p} < 0.367) = P(z < (0.367 - 0.45)/ \sqrt{[0.45(1 - 0.45)]/49}) = P(z < -1.17) = 0.5 - 0.379 = 0.121$

b. The maximum sampling error would occur when the highest proportion is observed above .45. This would be at about 3 standard deviations above .45. This point would be:
    $0.45 + 3 (\sqrt{[0.45(1 - 0.45)]/49} = .6632$. Then the maximum sampling error we might expect is $.6632 - .45 = .2132$.

6.77.

a. $\bar{p} = 250/625 = 0.40$

$P(\bar{p} \geq 0.4) = P(z \geq (0.40 - 0.37)/ \sqrt{[0.37(1 - 0.37)]/625}) = P(z \geq 1.55) = 0.5 - 0.4394 = 0.0606$

b. $P(\bar{p} < 0.5) = P(z < (0.50 - 0.37)/ \sqrt{[0.37(1 - 0.37)]/100}) = P(z < 2.69) = 0.5 + 0.4964 = 0.9964$

Thus, there is a .9964 chance that 50 mugs will be sufficient assuming that the mix of customers in the population is 37 percent college students.

6.79.

a. $P(\bar{p} \geq 0.3) = P(z \geq (0.30 - 0.27)/ \sqrt{[0.27(1 - 0.27)]/500}) = P(z \geq 1.51) = 0.5 - 0.4345 = 0.0655$

b. $P(\bar{p} \geq 0.3) = P(z \geq (0.30 - 0.29)/ \sqrt{[0.29(1 - 0.29)]/500}) = P(z \geq 0.49) = 0.5 - 0.1879 = 0.3121$

c. Students will probably conclude that it is greater than 0.27. The probability of getting a sample proportion of more than 30% if the true proportion is 27% is only 6.55%. The probability of getting a sample proportion of more than 30% if the true proportion is 29% is 31%. This should lead us to believe that the sample proportion is greater than 27% rather than less than 27%.

6.81.

$P(0.25 < \bar{p} < 0.29) = P[(0.25 - 0.27)/ \sqrt{[0.27(1 - 0.27)]/500}) < z < (0.29 - 0.27)/$

$\sqrt{[0.27(1 - 0.27)]/500})] = P(-1.01 < z < 1.01) = 2(0.3438) = 0.6876$

6.83.

a.

Count of Sales Plan	
Sales Plan	Total
Basic Plan	26.00%
Business Plan	74.00%
Grand Total	100.00%

The sample proportion of Business Plan customers is 0.74.

b. $P(\bar{p} \geq 0.74) = P(z \geq (0.74 - 0.7)/ \sqrt{[0.7(1 - 0.7)]/200}) = P(z \geq 1.23) = .50 - .3907 = .1093$

c. The owner might conclude, based on the small probability of .1093, that the 70% figure is low. However, more study may be warranted if the .1093 probability is not considered to be extremely small.

CHAPTER 7

ESTIMATING POPULATION VALUES

7.1.

    a. $t = 2.0595$

    b. $t = 1.6973$

    c. $t = 2.6245$

    d. $t = 2.8784$

    e. $t = 1.3253$

    f. $t = 1.7459$

7.3.

    a. $102.36 \pm 1.645(1.26/\sqrt{17})$; 101.8573 ----- 102.8627

    b. $56.33 \pm 1.7247(22.4/\sqrt{21})$; 47.8995 ----- 64.7605

7.5.

    a. $e = \pm 2.33(6.58/\sqrt{12})$; ± 4.4258

    b. $e = \pm 2.0860(2.33/\sqrt{21})$; ± 1.0606

    c. $e = \pm 1.28(15.6/\sqrt{500})$; ± 0.8930

7.7.

    a. $e = \pm 2.681(15.68/\sqrt{13})$; ± 11.6593

    b. $e = \pm 2.575(3.47/\sqrt{25})$; ± 1.7871

    c. Since the sample size is not given, we assume that the standard normal distribution is used to obtain the critical value. Thus:
        $e = \pm 2.33(2.356)$; ± 5.4895

7.9.

Since we don't know the population standard deviation and since the sample size is small, we must assume that the population is approximately normally distributed.

The interval estimate is given by: $\bar{x} \pm t\dfrac{s}{\sqrt{n}}$; $92.2 \pm 2.2622(15.562/\sqrt{10})$

92.2 ± 11.1326;   81.0674 ----------- 103.3326

7.11.

a. point estimate $= \bar{x} = \$4.22$

b. $\bar{x} \pm z \dfrac{s}{\sqrt{n}}$; $4.22 \pm 1.96(2.59/\sqrt{200}\,)$; $4.22 \pm .359$; $\$3.861$ -------- $\$4.579$

With 95 percent confidence and based on the sample data, we conclude that the true population mean amount spent on appetizers per receipt is between $3.86 and $4.60.

7.13.

a. $54.5 \pm 1.96(14.0/\sqrt{200}\,)$; 52.5597 ----- 56.4403 per car

b. The range of costs should be $(52.5597)(0.25)(200)$ ----- $(56.4403)(0.25)(200)$; $\$2,627.99$ ----- $\$2,822.02$; because the billing is lower than the lower limit they may want to investigate to make sure the location is not under-billing.

c. The margin of error is comprised of the critical value, the standard deviation of the population or sample and the sample size. If you decrease the confidence level (i.e. from 90% to 80%) you will decrease the margin of error. If you decrease the standard deviation you will decrease the margin of error. If you increase the sample size you will decrease the margin of error.

7.15.

a. $1.2 \pm 1.96(0.5/\sqrt{200}\,)$; 1.1307 ----- 1.2693

b. $1.2 \pm 1.645(0.5/\sqrt{200}\,)$; 1.1418 ----- 1.2582

c. The interval in b is more precise and because it is narrower it may be more useful in decision making. However, intervals formed with a 0.90 confidence coefficient contain the true mean a smaller proportion of the time.

7.17.

a. $311 \pm 1.645(72/\sqrt{144}\,)$; 301.13 ----- 320.87
Based upon the sample data with 90% confidence the officials can conclude that the mean time spent in the park is between 301.13 minutes and 320.87 minutes.

b. The margin of error is comprised of the critical value, the standard deviation of the population or sample and the sample size. If you decrease the confidence level (i.e. from 90% to 80%) you will decrease the margin of error. Park officials do not really control the standard deviation of length of stay so cannot really effect that. If you increase the sample size you will decrease the margin of error.

7.19.

a. $\bar{x} = \dfrac{\sum x}{n} = 67.0$; $s = \sqrt{\dfrac{\sum (x - \bar{x})^2}{n-1}} = 14.5285$

$67 \pm 1.7709(14.5285/\sqrt{14}\,)$; 67 ± 6.8762; 60.1238 -------- 73.8762

Based on the sample results, with 90% confidence we believe that the mean heart rate is between 60.1238 and 73.8762.

b.   No, the conclusions could apply to only those people that have heart rates higher than 55 when they begin taking the medication. Even then, care would need to be taken to assure that the sample was random.

c.   (1) It does look like heart rates did increase since the interval estimate for the mean heart rate, based on 90% confidence is estimate to be between 60.1 and 73.9 after taking the medication compared to the 55 or less baseline prior to taking the medication. (2) Using the point estimate of $\bar{x} = 67$ and assuming that the population mean prior to taking the medication was 55, we get:

$P(z \geq (67\text{-}55)/(14.5285/\sqrt{14}\,)) = P(z \geq 3.09) = .50\ \text{-}\ .50 = 0$

Thus, there is essentially a zero chance of getting a sample of 67 or more if the population mean stays at 55 for the heart rate. Again, we conclude that heart rates do increase.

7.21.

a.   Using Excel's function features students can calculate the mean and standard deviation of the sample. Mean = 2.505; s = 1.5071

$2.505 \pm 1.645(1.5071/\sqrt{200}\,);\ 2.3297\ \text{-----}\ 2.6803$

Based upon the sample results with 90% confidence the mean number of mutual funds is thought to be between 2.33 and 2.68.

b.   The margin of error is comprised of the critical value, the standard deviation of the population or sample and the sample size. If you decrease the confidence level (i.e. from 90% to 80%) you will decrease the margin of error. If you decrease the standard deviation you will decrease the margin of error. If you increase the sample size you will decrease the margin of error. The advantages of decreasing the confidence level is that there is no additional cost of sampling. The disadvantages are that you won't be as confident. Increasing sample size costs money but you won't have to reduce your confidence level.

7.23.

a. Students can use Excel's pivot table features to manipulate the data to obtain the information they need.

All Complaint Categories   Boise

Count of Dollar Claim Amount	78
Average of Dollar Claim Amount	268.4358974
StdDev of Dollar Claim Amount	50.89551041

$268.4359 \pm 1.9913(50.8955/\sqrt{78})$; 256.9605 ----- 279.9113

Boise

Corrosion		Count of Dollar Claim Amount	30
		Average of Dollar Claim Amount	274.1333333
		StdDev of Dollar Claim Amount	54.01962181

Corrosion:

$274.1333 \pm 2.0452(54.0196/\sqrt{30})$; 253.9623 ----- 294.3043

The corrosion estimate is less precise and centered at a higher value.

Malfunction:

Count of Dollar Claim Amount	31
Average of Dollar Claim Amount	273.6774194
StdDev of Dollar Claim Amount	42.61876511

Since $n \geq 30$, students could use either $z = 1.96$ or $t = 2.0423$

$273.68 \pm 2.0423(42.62/\sqrt{31})$; 258.05 ----- 289.31

Wiring:

Count of Dollar Claim Amount	13
Average of Dollar Claim Amount	265.2307692
StdDev of Dollar Claim Amount	53.76825868

$265.23 \pm 2.1788(53.77/\sqrt{13})$; 232.49 ----- 297.72

Sound:

Count of Dollar Claim Amount	4
Average of Dollar Claim Amount	195.5
StdDev of Dollar Claim Amount	28.34901527

$195.5 \pm 3.1824(28.35/\sqrt{4})$; 150.39 ----- 240.61

b. Student letters will vary but given the data it is difficult to conclude that one cause or the other is more serious in terms of dollar values. The interval estimates for the mean cost overlap. However, Sound seems to have lower average warranty costs.

7.25.

$$n = \frac{z^2\sigma^2}{e^2} = \frac{(1.96^2)(40^2)}{2.5^2} = 983.44 = 984$$

7.27.

$$s = \sqrt{\frac{\sum(x-\bar{x})^2}{n-1}} = 246.667; \quad n = \frac{z^2s^2}{e^2} = \frac{(1.645^2)(246.667^2)}{60^2} = 45.73 = 46$$

Note, the 10 values in the pilot sample can be used leaving an additional 36 items needed in the sample.

7.29.

a. $$n = \frac{z^2s^2}{e^2} = \frac{(1.645^2)(900^2)}{40^2} = 1,369.9 = 1,370$$

b. $$n = \frac{z^2s^2}{e^2} = \frac{(1.96^2)(900^2)}{40^2} = 1,944.8 = 1,945$$

   The percentage change is:

$$\frac{1,945-1370}{1,370}(100) = 41.97 = 41.97\% \text{ increase}$$

7.31.

a. The margin of error can be decreased by either decreasing the confidence level, or decreasing the population standard deviation, or some combination of both. Note, in most instance we have no control over the standard deviation.

b. If the confidence level is increased for a given size sample, the margin of error will be increased.

c. Both confidence level and margin of error can be decreased at the same time by increasing the required sample size or by reducing the population standard deviation.

7.33.

$n = (1.645)^2(0.80)^2/(0.2)^2 = 43.29 \text{ or } 44$

7.35.

a. $n = (1.96)^2(200)^2/(50)^2 = 61.4656 \text{ or } 62$ so you would need to sample $62-40 = 22$ more

b. cost of pilot with the 22 additional sampled $= (62)(\$10) = \$620$

   without pilot:

   $n = (1.96)^2(300)^2/(50)^2 = 138.29 \text{ or } 139 @ \$10 = \$1390$; so savings of $\$1390 - \$620 = \$770$

7.37.

$$s = \sqrt{\frac{\sum (x - \bar{x})^2}{n-1}} = 1.91; \quad n = \frac{z^2 s^2}{e^2} = \frac{(2.33^2)(1.91^2)}{.10^2} = 1,980.5 = 1,981$$

The pilot sample had n = 88 items so the additional required sample size is 1,981 – 88 = 1,893 items.

7.39.

Type	Commercial

Data	Total
Count of Loan Amount	171
Average of Loan Amount	61780.70175
StdDev of Loan Amount	35620.92299

a. $61780.7018 \pm 1.96(35620.9230/\sqrt{171})$; 56,441.6617 ----- 67,119.7419

Because $67,500 is outside the confidence interval the promotion was probably not a success.

b. The margin of error is currently 5339.04; 40% of that is 2135.616

$n = (1.96)^2(35620.9230)^2/(2135.616)^2 = 1,068.75$ or 1,069 – 171 current = 898 additional

c. He would need to change the confidence level. If he wants to cut the sample size by 15% he would need to sample 909 individuals. The confidence level critical value needed to maintain a margin of error of 2,135.6 is z = 1.81. This confidence level is 93%.

7.41.

$0.30 \pm 1.96(\sqrt{[(0.3)(1-0.3)]/400})$; 0.2551 ----- 0.3449

7.43.

$\bar{p} = 55/300 = .1833;$ $0.1833 \pm 1.645(\sqrt{[(0.1833)(1-0.1833)]/300})$; $.1833 \pm .0367$;
.1466 ----------- .2200

7.45.

$\bar{p} = 11/50 = .22;$ $n = \frac{z^2 p(1-p)}{e^2} = \frac{2.33^2(.22)(1-.22)}{.03^2} = 1,035.1 = 1,036$

Additional items needed = 1,036 – 50 = 986

7.47.

a. $n = \dfrac{z^2 p(1-p)}{e^2} = \dfrac{1.96^2(.70)(1-.70)}{.03^2} = 896.37 = 897$

b. $n = \dfrac{z^2 p(1-p)}{e^2} = \dfrac{1.96^2(.30)(1-.30)}{.03^2} = 896.37 = 897$

The sample size requirements are the same since the variation in the population is the same whether the population proportion is .70 or .30.

7.49.

$\bar{p} = 88/300 = 0.2933$

$0.2933 \pm 1.44(\sqrt{[(0.2933)(1-0.2933)]/300}\,);0.2554 \text{-----} 0.3312$

7.51.

$\bar{p} = 22/50 = 0.44$

$n = 1.645^2(0.44)(1-0.44)/(.05)^2 = 266.71 \text{ or } 267 - 50 \text{ pilot sample} = 217 \text{ more}$

7.53.

a. $\bar{p} = 13/130 = .10;\ 0.10 \pm 1.645(\sqrt{[(0.10)(1-0.10)]/130}\,);\ .10 \pm .0433;$

$0.0567 \text{-----} 0.1433$

b. To reduce the margin of error, the buyer can reduce the confidence level or take a larger sample size.

7.55.

a. Use 0.50 for the population proportion to provide a conservatively large sample size.

$n = \dfrac{z^2 p(1-p)}{e^2} = \dfrac{1.96^2(.50)(1-.50)}{.03^2} = 1{,}067.1 = 1{,}068$

b $\bar{p} = .18;\ 0.18 \pm 1.96(\sqrt{[(0.18)(1-0.18)]/1{,}068}\,);\ .18 \pm .0230;\ .1570 \text{-----} .2030$

c. The reason is that the sample size was computed based on the assumption that the population proportion is 0.50. However, the interval was computed using the sample proportion equal to 0.18. This implies that the population is less variable than assumed when the sample size was computed. They would have been wise to have selected a pilot sample to get a feel for what the population proportion might be before taking a sample as large as 1,068.

7.57.

a. $\bar{p}$ $= 643/900 = 0.7144$

$$0.7144 \pm 1.96(\sqrt{[(0.7144)(1-0.7144]/900}) = 0.6849 ----- 0.7439$$

b. If the proportion in the East is 0.75, they should use a different ratio for the West. The interval estimate for the West does not include 0.75.

c. The margin of error is $1.96(\sqrt{[(0.7144)(1-0.7144]/900}) = 0.0295$

d. The options available to reduce the margin of error are to reduce the confidence level or to increase the sample size.

7.59.

a. $0.23 \pm 1.645(\sqrt{[(0.23)(1-0.23]/499})$; $0.1990 ----- 0.2610$

Based on the sample data and with 90% confidence, we believe that the proportion of women who wear athletic shoes to work is between 0.1990 and 0.2610.

b. The point estimate would be 0.23 and the margin of error would be 0.031. Student paragraphs will differ but should contain this information.

c. The margin of error must be changed. We can solve for the new margin of error as follows:

$$e = \sqrt{\frac{z^2(p)(1-p)}{n}} = \sqrt{\frac{1.645^2(.23)(1-.23)}{300}} = 0.04$$

Thus, the margin of error must be increased from 0.031 to 0.04 if the sample size is to be reduced to 300. Note, this assumes that p = 0.23 will hold constant.

7.61.

The margin of error for a proportion is $z(\sqrt{[(\bar{p})(1-\bar{p}]/n})$. The only thing that is going to change is the numerator ($\bar{p}$)(1-$\bar{p}$). The larger the numerator, the larger the margin of error. If this is (0.5)(0.5) you will get a numerator of 0.25. If for example, you had (0.4)(0.6) = 0.24; the further you get from 0.5 the smaller this value gets (i.e. (0.1)(0.9) = 0.09)

7.63.

This is not correct. The average number of miles people commute is a single value. Therefore it has no probability. What the confidence interval is telling you is that if you want to produce all the possible confidence intervals using each possible sample mean from the population, 95% of these intervals would contain the population mean.

7.65.

a. $\bar{x} = \$178$

b. $1.96(27/\sqrt{48}) = 7.6383$

c. $170.3617 ----- 185.6383$

7.67.

Students can select any confidence level. The solution uses 95% confidence.

a. $1,345.78 \pm 1.96(257.90/\sqrt{300}\,)$; $1,316.5959 ----- $1,374.9641

Based on the sample data and with 95% confidence, we believe that the mean value of PC's purchased recently is between $1,316.60 and $1,374.96.

b.   The margin of error could be reduced by increasing the sample size and/or decreasing the confidence level.

c.   We typically think of the smallest and largest values being 3 standard deviations from the mean. Using this assumption the smallest population mean as specified by the confidence interval we get the lowest price to be $1,316.60 – 3(257.90) = $542.90; and the largest price would be $1,316.60 + 3(257.90) = $2,090.30   However, if we assumed that the population mean was at the upper limit of the confidence interval then the smallest value might be $1,374.96 – 3(257.90) = $601.26 and the largest price would be $1,374.96 + 3(257.90) = $2,148.66.

d.   You assume that the underlying distribution is approximately normally distributed.

7.69.

$$n = \frac{z^2\sigma^2}{e^2} = \frac{(1.96^2)7^2}{1^2} = 188.24 = 189$$

7.71.

n $= 1.88^2(0.5)(1 - 0.5)/(.04)^2 = 552.25$ or 553

7.73.

Using Excel's average and stdev functions the mean = 11.9991; standard deviation = 0.2002

$11.9991 \pm 1.96(0.2002/\sqrt{5000}\,)$; 11.9936 ----- 12.0046

The confidence interval does include the 12 ounces. However, it barely includes the 12 ounces and if you consider any weight for the can itself they may actually determine that the mean fluid in the can is not 12 ounces.

7.75.

a. $0.7 \pm 1.96\sqrt{[(0.7)(1-0.7)]/1024}$; 0.6719 ----- 0.7281

b.   One approach would be to use 0.5 for the estimate for the population proportion in the margin of error rather than the sample proportion. Doing this would give us a margin of error of

$1.96(\sqrt{(0.5)(1-0.5)/1024}\,)$; 0.0306

7.77.

a. and b. Student answers for a and b will vary depending upon the sample selected.

c.   The population mean is 63668.5714. At a 90% confidence interval you would expect 90% of your 10 samples which would be 9.

7.79.

a. $\bar{p}$ $= 546/758 = 0.7203$

$0.7203 \pm 1.96 \sqrt{[(0.7203)(1-0.7203)]/758}$; 0.6883 ----- 0.7523

Based on the sample information, with 95% confidence, you can conclude that the proportion of athletes who have gambled on sports is between .69 and .75.

b.   Number of males = 758 – 316 = 442; Number of males who have gambled = 546 – 187 = 359; $\bar{p}$ = 359/442 = 0.8122

$0.8122 \pm 2.575 \sqrt{[(0.8122)(1-0.8122]/442}$; 0.7644 ----- 0.8600

Based on the sample data, with 99% confidence, you can conclude that the proportion of males athletes who have gambled on sports is between .76 and .86.

c. $\bar{p}$ $= 22/442 = 0.0498$

$0.0498 \pm 1.96 \sqrt{[(0.0498)(1-0.0498]/442}$; 0.0295 ----- 0.0701

d.   Student answers will vary but they may want to discuss that a fairly large percent of student athletes say they have gambled and that it seems to be more prevalent in men than in women.

7.81.

a. $\bar{p}$ = 40/64 = 0.625

$0.625 \pm 2.575(\sqrt{[(0.625)(1-0.625]/64}$); 0.4692 ----- 0.7808

Based on these sample data, it appears that an vast majority of people prefer mint-flavored toothpaste so the marketing plan could emphasize that flavor.

b.   Student answers will vary but one approach might be that since 50% is within the range of the confidence interval they may want to produce half mint and half plain.

CHAPTER 8

INTRODUCTION TO HYPOTHESIS TESTING

8.1.

a.

$$H_o : \mu \leq 20$$
$$H_A : \mu > 20$$

b.

$$H_o : \mu = 50$$
$$H_A : \mu \neq 50$$

c.

$$H_o : \mu \geq 35$$
$$H_A : \mu < 35$$

d.

$$H_o : \mu \leq 87$$
$$H_A : \mu > 87$$

e

$$H_o : \mu \leq 6$$
$$H_A : \mu > 6$$

8.3.

If $\bar{x} > 205.2344$ reject H_o
If $\bar{x} \leq 205.2344$ do not reject H_o

$$\bar{x}_\alpha = 200 + 1.645(45/\sqrt{200}); \ \bar{x}_\alpha = 205.2344$$

If $z > 1.645$ reject H_o
If $z \leq 1.645$ do not reject H_o

a. $z = (204.50 - 200)/(45/\sqrt{200}) = 1.41$; Since $1.41 < 1.645$ do not reject H_o
Since $204.5 < 205.2344$ do not reject H_o

b. The alternative hypothesis. The burden of proof is always to on the alternative hypothesis.

8.5.

a. Even though the population standard deviation is unknown, since n = 100 is large, we can use the standard normal distribution to obtain the critical value.

$$\bar{x}_\alpha = 4{,}000 - 1.645(205/\sqrt{100}\,); \;\; \bar{x}_\alpha = 3966.2775$$

If $\bar{x} < 3966.2775$ reject H_o
If $\bar{x} \geq 3966.2775$ do not reject H_o

If p-value < .05, reject H_o
If p-value ≥ .05, do not reject H_o

b. Since 3980 > 3966.2775 do not reject H_o

p-value = $P(z < -.9756) = .50 - .3365 = .1635$

Since p-value = .1635 ≥ 0.05 do not reject H_o

c. The two research hypotheses that could have produced the null and alternative hypotheses are:

The population mean is less than 4,000.
The population mean is at least 4,000.

8.7.

a. Type I error

b. Type II error

c. Type I error

d. Type II error

8.9.

a. p-value = $2 * P(z > 2.36) = 2 * (.50 - .4909) = 0.0182$

b. p-value = $P(z < -1.85) = .50 - .4678 = 0.0322$

c. p-value = $P(z > .84) = .50 - .2995 = 0.2005$

d. p-value = $P(z > -2.06) = .50 + .4803 = 0.9803$

8.11.

a. $4,450 \pm 1.6991(940/\sqrt{30})$; 4,158.4 and 4,741.6

> Decision Rule:
> If $\bar{x} < 4,158.4$ reject H_o
> If $\bar{x} > 4,741.6$ reject H_o
> Otherwise, do not reject

b. Since $\bar{x} = 4,475.6$ is $> 4,158.4$ and $< 4,741.6$, do not reject the null hypothesis

8.13

a.
$$H_o : \mu \geq 30,000$$
$$H_A : \mu < 30,000$$

b. For alpha = .05 and a one tailed , lower tail test, the critical value is z = -1.645

c. $z = \dfrac{\bar{x} - \mu}{\dfrac{s}{\sqrt{n}}} = \dfrac{29,750 - 30,000}{\dfrac{2,500}{\sqrt{100}}} = \dfrac{-250}{250} = -1.00$

Since z = -1.00 > -1.645, do not reject the null hypothesis.

d. A Type II error could have been made since the null hypothesis was not rejected.

8.15.

a. H_o: $\mu \leq 6$ days
H_a: $\mu > 6$ days

b. $z = \dfrac{\bar{x} - \mu}{\dfrac{s}{\sqrt{n}}} = \dfrac{6.65 - 6.00}{\dfrac{1.5}{\sqrt{40}}} = \dfrac{.65}{.2372} = 2.7406$

$z_{.025} = 1.96$

Since 2.7406 > 1.96 reject H_o and conclude that the mail-order business is not achieving its goal.

c. The p-value = $P(z > 2.74)$ = (.50 - .4969) = .0031; Since .0031 < .025, reject the null hypothesis.

d. Must assume that the population standard deviation is 1.5 and that the sample size is set at 40.

$\bar{x}_\alpha = 6.00 + 1.96(1.5/\sqrt{40}) = 6.4649$

If $\bar{x} > 6.4649$, reject the null hypothesis

Otherwise, do not reject.

8.17.

a.
$$H_o : \mu \leq 4,000$$
$$H_A : \mu > 4,000$$

b.   The normality assumption can be examined by looking at a box and whiskers plot although with only 12 values, such a plot may not be conclusive. The box and whiskers plot is shown as

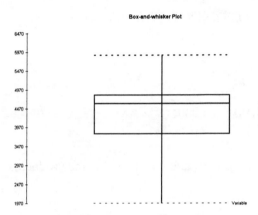

Box-and-whisker Plot

follows:

This plot dies is not all that consistent with what would be expected from a normal distribution, but the small sample size may be a problem. The t-test is fairly robust to the normality assumption so we will continue with it as a method for testing whether the population mean exceeds 4,000.

$\bar{x} = 4,366$ and s = 1000.849

$t = (4,366 - 4,000)/(1000.849/\sqrt{12}) = 1.2668$

The critical t for a one-tailed test with alpha = .05 and 11 degrees of freedom is 1.7959. Since t = 1.2668 < 1.7959, there is insufficient evidence to reject the null hypothesis. Thus, they cannot make the claim that mean life of a component exceeds 4,000 hours. A larger sample would be desirable.

8.19.

a. $H_o:$ $\mu \geq 40$
     $H_a:$ $\mu < 40$

b.   Students can use Excel's AVERAGE and STDEV functions to determine the sample mean and standard deviation.

$\bar{x} = 38.52$ s = 12.9965
$z = (38.52 - 40)/(12.9965/\sqrt{50}) = -0.8052$
$z_{.10} = -1.28$

Since z = -0.8052 > -1.28 do not reject H_o and conclude that the average age is not less than 40.

c.   Type II error. There is very little chance of ever being able to determine if the error has been made as that would require the company to know the age of every customer (ie. know the true population mean.)

8.21.

a. H_o: $\mu = 0.75$ inch
   H_a: $\mu \neq 0.75$ inch

b.   Students can use Excel' AVERAGE and STDEV functions to determine the sample mean and standard deviation.

$\bar{x} = 0.7532$ $s = 0.0337$

$z = (0.7532 - 0.75)/(0.0337/ \sqrt{100}\,) = 0.9496$
$z_{.01/2} = \pm 2.58$

Since $z = 0.9496 < 2.58$, do not reject H_o and conclude that the product is meeting the thickness specifications.

c.   Assuming that the population standard deviation is 0.0337 and that the sample size is n = 100, the following will provide the rule for the manager:

$\bar{x}_\alpha = .75 \pm 2.58(0.0337/ \sqrt{100}\,)$; $\bar{x}_\alpha = 0.75 \pm .0087$; 0.7413 and 0.7587
If $\bar{x} < 0.7413$, reject the null hypothesis
If $\bar{x} > 0.7586$, reject the null hypothesis
Otherwise, do not reject the null hypothesis

d.   Since the sample data did not lead to rejecting the null hypothesis, a Type II error could have been made. Short of measuring every sheet of plywood, there is no way to know whether a Type II error was made since to know that requires that we know the true population mean.

8.23.

a. $z_\alpha = 1.645$; $p + z\left(\sqrt{\dfrac{p(1-p)}{n}} \right) = 0.40 + 1.645\left(\sqrt{\dfrac{0.40(1-0.40)}{150}} \right) = 0.4658$

b. $z_\alpha = -1.28$; $p + z\left(\sqrt{\dfrac{p(1-p)}{n}} \right) = 0.70 - 1.28\left(\sqrt{\dfrac{0.70(1-0.70)}{200}} \right) = 0.6585$

c. $z_\alpha = 1.645$; $p \pm z\left(\sqrt{\dfrac{p(1-p)}{n}} \right) = 0.85 \pm 1.645\left(\sqrt{\dfrac{0.85(1-0.85)}{100}} \right) = 0.7913$ and 0.9087

8.25.

$$z = \frac{\bar{p} - p}{\sqrt{\frac{p(1-p)}{n}}} = \frac{.64 - .70}{\sqrt{\frac{.70(1-.70)}{100}}} = -1.31$$

p-value $= 2*P(z < -1.31) = 2*(0.50 - 0.4049) = 0.1902$

Decision Rule: If p-value $< .07$, reject the null hypothesis
Otherwise, do not reject the null hypothesis

Since $0.1902 > 0.07$, do not reject the null hypothesis.

8.27.

a. $\bar{P}_\alpha = p + z\sqrt{\frac{p(1-p)}{n}} = .24 + 1.645\sqrt{\frac{.24(1-.24)}{100}} ; .3103$

If $p > .3103$, reject the null hypothesis
Otherwise, do not reject

Since $.27 < .3103$, do not reject the null hypothesis

b. $z = \frac{\bar{p} - p}{\sqrt{\frac{p(1-p)}{n}}} = \frac{.27 - .24}{\sqrt{\frac{.24(1-.24)}{100}}} = .7024$

If $z > 1.645$, reject the null hypothesis
Otherwise, do not reject

Since $.7024 < 1.645$, do not reject

8.29.

a. H_o: $p \geq 0.70$
H_a: $p < 0.70$

$\bar{p} = 63/100 = 0.63$

$z = (0.63 - 0.70)/ \sqrt{(0.70)(1 - 0.70)/100} = -1.5275$

Decision Rule:

If $z < -1.645$ reject H_o, otherwise do not reject

Since $z = -1.5275 > -1.645$ do not reject and conclude that the difficulty of the test seems to be appropriate

b. A Type II error in this problem would mean that the proportion of students passing the test is actually less than 0.70 but the sample results lead the administrators to believe that it is actually 70% or better. This would mean that a test that must be too difficult would continue to be administered.

8.31.

a. H_o: $p \geq 0.01$
    H_a: $p < 0.01$
    $\bar{p}$ $= 6/800 = 0.0075$

    $z = (0.0075 - 0.01)/ \sqrt{(0.01)(1-0.01)/800} = -0.7107$

Decision Rule:

If z < -1.645 reject H_o, otherwise do not reject

Since z = -0.7107 > -1.645 do not reject and conclude that the percentage of lost luggage is 1% or more.

b. $0.0075 \pm 1.96(\sqrt{(0.0075)(1-0.0075)/800}\ )$; $.0075 \pm .006$; 0.0015 ---------- 0.0135

8.33.

a. H_o: $p \leq 0.30$
    H_a: $p > 0.30$

b. $\bar{p}$ $= 66/200 = .33$

$$z = \frac{\bar{p} - p}{\sqrt{\dfrac{p(1-p)}{n}}} = \frac{.33 - .30}{\sqrt{\dfrac{.30(1-.30)}{200}}} = .9258$$

Since z = .9258 < 1.28, do not reject the null hypothesis.

Based upon these sample data, the claim made by the University administrators is not supported since there is not enough evidence to reject the null hypothesis.

8.35.

a. H_o: $p \leq 0.50$
    H_a: $p > 0.50$

b. $\bar{p}$ $= .67$

$$z = \frac{\bar{p} - p}{\sqrt{\dfrac{p(1-p)}{n}}} = \frac{.67 - .50}{\sqrt{\dfrac{.50(1-.50)}{300}}} = 5.889$$

Since z = 5.889 > 1.645, reject the null hypothesis.
Since z = 5.889, the p-value as approximately zero.

8.37.

a. H_o: $p \le 0.80$
    H_a: $p > 0.80$

b.

Count of Call Answered < 5 minutes	
Call Answered < 5 minutes	Total
$\ge$ 5 minutes	7
< 5 minutes	63
Grand Total	70

$\bar{p}$ $= 63/70 = 0.90$

$z = (0.9 - 0.80)/\sqrt{(0.80)(1-0.80)/100} = 2.50$

Decision Rule:

If z > 1.28 reject H_o, otherwise do not reject

Since z = 2.5 > 1.28 reject and conclude that the proportion of calls answered within 5 minutes is greater than 80%

c. $0.9 \pm 1.645(\sqrt{(0.90)(1-0.90)/70}$; 0.8410 ----- 0.9590

Because the sample proportion 0.80 is not between 0.8410 and 0.9590 this would be consistent with the conclusion that the proportion exceeds .80

8.39.

a. As long as the sample size is sufficiently large such that np and n(1-p) are both greater than 5, you are justified in using the standard normal when estimating a population proportion. In this case, we have .2537(67) > 5 and (1-.2537)(5) > 5 so we are okay.

b. Use Excel's Pivot Table – use percent of rows option and group handicaps as shown below. Note there are 67 golfers with handicaps of 20 or more.

Count of Club Status	Club Status		
USGA Handicap	Copy	Original	Grand Total
0-19.99	27.31%	72.69%	100.00%
20.00-39.98	25.37%	74.63%	100.00%
Grand Total	26.87%	73.13%	100.00%

H_o: $p \geq 0.40$
H_a: $p < 0.40$

$z = (0.2537 - 0.40) / \sqrt{(0.40)(1 - 0.40)/67}$ = -2.4444

Decision Rule:

If $z < -1.645$ reject H_o, otherwise do not reject

Since $z = -2.4444 < -1.645$ reject H_o and conclude that the "knock-offs" is less than 40% in the high handicap players.

8.41.

a. $\overline{x}_{\alpha U} = 1.2 + 1.645(0.5/\sqrt{60})$; $\overline{x}_{\alpha U} = 1.3062$
$\overline{x}_{\alpha L} = 1.2 - 1.645(0.5/\sqrt{60})$; $\overline{x}_{\alpha L} = 1.0938$

Beta = $P[(1.0938 - 1.25)/(0.5/\sqrt{60}) < z < (1.3062 - 1.25)/(0.5/\sqrt{60})] = P(-2.42 < z < 0.87) =$ $0.4922 + 0.3078 = 0.80$

b.   Power of the test = $1 - 0.80 = 0.20$

c. The power increases, and beta decreases, as the sample size increases. We could also increase alpha since alpha and beta are inversely related.

d. If $\overline{x} > 1.3062$ or $\overline{x} < 1.0938$ reject H_o
Otherwise, do not reject H_o

Since $\overline{x} = 1.23$ then $1.0398 < 1.23 < 1.3062$ do not reject H_o

8.43.

a. $\overline{x}_\alpha = 4,350 - 1.645(200/\sqrt{100})$; $\overline{x}_\alpha = 4,317.10$

$P(z > (4317.10 - 4345)/(200/\sqrt{100})$; $= P(z > -1.40) = 0.5 + 0.4192 = 0.9192$

b. Power = $1 -$ Beta $= 1 - 0.9192 = 0.0808$

c. The power increases, and beta decreases, as the sample size increases. We could also increase alpha since alpha and beta are inversely related.

d. If $\bar{x} < 4{,}317.10$, reject the null hypothesis
Otherwise, do not reject the null hypothesis

Since $\bar{x} = 4{,}337.5 > 4{,}317.1$, do not reject the null hypothesis.

8.45.

$$H_o: \mu \geq 18.0$$
$$H_a: \mu < 18.0$$

a. $\bar{x}_\alpha = 18 - 1.88(2.4/\sqrt{60})$; $\bar{x}_\alpha = 17.4175$

$P(z > (17.4175 - 16.5)/ (2.4/\sqrt{60})) = P(z > 2.96) = 0.5 - 0.4985 = 0.0015$

b. $P(z > (17.4175 - 17.3)/ (2.4/\sqrt{60})) = P(z > .38) = .50 - .1480 = .352$

c. The probability of a Type II error would be smaller.

d. The probabilities of Type II errors would be reduced for larger sample sizes.

8.47.

a. $\bar{x}_{\alpha U} = 24 + 1.96(0.65/\sqrt{16})$; $\bar{x}_{\alpha U} = 24.3185$
$\bar{x}_{\alpha L} = 24 - 1.96(0.65/\sqrt{16})$; $\bar{x}_{\alpha L} = 23.6815$

$P(z < (23.6815 - 24.5)/ (0.65/\sqrt{16})) + P(z > (24.3185 - 24.5)/ (0.65/\sqrt{16}))$
$= P(z < -5.04) + P(z > -1.12) = 0.0 + (0.5 + 0.3686) = 0.8686$

b. There is an 87% chance that you would reject the null hypothesis if the population mean actually equals 24.5. I would not make any changes.

8.49.
A Type I error occurs when the decision maker rejects a true null hypothesis. A Type II error occurs when a false null hypothesis is accepted. Business examples of these two types of error will vary.

8.51.
The critical value is the cut-off point or demarcation between acceptance and rejection regions in a hypothesis test. It may be expressed in terms of a value of the sample mean or as a z value.

8.53.
The probability of committing a Type I error is denoted by alpha (α) and is usually specified by the decision maker. The choice of alpha reflects the cost of making a Type I error. If the cost is high, alpha will be set at a lower value than if the cost of committing the error is low.

8.55.
You use the population proportion to calculate the standard error. If you were testing that the population proportion were 0 then the standard error would be 0. This would make it impossible to make a logical calculation.

8.57.

    a. H_o: $\mu \leq 100$
    H_a: $\mu > 100$

$$z = (114 - 100)/(50/\sqrt{50}) = 1.98$$
$$z_{.10} = 1.28$$

Since $z = 1.98 > 1.28$ reject H_o and conclude that the sample data do refute the director's claim.

b. $1.28 = (\bar{x} - 100)/50/\sqrt{50}$; $\bar{x} = 109.051$

8.59.

    a. H_o: $\mu \geq 20$
    H_a: $\mu < 20$

$$z = (19.62 - 20)/(0.5/\sqrt{70}) = -6.3586$$
$$z_{.\alpha} = -1.645$$

Since $-6.3586 < -1.645$ reject H_o and conclude that the average is less than 20 and under filling is occurring

b. $P(z < (19.62 - 20)/(0.5/\sqrt{70})) = P(z < -6.36) = .50 - .50 = 0$; this is called the p-value. There is essentially no chance of this happening if the population mean is 20 pounds.

c.   From the warehouse manager's perspective a Type II error might be the most important since he would not want to pay for light boxes of cherries. He does not want to go on thinking that that the boxes average 20 or more pounds when they don't.

d.   From the grower's perspective, he does not want to be falsely accused so the Type I error would be more important.

8.61.

    a. H_o: $\mu \leq 10$
    H_a: $\mu > 10$

Reject H_o if $z > 1.645$; otherwise do not reject H_o

$$z = (10.32 - 10)/(2.9/\sqrt{200}) = 1.56$$

Since $1.56 < 1.645$ do not reject H_o and conclude that the average fill is less than or equal to 10 gallon

b. $10.32 \pm 1.96(2.9/\sqrt{200})$; 9.9181 ----- 10.7219

8.63.

a. H_o: $\mu \le 3$
    H_a: $\mu > 3$ research from Union perspective

A Type I error would mean that we reject the personnel manager's statement when it was in fact true. A Type II error means that we would accept the personnel manager's statement even though it is not true and the true overtime hours exceeds three on average.

b. Decision Rule:

If $z > 2.33$ reject H_o, otherwise do not reject H_o

c. $z = (3.15 - 3)/(1.2/\sqrt{250}) = 1.98$

Since $z = 1.98 < 2.33$ do not reject H_o and conclude that overtime is actually less than or equal to 3 hours per week.

8.65.

a. H_o: $\mu \ge 40$
    H_a: $\mu < 40$

b. $z = (38.98 - 40)/(5.3/\sqrt{300}) = -3.3334$

Decision Rule:

If $z < -1.28$ reject H_o, otherwise do not reject

Since $z = -3.3334 < -1.28$ reject H_o and conclude that the average rating is less than 40

c. A Type I error would cause you to believe that your rating was less than 40 when it was actually greater than 40. The cost of this would be to advertise to improve your rating when you didn't actually need to. A Type II error would cause you to accept that your rating was above 40 when in fact it was less than 40. This would mean that you would not try to improve your image when in fact you needed to. In this case it would seem the Type II error would be more serious. You wouldn't improve your image when in fact you needed to.

8.67.

a. H_o: $\mu \le 417$
    H_a: $\mu > 417$

b. This test is one tailed since we will reject the null hypothesis only if the sample mean is larger than a critical level for the specified alpha level.

c. $z = (433 - 417)/(200/\sqrt{100}) = 0.80$
    Decision Rule:
    If $z > 1.645$ reject H_o, otherwise do not reject

Since $z = 0.80 < 1.645$ do not reject H_o and conclude that the average health-care benefits is less than or equal to \$417

8.69.

a. H_o: $\mu \leq 3$
H_a: $\mu > 3$

$t = (3.15 - 3.0)/(.2/\sqrt{20}) = 3.35$

If $t > 1.3277$, reject the null hypothesis
Otherwise, do not reject the null hypothesis

Since $t = 3.35 > 1.3277$, reject and conclude that the mean exceeds 3 tries.

b.   The group would likely be most interested in avoiding a Type II error (believing that the product will light within three tries if it actually will take more than 3 tries on average.

8.71.

a. H_o: $\mu \geq 10$
H_a: $\mu < 10$

b.   Decision Rule:
If $z < -1.28$ reject H_o, otherwise do not reject H_o

c. $z = (9.5 - 10)/(3/\sqrt{70}) = -1.3944$
Since $z = -1.3944 < -1.28$ reject H_o and conclude that the average savings is less than 10 ounces.

d.   Since the company rejected the null hypothesis, it might have committed a Type I error, or rejected a true null hypothesis. If the claim is actually true, the company may miss out on a good advertising approach.

8.73.

a. H_o: $\mu \leq \$3$
H_a: $\mu > \$3$

b.   Decision Rule:

If $z < -1.645$ reject H_o, otherwise do not reject H_o

Students can use Excel's AVERAGE and STDEV functions to determine the sample mean and standard deviation.
$\bar{x} = 3.4232$ $s = 4.8992$

$z = (3.4232 - 3)/(4.8992/\sqrt{50}) = .6108$

Since $z = .6108 < 1.645$ do not reject H_o and conclude that the average savings is less than or equal to $3 which does not support Inland's advertising campaign

c.   The consumer group would be more concerned with a Type I error because they would not want to tell consumers they will save more than $3 when in fact they will not. The company would be more concerned with a Type II error because they would not want consumers thinking they would not save at least $3 when in fact that savings are $3 or more.

8.75.

a. $H_o: p \le 0.30$
    $H_a: p > 0.30$

Decision Rule:
If z > 1.28 reject H_o, otherwise do not reject

$$\bar{p} = 74/200 = 0.37$$

$$z = (0.37 - 0.30)/\sqrt{(0.30)(1 - 0.30)/200} = 2.1602$$

Since 2.1602 > 1.28 reject H_o and conclude that greater than 30% of coupons are being redeemed.

b. $0.37 \pm 1.645\sqrt{(0.37)(1 - 0.37)/200}$; .37 $\pm$ .0562 ; 0.3138 ----- 0.4262

(0.3138)($0.10)(5000) ----- (0.4262)($0.10)(5000); $156.90 ----- $213.10

8.77.

$H_o: \mu \ge 25,000$
$H_a: \mu < 25,000$

Decision Rule:
If z < - 1.645 reject H_o, otherwise do not reject H_o

Students can use Excel's AVERAGE and SDEV functions to determine the sample average and sample standard deviation

$\bar{x} = 24,117.0606$ s = 2,747.3981
$z = (24,117.0606 - 25,000)/(2,747.3981/\sqrt{33}) = -1.8461$

Since z = -1.8461 < -1.645 reject H_o and conclude that the average white-collar 1998 earnings in U.S. cities is less than $25,000

8.79.

Count of Make	
Make	Total
Ericsson	52.00%
Motorola	4.00%
Nokia	42.00%
Philips	2.00%
(blank)	0.00%
Grand Total	100.00%

H_o: $p \leq 0.35$
H_a: $p > 0.35$

$$z = (0.42 - 0.35)/\sqrt{(0.35)(1-0.35)/50} = 1.0377$$

Reject H_o if $z > 1.645$ otherwise do not reject H_o

Since $1.0377 < 1.645$ do not reject H_o and conclude that the proportion of cell phone owners using the Nokia brand is no greater than 35%.

CHAPTER 9

ESTIMATION AND HYPOTHESIS TESTING FOR TWO POPULATION PARAMETERS

9.1.

a. $(65 - 50) \pm 1.645 \sqrt{(64/150) + (36/100}$; 13.541 ----- 16.459; This indicated the range, at the 90% confidence level, of the difference between the two population means.

b. $(65 - 50) \pm 2.33 \sqrt{(64/150) + (36/100}$; 12.933 ----- 17.067; This indicated the range, at the 98% confidence level, of the difference between the two population means.

c. The advantage is you are less likely to make the error of not including the true difference in means in your estimate. The disadvantage is that there is a larger error margin since the interval is wider.

9.3.

a. The formula for the confidence interval is: $\overline{d} \pm t_{\alpha/2} \dfrac{s_d}{\sqrt{n}}$

b. 95% confidence interval: $344 \pm 2.0739 \dfrac{34}{\sqrt{23}}$; 329.297 -------358.703. If many random samples of this size were taken and intervals constructed, 95% of them would contain the true population mean.

c. A 90% confidence interval: $344 \pm 1.7171 \dfrac{34}{\sqrt{23}}$; 331.827 -------356.173. If many random samples of this size were taken and intervals constructed, 90% of them would contain the true population mean.

d. A lower confidence level gives a more precise, narrower, interval. However, the chances of an interval not containing the true population mean are increased.

9.5.

a. $(2,456 - 2,460) \pm 1.645 \sqrt{(32^2/36) + (80^2/45)}$; -25.49 ----- 17.49

b. $(2,456 - 2,460) \pm 2.33 \sqrt{(32^2/36) + (80^2/45)}$; -34.439 ----- 26.439

9.7.

a. $s_p = \sqrt{\dfrac{(14-1)2.5^2 + (14-1)1.8^2}{14+14-2}} = 2.1783$

$(17.2 - 15.9) \pm 1.7056(2.1783)\sqrt{(1/14)+(1/14)}$; -0.1043 ----- 2.7043; No because the interval contains the value 0 you cannot say that there is a difference setup time for the two additives.

b. No because again you cannot say that there is a difference in the setup time for the two additives.

9.9.

Manufacturing Plant	Data	Total
Boise	Average of Dollar Claim Amount	268.4358974
	StdDev of Dollar Claim Amount	50.89551041
	Count of Dollar Claim Amount	78
Atlanta	Average of Dollar Claim Amount	277.3333333
	StdDev of Dollar Claim Amount	62.64299584
	Count of Dollar Claim Amount	24

$$s_p = \sqrt{\dfrac{(78-1)50.8955^2 + (24-1)62.6430^2}{78+24-2}} = 53.8249$$

$(277.3333 - 268.4359) \pm 2.3642(53.8249)\sqrt{(1/78)+(1/24)}$; -20.8069 ----- 38.6011

No, since the confidence interval includes the value of 0 you cannot conclude that there is a difference between the two plants. Because of the sample sizes you must use Excel's TINV function.

9.11.

a.

Credit Card Balances - Male	
Mean	746.512931
Standard Error	19.33632279
Median	738.5
Mode	1018
Standard Deviation	294.5220941
Count	232

Credit Card Account Balance - Female	
Mean	778.1323529
Standard Error	35.80014705
Median	737
Mode	600
Standard Deviation	295.2155754
Count	68

Since the sample size for both male and female are greater than 30 determine the confidence interval using:

$$(778.1324 - 746.5129) \pm 1.96\sqrt{\frac{87,152.2505}{68} + \frac{86,743.2639}{232}} \; ; \; -48.13 \text{ ----- } 111.37$$

b. Student answers will vary but should include comments that based upon this confidence interval it cannot be concluded that there is a difference between male and female credit card balances because the interval includes the value 0.

9.13.

Since the dataset has SAT and ACT scores together for both city and suburb you must separate out the ACT scores and the SAT scores. The SAT scores are the larger numbers. You must also remove all -99 data.

a.

Average of SAT Suburb	946.9545
Average of SAT City	854.7143

Point average of differences = 946.9545 – 854.7143 = 94.2402; no, because the only number you have is 94.2402

b.

	SAT - City	SAT - Suburb
Average	854.7143	946.9545
Standard Deviation	81.5	61.1

Count of SAT Suburb	22
Count of SAT City	21

$$s_p = \sqrt{\frac{(21-1)81.5^2 + (22-1)61.1^2}{21+22-2}} = 71.8$$

$(946.9545 - 854.7143) \pm 2.0195(71.8)\sqrt{(1/22) + (1/21)}$; 48 ----- 136.5; based on this confidence interval you could not conclude that it might be as high as 150 because this interval does not contain the value 150. Excel's TINV function is used to find the t value.

c. $(946.9545 - 854.7143) \pm 1.3025(71.8)\sqrt{(1/22) + (1/21)}$; 63.7 ----- 120.8 it has reduced the width of the confidence interval because you have reduced the confidence level and increased the probability the interval will not contain the population mean.

9.15.

a. $(41.5 - 39) \pm 1.96\sqrt{(25/200) + (12.96/200)}$; 1.6461 ----- 3.3539; yes because the interval does not contain the value 0 which would indicated no difference.

b.   Company A:

-1.645 = $(\bar{x} - 41.5)/(3.6/\sqrt{200})$; $\bar{x} = 41.0813$

Company B:

-1.645 = $(\bar{x} - 39)/(5/\sqrt{200})$; $\bar{x} = 38.4184$

9.17.

The hypotheses are: H_0: $\mu_1 = \mu_2$
                             H_A: $\mu_1 \neq \mu_2$

Reject H_0 if t < -1.7341 or t > 1.7341.

$$s_p = \sqrt{\frac{(10-1)2.898^2 + (10-1)2.703^2}{10+10-2}} = 2.802$$

$$t = \frac{(19.53 - 19.59) - 0}{2.802\sqrt{\frac{1}{10} + \frac{1}{10}}} = -.0479: \text{ Do not reject } H_0.$$

9.19.

a.   The hypotheses are: H_0: $\mu_1 \geq \mu_2$
H_A: $\mu_1 < \mu_2$

$$s_p = \sqrt{\frac{(16-1)32^2 + (25-1)30^2}{16+25-2}} = 30.785$$

Using Excel's TINV function, the test for the hypothesis about equality of means becomes:

Reject H_0 if t < -1.6849

b.

$$t = \frac{(2{,}456 - 2{,}460) - 0}{30.785\sqrt{\frac{1}{16} + \frac{1}{25}}} = -.4058: \text{ Do not reject } H_0.$$

9.21.

a.   The hypotheses are: H_0: $\mu_1 = \mu_2$
H_A: $\mu_1 \neq \mu_2$

$$df = 125 + 120 - 2 = 143$$

The Decision Rule is: If z > 1.96 or z < -1.96 reject H_0, otherwise do not reject H_0

b.

$$z = \frac{(130 - 105) - 0}{\sqrt{\frac{31^2}{125} + \frac{38^2}{120}}} = 5.630$$

Since 5.630 > 1.96 reject H_0

9.23.

a.   If the difference is Sample 1 – Sample 2, the hypotheses are:

$$H_0:\ \mu_d \geq 0$$
$$H_A:\ \mu_d < 0$$

b.   The differences are:

Sample 1	Sample 2	Difference
4.4	3.7	0.7
2.7	3.5	-0.8
1	4	-3
3.5	4.9	-1.4
2.8	3.1	-0.3
2.6	4.2	-1.6
2.4	5.2	-2.8
2	4.4	-2.4
2.8	4.3	-1.5

Using these values find: $\bar{d} = -1.456$

$s_d = 1.2$

The Decision Rule is: Reject if $t < -1.3968$. Using Equation 9-18:

$$t = \frac{-1.456 - 0}{\dfrac{1.2}{\sqrt{9}}} = -3.64$$

Since $-3.64 < -1.3968$, reject H_0.

Using the p-value approach, the calculated value of -3.64 is less than -3.3544, the smallest value in the t table (adjusting for a lower tail test). Therefore, the p-value $< 0.01 < 0.10 = \alpha$ and the null hypothesis is rejected.

c.   The 90% confidence interval is:

$$-1.456 \pm 1.8595(1.2/\sqrt{9} = -2.1998 \ \text{-----} \ -.7122$$

This confidence interval does not contain 0. Therefore, a value of 0 is not a plausible value for μ_d as was concluded by the hypothesis test.

9.25.

$$H_0:\ \mu_F - \mu_M \leq 1$$
$$H_A:\ \mu_F - \mu_M > 1$$

$$df = 60 + 60 - 2 = 118$$

$$z = \frac{(14.65 - 13.24) - 1}{\sqrt{\dfrac{1.2^2}{60} + \dfrac{1.56^2}{60}}} = 1.6136$$

Since $1.6136 < 1.645$ do not reject H_0 and conclude that the difference is not greater than 1.

9.27.

a. H_0: $\mu_N - \mu_O \leq 0$
    H_A: $\mu_N - \mu_O > 0$

If z > 1.28 reject H_0, otherwise do not reject H_0

$$z = \frac{(288 - 279) - 0}{\sqrt{\dfrac{16.23^2}{35} + \dfrac{15.91^2}{32}}} = 2.2907$$

Since 2.2907 > 1.28 reject H_0 and conclude that the new cartridge will result in a longer lasting product.

b. 90% confidence interval:

$$(288 - 279) \pm 1.645 \sqrt{\frac{16.23^2}{35} + \frac{15.91^2}{32}}$$ 2.537 ----- 15.463; yes this is consistent with the results in

part a since the interval does not contain 0. Thus, 0 is not a plausible value for the difference between the two means.

9.29.

a. Ho: $\mu_B - \mu_A \leq 0.35$
    Ha: $\mu_B - \mu_A > 0.35$

df = 20 + 20 − 2 = 38

If t > 2.4286 reject H_0, otherwise do not reject H_0

Students can use Excel's data analysis tool to conduct the t-test assuming equal variances

t-Test: Two-Sample Assuming Equal Variances

	Brochure B	Brochure A
Mean	11.881	9.3225
Variance	75.56685158	50.943725
Observations	20	20
Pooled Variance	63.25528829	
Hypothesized Mean Difference	0.35	
df	38	
t Stat	**0.878110123**	
P(T<=t) one-tail	0.192701262	
t Critical one-tail	**2.428569132**	
P(T<=t) two-tail	0.385402525	
t Critical two-tail	2.711567504	

Since 0.8781 < 2.4286 do not reject H_0 and conclude that the difference in sales does not make up for the difference in the cost of the brochures

b. You have to assume independent samples, and that each population has a normal distribution.

9.31.

a. Ho: $\mu_D - \mu_S \leq 0$
    Ha: $\mu_D - \mu_S > 0$

    df $= 15 + 21 - 2 = 34$

    If t > 1.6909 reject H_o, otherwise do not reject H_o

    Students can use Excel's data analysis tool to conduct the t-test assuming equal variances

t-Test: Two-Sample Assuming Equal Variances

	Day Care	Stay Home
Mean	15.12380952	13.02
Variance	3.988904762	4.181714286
Observations	21	15
Pooled Variance	4.068296919	
Hypothesized Mean Difference	0	
df	34	
t Stat	3.085347764	
P(T<=t) one-tail	0.002012187	
t Critical one-tail	1.690923455	
P(T<=t) two-tail	0.004024374	
t Critical two-tail	2.032243174	

Since 3.0853 > 1.6909 reject H_0 and conclude that the children who have been in day care have a higher mean time in interactive situations than the stay-at-home children.

b. Since you rejected the null hypothesis the error that could occur is that you rejected a true null hypothesis which is a Type I error.

9.33.

a. This is a paired difference test problem:
    H_0: $\mu_d = 0$
    H_A: $\mu_d \neq 0$

t-Test: Paired Two Sample for Means

	Physician	Monitor
Mean	120.2	120.7333333
Variance	127.3142857	63.78095238
Observations	15	15
Pearson Correlation	0.043437863	
Hypothesized Mean Difference	0	
df	14	
T Stat	-0.152581759	
P(T<=t) one-tail	0.440452661	
T Critical one-tail	1.76130925	
P(T<=t) two-tail	0.880905322	

T Critical two-tail	2.144788596

Decision Rule:

If t > 2.1448 or t < -2.1448 reject H_0, otherwise do not reject H_0

Since −0.1526 > -2.1448 do not reject H_0 and conclude that there is no difference between the Sunbeam monitor and the physician.

b. Yes, you might be concerned that the machine always reads to high or reads to low. A solution to this would be to develop a confidence interval.

c.

Difference	
Mean	-0.533333333
Standard Error	3.495393794
Median	0
Mode	#N/A
Standard Deviation	13.53760195
Sample Variance	183.2666667
Kurtosis	-0.566797952
Skewness	-0.008323213
Range	47
Minimum	-24
Maximum	23
Sum	-8
Count	15
Confidence Level(95.0%)	**7.496880747**

95% confidence interval:

-0.5333 $\pm$ 7.4969; -8.0302 ----- 6.9636; yes since this includes the value 0

d. Sometimes different conclusions can be reached. Since a paired difference test removes one source of variation, it can determine significant differences when independent samples will not.

9.35.

Decision Rule:

If z > 1.645 or z < -1.645 reject H_0, otherwise do not reject H_0

$\bar{p}$ = (87+80)/(200+150) = 0.4771

$\bar{p}_1$ = 87/200 = 0.435
$\bar{p}_2$ = 80/150 = 0.5333

z = [(0.435 – 0.533)-0.0]/ $\sqrt{(0.435(1-0.435)/200) + (0.533(1-0.533)/150)]}$ = -1.82

Since z = -1.82 < -1.645 reject H_0, and conclude that the difference in the population proportions is not equal to 0.05.

9.37.

a. Decision Rule:

If z > 2.05 reject H_0, otherwise do not reject H_0

$\bar{p}$ = (30+24)/(60+80) = 0.3857

$\bar{p}_1$ = 30/60 = 0.5
$\bar{p}_2$ = 24/80 = 0.3

z = [(0.5 – 0.3)-0]/ $\sqrt{(0.3857)(1-.3857)[(1/60) + (1/80)]}$ = 2.4059

Since z = 2.4059 > 2.05 reject H_0, and conclude there is a difference in the population proportions.

b. Looking in the standard normal table we see area associated with z = 2.41 is .4920. So the p-value is .00800 which is less than α = .02 and again reject H_0.

9.39.

a. $n_1 \bar{p}_1 = 0.62(745) = 462 > 5$; $n_1(1 - \bar{p}_1) = 745(1 - 0.62) = 283 > 5$
    $n_2 \bar{p}_2 = 0.49(455) = 223 > 5$; $n_2(1 - \bar{p}_2) = 455(1 - 0.49) = 232 > 5$ Since both are greater than 5, the normal approximation is appropriate.

b. H_0: $p_1 - p_2 = 0$
    H_A: $p_1 - p_2 \neq 0$

    Decision Rule:
    If $z > 1.96$ or $z < -1.96$ reject H_0, otherwise do not reject H_0

    $\bar{p} = (462 + 223)/(745 + 455) = 0.5708$

    $z = [(0.62 - 0.49) - 0] / \sqrt{(0.5708)(1 - .5708)[(1/745) + (1/455)]} = 4.414$

    Since $z = 4.414 > 1.96$ reject H_0, and conclude that there is a difference in the proportion of homes that watch a national news broadcast.

9.41.

$n_1 \bar{p}_1 = 123 > 5$; $n_1(1 - \bar{p}_1) = 473 > 5$

$n_2 \bar{p}_2 = 181 > 5$; $n_2(1 - \bar{p}_2) = 223 > 5$

$\bar{p}_{\geq 2} = 123/596 = 0.2064$
$\bar{p}_{<2} = 181/404 = 0.4480$

$(0.4480 - 0.2064) \pm 1.96 \sqrt{\dfrac{(0.4480)(1 - 0.4480)}{404} + \dfrac{(0.2064)(1 - 0.2064)}{596}}$; 0.1832 --- 0.3000

This indicates that a larger proportion of the passengers traveling with less than two bags are in favor of the airline limiting carry-on bags to one. No, this does not surprise me.

9.43.

H_0: Response to question 1 is independent of the response to question 2.
H_A: Response to question 1 is not independent of the response to question 2.
$\alpha = .05$

The expected frequencies are calculated by multiplying the row total by the column total and then dividing by the grand total. For instance for the YES, YES cell, we get $(17 \times 17)/30 = 7.37$

Observed Frequencies			
Question 1	Question 2		
	Yes	No	Total
Yes	6	11	17
No	7	6	13
Total	13	17	30

Expected Frequencies			
Question 1	Question 2		
	Yes	No	Total
Yes	7.37	9.63	17
No	5.63	7.37	13
Total	13	17	30

The calculated chi-square is:

$$\chi^2 = \sum\sum \frac{(o-e)^2}{e} = \frac{(6-7.37)^2}{7.37} + \frac{(11-9.63)^2}{9.63} + \frac{(7-5.63)^2}{5.63} + \frac{(6-7.37)^2}{7.37} = 1.037$$

The critical value of the chi-square test statistic for $\alpha = 0.05$ and $(2-1)(2-1) = 1$ d.f. is 3.8415. Since the calculated value of $1.0377 < 3.8415$, we do not reject the null hypothesis and conclude that the response to question 1 is independent of the response to question 2.

9.45.

a. H_0: Data indicate the proportion of bad calls is the same for each official.
    H_A: Data indicate the proportion of bad calls is not the same for each official.

One approach is to test the hypothesis using the standard normal distribution procedure introduced in Chapter 9. Assume and $\alpha = 0.05$.

The test statistic based on the normal distribution (as an approximation) is

$$z = \frac{\dfrac{51}{514} - \dfrac{38}{556}}{\sqrt{\dfrac{89}{1070}\left(\dfrac{981}{1070}\right)\left(\dfrac{1}{514} + \dfrac{1}{556}\right)}} = 1.83$$

The critical value for a two-sided hypothesis test is 1.96. Since the critical value of 1.83 is smaller than 1.96), the null hypothesis is not rejected. We cannot conclude that the proportion of bad calls differs between the two officials.

b. H_0: Data indicate the proportion of bad calls is the same for each official.
H_A: Data indicate the proportion of bad calls is not the same for each official.
$\alpha = 0.05$

Observed Frequencies			
Call	Official		
	A	B	Total
Good	463	518	981
Bad	51	38	89
Total	514	556	1070

Expected Frequencies			
Call	Official		
	A	B	Total
Good	471.25	509.75	981
Bad	42.75	46.25	89
Total	514	556	1070

$$\chi^2 = \sum\sum \frac{(o-e)^2}{e} = \frac{(463-471.25)^2}{471.25} + \frac{(518-509.75)^2}{509.75} + \frac{(51-42.75)^2}{42.75} + \frac{(38-46.25)^2}{46.25} = 3.339$$

The calculated chi-square test statistic is $0.144 + 0.133 + 1.591 + 1.471 = 3.339$. The critical value of the chi-square test statistic for $\alpha = 0.05$ and 1 d.f. is 3.8415. Since the calculated value of $3.339 < 3.8415$, we do not reject the null hypothesis and conclude that the data indicate the proportion of bad calls is the same for each official.

c. The chi-square test statistic developed in part b is (within the limits of round off error) the square of the z test statistic developed in part a, i.e., $\chi^2 = 3.339 \approx (1.83)^2 = z^2$

9.47.

a. H_0: Type of car owned is independent of union membership.
H_A: Type of car owned is not independent of union membership.
$\alpha = 0.05$

Observed Frequencies			
	Union Membership		
Car	Yes	No	Total
Domestic	155	470	625
Foreign	40	325	365
Total	195	795	990

Expected Frequencies			
	Union Membership		
Car	Yes	No	Total
Domestic	123.1061	501.8939	625
Foreign	71.8939	293.1061	365
Total	195	795	990

The calculated chi-square test statistic is $8.2630 + 2.0268 + 14.1489 + 3.4705$ $= 27.9092$. The critical value of the chi-square test statistic for $\alpha = 0.05$ and 1 d.f. is 3.8415. Since the calculated value of $27.9092 > 3.8415$, we reject the null hypothesis and conclude that type of car owned is not independent of union membership.

b.   The p-value can be found using Excel's CHITEST function or Excel's CHIDIST function. The form of the CHITEST function is =CHITEST(Actual_range, Expected_range). The function returns the p-value. The p-value for this test is 0.0000001271442. Small p-values provide strong evidence to reject the null hypothesis. The form of the CHIDIST function is =CHIDIST(Chi-Square, Degrees of freedom) or CHIDIST(27.9092, 1) which gives .0000000127, the same value as the CHITEST function

9.49.

a. H_0: The number of citations issued and the gender of the driver are independent.
H_A: The number of citations issued and the gender of the driver are not independent.
$\alpha = 0.05$

Observed Frequencies

Citations Issued	Male	Female	Total
0	240	160	400
1	80	40	120
2	32	18	50
3	11	9	20
Over 3	5	4	9
Total	368	231	599

Expected Frequencies

Citations Issued	Male	Female	Total
0	245.7429	154.2571	400
1	73.72287	46.27713	120
2	30.71786	19.28214	50
3	12.28715	7.712855	20
Over 3	5.529215	3.470785	9
Total	368	231	599

The critical value of the test statistic with alpha = 0.05 and $(r-1)(c-1) = (5-1)(2-1) = 4$ d.f. is 9.4877. If the calculated chi-square value is greater than 9.4877, then reject the null hypothesis. Otherwise do not reject.

$$\chi^2 = \sum\sum \frac{(o-e)^2}{e} = \frac{(240-245.74)^2}{245.74} + \frac{(160-154.26)^2}{154.26} + \cdots + \frac{(4-3.47)^2}{3.47} = 2.356$$

The calculated chi-square value is 2.3536. Because the calculated value is less than the critical value for alpha = .05 and $(r-1)(c-1) = (5-1)(2-1) = 4$ degrees of freedom = 9.4877 we do not reject the null hypothesis, and conclude that the two variables, gender of driver and citations issued are independent. Note that one of the expected frequency cells have values less than 5. However, since we did not reject the null hypothesis there is no chance that we have committed a Type I Error. Therefore, it is not necessary for us to group categories and rerun the test.

b. The probability of being female is $P(F) = 231/599$. The probability of having more than 1 citation issued is $P(\text{Citations} > 1) = (32+18+11+9+5+4)/599$, or, $79/599$. The probability of more than one citation given that the driver is female is $(18 + 9 + 4)/231$, or $31/231$. Therefore, the probability that the driver is female given that more than one citation was issued is

$$P(F \mid \text{Citations} > 1) = \frac{P(F \cap \text{Citations} > 1)}{P(\text{Citations} > 1)} = \frac{(231/599)(31/231)}{79/599} = 0.39241.$$

9.51.

a. H_0: Strike Length Tolerance is independent of Time with Company
    H_A: Strike Length Tolerance is not independent of Time with Company.
    $\alpha = .05$

Observed Frequencies:

Time with Company	Under 1 Week	1-4 Weeks	Over 4 Weeks	Total
Under 1 Year	23	6	3	**32**
1-2 Years	19	15	8	**42**
2-5 Years	20	23	19	**62**
5-10 Years	4	21	29	**54**
Over 10 Years	2	5	18	**25**
Total	**68**	**70**	**77**	**215**

Expected Frequencies:

Time with Company	Under 1 Week	1-4 Weeks	Over 4 Weeks	
Under 1 Year	10.12093023	10.418605	11.46046512	32
1-2 Years	13.28372093	13.674419	15.04186047	42
2-5 Years	19.60930233	20.186047	22.20465116	62
5-10 Years	17.07906977	17.581395	19.33953488	54
Over 10 Years	7.906976744	8.1395349	8.953488372	25
	68	70	77	215

Decision Rule:

If $\chi^2 > 15.5073$ reject H_0, otherwise do not reject H_0.

$$\chi^2 = \sum\sum \frac{(o-e)^2}{e} = \frac{(23-10.12)^2}{10.12} + \frac{(6-10.42)^2}{10.42} + \cdots + \frac{(18-8.95)^2}{8.95} = 61.5267$$

Since $61.5267 > 15.5073$ reject H_0 and conclude that strike length tolerance is not independent of time with company.

b. H_o: $\pi_{\le 5} \le \pi_{>10}$ or $\pi_{<5} - \pi_{>10} \le 0$
     H_a: $\pi_{\le 5} > \pi_{>10}$ or $\pi_{<5} - \pi_{>10} > 0$

You can use the standard normal distribution test for two population proportions introduced in Chapter 9 to answer this question.

$$\bar{p} = (74+23)/(136+25) = 0.6025$$

$p_{<5\ yr\ \&\ >1\ week} = 74/136 = 0.5441$
$p_{>10\ yr\ \&\ >1\ week} = 23/25 = 0.92$

$$z = (0.5441 - 0.92)/\sqrt{(0.6025)(1-0.6025)(1/136+1/25)} = -3.53$$

Note, the sample information directly supports the null hypothesis. The difference in proportions is in the lower tail of the sampling distribution. There is no chance that the difference in proportions can be in the rejection region. Therefore, the p-value = is essentially 1.0

Because of the large p-value do not reject the null hypothesis; do not conclude that the proportion of employees that would be willing to stay out on strike for at least a week if a strike were called is larger for the first group.

9.53.

H_0: Shift and type of accident are independent.
H_A: Shift and type of accident are not independent.
$\alpha = 0.01$

		Observed Frequencies		
		Accident Type		
		Behavior Based	Equipment Related	Total
Shift	Day	270	80	350
	Swing	190	25	215
	Graveyard	96	24	120
	Total	556	129	685

		Expected Frequencies		
		Accident Type		
		Behavior Based	Equipment Related	Total
Shift	Day	284.0876	65.9124	350
	Swing	174.5109	40.4891	215
	Graveyard	97.4015	22.5985	120
	Total	556	129	685

$$\chi^2 = \sum\sum \frac{(o-e)^2}{e} = \frac{(270-284.09)^2}{284.09} + \frac{(80-65.91)^2}{65.91} + \cdots + \frac{(24-22.60)^2}{22.60} = 11.1167$$

The critical value of the test statistic for $\alpha = 0.01$ and 2 d.f. is 9.2104. Since the calculated test statistic = 11.1167 is greater than 9.21035, reject the null hypothesis and conclude that the type of accident and the shift are not independent. There is a relationship between the two.

9.55.

H_0: Account balance and model of washer purchased are independent.
H_A: Account balance and model of washer purchased are not independent.
$\alpha = 0.02$

		Observed Frequencies				
		Washer Model Purchased				
		Standard	Deluxe	Superior	XLT	Total
Credit Balance	Under $200	10	16	40	5	71
	$200-800	8	12	24	15	59
	Over $800	16	12	16	30	74
	Total	34	40	80	50	204

		Expected Frequencies				
		Washer Model Purchased				
		Standard	Deluxe	Superior	XLT	Total
Credit Balance	Under $200	11.8333	13.9216	27.8431	17.4020	71
	$200-800	9.8333	11.5686	23.1373	14.4608	59
	Over $800	12.3333	14.5098	29.0196	18.1373	74
	Total	34	40	80	50	204

$$\chi^2 = \sum\sum \frac{(o-e)^2}{e} = \frac{(10-11.83)^2}{11.83} + \frac{(16-13.92)^2}{13.92} + \cdots + \frac{(30-18.13)^2}{18.13} = 30.2753$$

The p-value for a chi-square value of 30.2753 and 6 d.f. is 0.00003484. Since the p-value is less than $\alpha = 0.02$, we reject the null hypothesis and conclude that account balance and model of washer purchased are not independent.

c. H_0: Type of warranty problem and shift are independent.
H_A: The of warranty problem and shift are not independent

Expected Frequencies — Plant

Type of Complaint	Day	Swing	Graveyard	Total
Corrosion	23.8636364	9.545454545	1.59090909	35
Cracked Lens	30.6818182	12.27272727	2.04545455	45
Wiring	15.6818182	6.272727273	1.04545455	23
Sound	4.77272727	1.909090909	0.31818182	7
Total	75	30	5	110

Since several of the expected frequencies are less than 5 we need to combine swing and graveyard and combine wiring and sound.

Observed Frequencies: — Shift

Type of Complaint	Day	Swing and Graveyard	Total
Corrosion	23	12	35
Cracked Lens	32	13	45
Wiring & Sound	20	10	30
Total	75	35	110

Expected Frequencies: — Shift

Type of Complaint	Day	Swing and Graveyard	Total
Corrosion	23.86364	11.13636364	35
Cracked Lens	30.68182	14.31818182	45
Wiring & Sound	20.45455	9.545454545	30
Total	75	35	110

Chi-Square Calculation — Shift

Type of Complaint	Day	Swing and Graveyard
Corrosion	0.031255	0.066975881
Cracked Lens	0.056633	0.121356421
Wiring & Sound	0.010101	0.021645022

Chi-Square Critical	5.991476
Chi-Square Calculated	0.307967
p-value	0.857286

Since $0.307967 < 5.9915$ do not reject H_0 and conclude that type of warranty problem and shift are independent.

9.57.

H_0: $\mu_W - \mu_O = 0$

H_A: $\mu_W - \mu_O \neq 0$

df = 65 + 85 − 2 = 148

If p-value is less than 0.05 reject H_0, otherwise do not reject H_0

$$z = \frac{(58740 - 54900) - 0}{\sqrt{\dfrac{24800^2}{65} + \dfrac{27920^2}{85}}} = 0.8895$$

Using the standard normal table, for z = .8895 the p-value = 0.3738 > 0.05 so do not reject H_0 and conclude that there is no difference in the average whole life insurance coverage for clients in Wisconsin and Ohio.

9.59.

$n_1 \bar{p}_1 = 144 > 5$; $n_1(1 - \bar{p}_1) = 56 > 5$

$n_2 \bar{p}_2 = 402 > 5$; $n_2(1 - \bar{p}_2) = 98 > 5$

H_0: $p_A - p_N = 0$

H_A: $p_A - p_N \neq 0$

Decision Rule:

If z > 1.96 or z < -1.96 reject H_0, otherwise do not reject H_0

$\bar{p}_A = 144/200 = 0.72$

$\bar{p}_N = 402/500 = 0.804$

$\bar{p} = (144+402)/(200+500) = 0.78$

$z = [(0.72 - 0.804)-0]/\sqrt{(.78)(1 - .78)[(1/200) + (1/500)]} = -2.4237$

Since −2.4237 < -1.96 reject H_0 and conclude that there is a difference in graduation rates.

9.61.

$n_1 \bar{p}_1 = 62 > 5$; $n_1(1 - \bar{p}_1) = 38 > 5$

$n_2 \bar{p}_2 = 36 > 5$; $n_2(1 - \bar{p}_2) = 39 > 5$

H_0: $p_{ci} - p_{co} \leq 0$
H_A: $p_{ci} - p_{co} > 0$

Decision Rule:
If z > 1.28 reject H_o, otherwise to not reject H_o

$\bar{p}_{ci} = 62/100 = 0.62$
$\bar{p}_{co} = 36/75 = 0.48$

$\bar{p} = (62+36)/(100+75) = 0.56$

$z = [(0.62 - 0.48)\text{-}0] / \sqrt{(0.56)(1 - 0.56)[(1/100) + (1/75)]} = 1.8464$

Since 1.8464 > 1.28 reject Ho and conclude that there the proportion of city residents who favor this proposal is greater than the proportion of county residents who favor the proposal.

9.63.

a.   You must assume that the populations are normally distributed.
b. H_0: $\mu_A - \mu_B \leq 0$
      H_A: $\mu_A - \mu_B > 0$

Note, no alpha level was specified. Students should select alpha. The solution below assumes that an alpha = .05 is used. If a different alpha level is selected, the critical t value will change. However, for any reasonable alpha level the same general conclusion will be reached.

$df = 7 + 7 - 2 = 12$

Using Excel's average and stdev functions students can determine the sample mean and sample standard deviation of each of the samples

Before:	After:
Mean = 1991.571	Mean = 2137.286
St. Dev. = 620.5395	St. Dev. = 578.6161

If t > 1.7823 reject H_0, otherwise do not reject H_0

$$S_p = \sqrt{\frac{(7-1)620.5395^2 + (7-1)578.6161^2}{7+7-2}} = 599.9441$$

$t = (2137.286 - 1991.571)/(599.9441 \sqrt{(1/7) + (1/7)}) = 0.4544$

Since 0.4544 < 1.7823 do not reject H_0 and conclude that there is no difference in average sales before and after the ad.

9.65.

a. $n_m \bar{p}_m = (81/280)(280) = 81 > 5$; $n_m(1 - \bar{p}_m) = 280(1 - 0.2893) = 199 > 5$

   $n_w \bar{p}_w = (74/280)(280) = 74 > 5$; $n_w(1 - \bar{p}_w) = 280(1 - 0.2643) = 206 > 5$

b. H_0: $p_m - p_w = 0$

   H_A: $p_m - p_w \neq 0$

   Decision Rule:

   If $z > 1.645$ or $z < -1.645$ reject H_0, otherwise to not reject H_0

   $\bar{p}_m = 81/280 = 0.2893$

   $\bar{p}_w = 74/280 = 0.2643$

   $\bar{p} = (81 + 74)/(280 + 280) = 0.2768$

   $z = [(0.2893 - 0.2643) - 0]/\sqrt{(0.2768)(1 - 0.2768)[(1/280) + (1/280)]} = 0.6611$

   Since $0.6611 < 1.645$ do not reject H_0 and conclude that there is no difference between men and women.

9.67.

a. H_o: Gross Income and Taxes Paid are independent
   H_a: Gross Income and Taxes Paid are not independent
   $\alpha = .05$

Observed Frequency:

Gross **Income**	$0 - $3,000	$3,001 - $5,000	$5,001 - $10,000	Over $10,000	Total
		Taxes			
$0 - $10,000	50	0	0	0	50
$10,001 - $20,000	42	30	0	0	72
$20,001 - $40,000	40	65	33	28	166
Over $40,000	28	52	47	39	166
Total	160	147	80	67	454

Expected Frequency

Gross **Income**	$0 - $3,000	$3,001 - $5,000	$5,001 - $10,000	Over $10,000	Total
		Taxes			
$0 - $10,000	17.62	16.19	8.81	7.38	50
$10,001 - $20,000	25.37	23.31	12.69	10.63	72
$20,001 - $40,000	58.50	53.75	29.25	24.50	166
Over $40,000	58.50	53.75	29.25	24.50	166
Total	160	147	80	67	454

Chi-Square Calculation

Gross **Income**	$0 - $3,000	$3,001 - $5,000	$5,001 - $10,000	Over $10,000
		Taxes		
$0 - $10,000	59.50	16.19	8.81	7.38
$10,001 - $20,000	10.89	1.92	12.69	10.63
$20,001 - $40,000	5.85	2.36	0.48	0.50
Over $40,000	15.90	0.06	10.77	8.59

Chi-Square Critical	16.9190
Chi-Square Calculated	172.50
p-value	1.85764E-32

Since 172.50 > 16.9190 reject Ho and conclude that Taxable Income and Taxes Paid are not independent

b. There is a relationship between income earned and taxes paid. As income increases the amount of taxes paid also increases.

9.69.

a. $n_1 \bar{p}_1 = 11 > 5$; $n_1(1 - \bar{p}_1) = 79 > 5$

$n_2 \bar{p}_2 = 15 > 5$; $n_2(1 - \bar{p}_2) = 75 > 5$

H_0: $p_T - p_B = 0$
H_A: $p_T - p_B \neq 0$

Decision Rule:
If p-value is < 0.05 reject H_0, otherwise to not reject H_0

$\bar{p}_T = 11/90 = 0.122$
$\bar{p}_B = 15/90 = 0.167$

$\bar{p} = (11+15)/(90+90) = 0.1444$

$z = [(0.167 - 0.122)-0] / \sqrt{(0.1444)(1 - 0.1444)[(1/90) + (1/90)]} = 0.86$

p-value = $(0.5 - 0.3051)2 = 0.3898 > 0.05$ so do not reject H_0 and conclude that there will be no difference in the proportion of people returning the tune-up coupon and those returning the brake work coupon.

b. A Type I error would be if there is no difference but we concluded there was a difference. A Type II error would be if there is a difference but we concluded there was not a difference. The relative cost of a Type I error would be that you might send out more of one coupon than the other and would lose business because of not enough people receiving the coupon. The cost of a Type II error would be that you sent out equal numbers of each coupon when one coupon would be redeemed more frequently. A type II error could have been committed in this problem.

9.71.

a. H_0: $\mu_{BB} - \mu_S \leq 0$
H_A: $\mu_{BB} - \mu_S > 0$

b. If $z > 2.33$ reject H_0, otherwise do not reject H_0

$z = \dfrac{(653 - 691) - 0}{\sqrt{\dfrac{112^2}{50} + \dfrac{105^2}{50}}} = -1.7502$

Since $-1.7502 < 2.33$ do not reject H_0 and conclude that the Bounce Back backboards is not as durable, on the average, as the Swoosh Company backboards.

c. In this case it would not change the data since we are testing the alternative of greater than but based on this sample our calculated value is negative so our decision will not changed.

9.73.

H_0: $\mu_M - \mu_F = 0$
H_A: $\mu_M - \mu_F \neq 0$

Credit Card Account Balance – Female	
Mean	778.1323529
Standard Error	35.80014705
Median	737
Mode	600
Standard Deviation	295.2155754
Count	68

Credit Card Balances – Male	
Mean	746.512931
Standard Error	19.33632279
Median	738.5
Mode	1018
Standard Deviation	294.5220941
Count	232

$$df = 68 + 232 - 2 = 298$$

If z > 1.96 or z < -1.96 reject H_0, otherwise do not reject H_0

$$z = \frac{(778.1324 - 746.5129) - 0}{\sqrt{\dfrac{295.2156^2}{68} + \dfrac{294.5221^2}{232}}} = 0.7771$$

Since 0.7771 < 1.96 do not reject H_0 and conclude that there is no difference between the mean credit card balances between female and male customers.

9.75.

a. $n_1 \bar{p}_1 = 26 > 5$; $n_1(1-\bar{p}_1) = 34 > 5$
     $n_2 \bar{p}_2 = 46 > 5$; $n_2(1-\bar{p}_2) = 34 > 5$

  H_0: $p_U - p_G \leq 0$
  H_A: $p_U - p_G > 0$

  Decision Rule:
  If $z > 1.645$ reject H_0, otherwise do not reject H_0

  $\bar{p}_G = 26/60 = 0.4333$
  $\bar{p}_U = 46/80 = 0.575$

  $\bar{p} = (26+46)/(60+80) = 0.5143$

  $z = [(0.575 - 0.4333)-0]/\sqrt{(0.5143)(1-0.5143)[(1/60)+(1/80)]} = 1.66$

  Since $1.66 > 1.645$ reject H_0 and conclude that the percentage of undergraduates who will attend graduation does exceed the percentage of graduate students who will attend graduation.

b.   Using the sample as a point estimate you could recommend that they reserve $0.4333(500) = 216.65$ or 217 seats for the graduates and $0.575(2000) = 1,150$ seats for the undergraduates. This is a point estimate. Confidence intervals can be determined to find the minimum and maximum number of seats to reserve for both types of students. We use 95% confidence intervals here.

  $0.4333 \pm 1.96 \sqrt{\dfrac{0.4333(0.5667)}{60}} = 0.4333 \pm 0.1254 = 0.3079 \text{----- } 0.5587$
  Graduate minimum/maximum number of seats $= 500(0.3079) = 154$ to $500(0.5587) = 279$

  $0.575 \pm 1.96 \sqrt{\dfrac{0.575(0.425)}{80}} = 0.575 \pm 0.1083 = 0.4667 \text{----- } 0.6833$
  Undergraduate minimum/maximum number of seats $= 2000(0.4667) = 934$ to $2000(0.6833) = 1,367$

CHAPTER 10

HYPOTHESIS TESTS FOR ONE AND TWO POPULATION VARIANCES

10.1.

    a. $\chi^2 = 16.919$

    b. $\chi^2 = 32.8523$

    c. $\chi^2 = 16.919$

10.3.

    a. $\chi^2 = \dfrac{(n-1)s^2}{\sigma^2} = \dfrac{(13-1)4.5^2}{12} = 20.25$

       If $\chi^2 = > 18.5493$, reject the null hypothesis

       Since $\chi^2 = 20.25 > 18.5493$, reject the null hypothesis

    b. $\chi^2 = \dfrac{(n-1)s^2}{\sigma^2} = \dfrac{(30-1)21}{12} = 50.75$

       If $\chi^2 = > 42.5569$, reject the null hypothesis

       Since $\chi^2 = 50.75 > 42.5569$, reject the null hypothesis

10.5.

    a. $\chi^2 = [(20-1)(20)^2]/300 = 25.3333$

       If $\chi^2 > 30.1435$, reject H_o, otherwise do not reject H_o

       Since $25.3333 < 30.1435$ do not reject Ho and conclude that the population variance is less than 300

    b. $\chi^2 = [(15-1)(367)]/300 = 17.1267$

       Decision Rule:
       If $\chi^2 > 21.0641$, reject H_o, otherwise do not reject H_o

       Since $17.1267 < 21.0641$ do not reject Ho

10.7.

a. H_o: $\sigma^2 \leq 2{,}025$
    H_a: $\sigma^2 > 2{,}025$

b. $\chi^2 = \dfrac{(n-1)s^2}{\sigma^2} = \dfrac{(20-1)3{,}000}{2{,}025} = 28.1481$

If $\chi^2 > 27.2036$, reject the null hypothesis

Since $28.1481 > 27.2036$, reject the null hypothesis and conclude the variance is greater than 2,025.

10.9.

a. H_o: $\mu = 0$
    H_a: $\mu \neq 0$

Using Excel's AVERAGE and STDEV functions

$\overline{x} = 1.6667$ $s = 4.9787$

$t = (1.6667 - 0)/(4.9787/\sqrt{12}) = 1.1597$
$t_{.05/2} = \pm 2.2010$

Since $t = 1.1597 < 2.2010$ do not reject H_o and conclude that the average arrival time is on time. Because this is a t-distribution you must assume that the underlying population is normally distributed.

b. H_o: $\sigma^2 \leq 4$
    H_a: $\sigma^2 > 4$

$\chi^2 = [(12\text{-}1)(4.9787)^2]/4 = 68.1655$

Decision Rule:
If $\chi^2 > 19.6752$, reject H_o, otherwise do not reject H_o

Since $68.1655 > 19.6752$ do reject Ho and conclude that the population variance is greater than 4

c. From part a and b airlines should conclude that on the average the planes arrive on time but with variance greater than 4

10.11.

H_o: $\mu \le 14.25$
H_a: $\mu > 14.25$

Using Excel's AVERAGE and STDEV functions

$\bar{x} = 15.8373$ s = 7.1624

z = $(15.8373 - 14.25)/(7.1624/\sqrt{166}) = 2.8553$
$z_\alpha = 1.645$

Decision Rule:
If z > 1.645 reject H_o, otherwise do not reject H_o

Since 2.8553 > 1.645 reject H_o and conclude that the mean dollar contribution is greater than 14.25

H_o: $\sigma^2 \ge 41.4736$
H_a: $\sigma^2 < 41.4736$

$\chi^2 = [(166-1)(7.1625)^2]/41.4736 = 204.0993$

Decision Rule:

If $\chi^2 < 136.2992$ (found using CHIINV in Excel with df=165), reject H_o, otherwise do not reject H_o

Since 204.0936 > 136.2992 do not reject Ho and conclude that the population variance is greater than or equal 41.4736. Thus, the standard deviation has not been reduced.

10.13.

a. Using the F distribution in Appendix H, F = 3.619

b. Using the F distribution in Appendix H, F = 3.106

c. Using the F distribution in Appendix H, F = 3.051

10.15.

a.   Using Appendix H: If the calculated F > 2.865, reject H_0, otherwise do not reject H_0

b.   F = $230^2/210^2 = 1.1995$

Since 1.1995 < 2.865 do not reject H_0

10.17.

a.   Using Appendix H: If the calculated F >3.858, reject H_0, otherwise do not reject H_0

b.   F = 345.7/745.2 = 0.46390

Since 0.46390 < 3.858 do not reject H_0

10.19.

$H_0: \sigma_d^2 = \sigma_w^2$

$H_A: \sigma_d^2 \neq \sigma_w^2$

Using Appendix H with $D_1 = 12$ and $D_2 = 8$: If the calculated $F > 3.284$, reject H_0, otherwise do not reject H_0

$F = 2^2/1.2^2 = 2.7778$

Since $2.7778 < 3.284$ do not reject H_0 and conclude that there is no difference in the standard deviations

10.21.

$s_A = 7.1375 \qquad s_B = 8.6929$

$H_0: \sigma_A^2 = \sigma_B^2$

$H_A: \sigma_A^2 \neq \sigma_B^2$

Using Appendix H with D_1 and D_2 both equal to 19: If the calculated $F > 3.0274$, reject H_0, otherwise do not reject H_0

$F = 8.6929^2/7.1375^2 = 1.4833$

Since $1.4833 < 3.0274$ do not reject H_0 and conclude that there is no difference in the standard deviation of dollars returned between the two brochures.

Excel or Minitab could be used to find the exact p-value = .199. Using the Appendix, the F value is less than the F for $\alpha = .05$ of 2.168. So the p-value must be greater than .05.

10.23.

$H_0: \sigma_c^2 \leq \sigma_n^2$

$H_A: \sigma_c^2 > \sigma_n^2$

Using Appendix H with $D_1 = 20$ and $D_2 = 16$: If the calculated $F > 2.276$, reject H_0, otherwise do not reject H_0

$F = 3.45^2/2.87^2 = 1.445$

Since $1.445 < 2.276$ do not reject H_0 and conclude there is not sufficient evidence to conclude the new ribbon is more consistent than the current ribbon.

10.25.

a. $H_0: \sigma_A^2 \le \sigma_T^2$
$H_A: \sigma_A^2 > \sigma_T^2$

If the calculated $F > 2.534$, reject H_0, otherwise do not reject H_0

$F = 0.202^2/0.14^2 = 2.0818$

Since $2.0818 < 2.534$ do not reject H_0 and conclude that the Trenton plant is not less variable than the Atlanta plant.

b.   You would have rejected a true null hypothesis, which is a Type I, error. You could decrease the alpha level to decrease the probability of a Type I error or you could increase the sample sizes.

10.27.

$H_o: \sigma_A^2 = \sigma_Z^2$
$H_a: \sigma_A^2 \ne \sigma_Z^2$

$\alpha = 0.05$ $n_A = 24$ $n_Z = 32$

$$F = = \frac{41.3^2}{37.5^2} = 1.2129$$

If $F > 2.231$, reject the null hypothesis

Since $1.2129 < 2.231$, do not reject the null hypothesis and conclude there is no evidence of differences in the variability of the effect time for the 2 drugs.

10.29

$H_o: \sigma^2 \le 0.90^2$
$H_a: \sigma^2 > 0.90^2$

$\alpha = 0.05$ $n = 27$ $df = 27 - 1 = 26$

$$\chi^2 = \frac{(n-1)s^2}{\sigma^2} = \frac{(27-1)1.15^2}{0.90^2} = 42.451$$

If $\chi^2 > 38.885$, reject the null hypothesis

Since $42.451 > 38.885$, reject the null hypothesis and conclude that there has been an increase in the variability of the toffee cooking temperatures.

10.31

H_o: $\sigma^2_1 \leq \sigma^2_2$

H_a: $\sigma^2_1 > \sigma^2_2$

$\alpha = 0.10$ $n_1 = 29$ $n_2 = 33$

$$F = = \frac{0.0061^2}{0.00593^2} = 1.0582$$

If F > 1.599, reject the null hypothesis

Since 1.0582 < 1.599, do not reject the null hypothesis and conclude that boards cut with Saw 1 are not significantly more variable than those cut with Saw 2.

10.33

H_o: $\sigma^2 \geq 29.2^2$

H_a: $\sigma^2 < 29.2^2$

$\alpha = 0.05$ $n = 45$ $df = 45 - 1 = 44$

$$\chi^2 = \frac{(n-1)s^2}{\sigma^2} = \frac{(45-1)22.8^2}{29.2^2} = 26.826$$

Since the table in the book does not contain df = 44, use Excel's CHIINV function to find the critical value. If $\chi^2 < 29.788$, reject the null hypothesis

Since 26.826 < 29.788, reject the null hypothesis and conclude that the variation in the number of daily checks cleared has been reduced.

10.35

H_o: $\sigma^2_N \geq \sigma^2_C$

H_a: $\sigma^2_N < \sigma^2_C$

$\alpha = 0.05$ $n_N = 43$ $n_C = 34$

$$F = = \frac{6.1^2}{4.2^2} = 2.109$$

If F > 1.748, reject the null hypothesis

Since 2.109 > 1.748, reject the null hypothesis and conclude that the new supplement significantly reduces variation in chicken weights.

10.37.

H_o: $\sigma^2 \leq 3,900^2$

H_a: $\sigma^2 > 3,900^2$

$\alpha = 0.10$ $s = 3,934.5589$ $n = 200$ $df = 200 - 1 = 199$

$$\chi^2 = \frac{(n-1)s^2}{\sigma^2} = \frac{(200-1)3,934.5589^2}{3,900^2} = 202.5424$$

Since the table in the book does not contain df = 199, use Excel's CHIINV function to find the critical value. If $\chi^2 > 224.9568$, reject the null hypothesis

Since 202.5424 < 224.9568, do not reject the null hypothesis and conclude that the manager is correct in the consistency of the current routes so he does not need to reroute trucks.

10.39.

a. H_o: $\sigma^2_{1998} \leq \sigma^2_{1997}$

H_a: $\sigma^2_{1998} > \sigma^2_{1997}$

$\alpha = 0.05$ $n_{1997} = 4$ $s_{1997} = 3,306.946$ $n_{1998} = 4$ $s_{1998} = 3,949.3898$

$$F = = \frac{3,949.3898^2}{3,306.946^2} = 1.4263$$

If $F > 9.2766$, reject the null hypothesis

Since 1.4263 < 9.2766, do not reject the null hypothesis and conclude that February sales for discounters are not less variable in 1997 than in 1998.

b. H_o: $\sigma^2_{Dept} \leq \sigma^2_{Misc}$

H_a: $\sigma^2_{Dept} > \sigma^2_{Misc}$

$\alpha = 0.05$ $n_{Dept} = 8$ $s_{Dept} = 608.0617$ $n_{amisc} = 6$ $s_{Misc} = 571.5125$

$$F = = \frac{606.0617^2}{571.5125^2} = 1.132$$

If $F > 4.8759$, reject the null hypothesis

Since 1.132 < 4.8759, do not reject the null hypothesis and conclude that 1998 Miscellaneous sales are not less variable than 1998 Department store sales.

10.41

a.

H_o: $\sigma^2_H \geq 2.5^2$	H_o: $\sigma^2_{SD} \geq 2.5^2$	H_o: $\sigma^2_B \geq 2.5^2$
H_a: $\sigma^2_H < 2.5^2$	H_a: $\sigma^2_{SD} < 2.5^2$	H_a: $\sigma^2_B < 2.5^2$

H_o: $\sigma^2_R \geq 2.5^2$	H_o: $\sigma^2_{TW} \geq 2.5^2$
H_a: $\sigma^2_R < 2.5^2$	H_a: $\sigma^2_{TW} < 2.5^2$

$\alpha = 0.10$ n = 25 for each courier   df = 25 − 1 = 24

$s_H = 2.2361$ $s_{SD} = 2.4503$ $s_B = 1.7295$ $s_R = 2.2696$ $s_{TW} = 1.8271$

$$\chi^2_H = \frac{(n-1)s^2}{\sigma^2} = \frac{(25-1)2.2361^2}{2.5^2} = 19.2005 > 15.6587 \text{ Do not reject}$$

$$\chi^2_{SD} = \frac{(n-1)s^2}{\sigma^2} = \frac{(25-1)2.4503^2}{2.5^2} = 23.0552 > 15.6587 \text{ Do not reject}$$

$$\chi^2_B = \frac{(n-1)s^2}{\sigma^2} = \frac{(25-1)1.7295^2}{2.5^2} = 11.4861 < 15.6587 \text{ Reject}$$

$$\chi^2_R = \frac{(n-1)s^2}{\sigma^2} = \frac{(25-1)2.2696^2}{2.5^2} = 19.7802 > 15.6587 \text{ Do not reject}$$

$$\chi^2_{TW} = \frac{(n-1)s^2}{\sigma^2} = \frac{(25-1)1.8271^2}{2.5^2} = 12.8191 < 15.6587 \text{ Reject}$$

If $\chi^2 < 15.6587$, reject the null hypothesis

Based upon the above results conclude that only Blazer and Time Warp couriers are meeting the requirements of Solontactics that the standard deviation of delivery times be less than 2.5 minutes

b. H_o: $\sigma^2_{TW} \leq \sigma^2_B$
     H_a: $\sigma^2_{TW} > \sigma^2_B$

$\alpha = 0.10$ $n_{TW} = 25$ $s_{TW} = 1.8271$ $n_B = 25$ $s_B = 1.7295$

$$F = = \frac{1.8271^2}{1.7295^2} = 1.1160$$

If F > 1.7019, reject the null hypothesis

Since 1.1160 < 1.7019, do not reject the null hypothesis and conclude that Blazers delivery times are not less variable than TimeWarp's delivery times.

10.43

a. H_o: $\sigma^2 \geq 10^2$
    H_a: $\sigma^2 < 10^2$

$\alpha = 0.05$ n = 48   df = 48 – 1 = 47

$$\chi^2 = \frac{(n-1)s^2}{\sigma^2} = \frac{(48-1)7.8764^2}{10^2} = 29.1577$$

Since the table in the book does not contain df = 47, use Excel's CHIINV function to find the critical value. If $\chi^2 < 32.2676$, reject the null hypothesis

Since 29.1577 < 32.2676, reject the null hypothesis and conclude that the variability of internet sales as measured by the standard deviation is less than $10.

b. H_o: $\sigma^2_{P/C} = \sigma^2_{IS}$
    H_a: $\sigma^2_{P/C} \neq \sigma^2_{IS}$

$\alpha = 0.05$ $n_{P/C} = 46$ $s_{P/C} = 6.7291$ $n_{IS} = 44$ $s_{IS} = 6.9933$

$$F = = \frac{6.9933^2}{6.7291^2} = 1.0801$$

If F > 1.8163, reject the null hypothesis

Since 1.0801 < 1.8163, do not reject the null hypothesis and conclude that there is no difference in the variability of sales between the two sales channels.

10.45.

a. H_o: $\sigma^2_B \leq 1.5^2$
    H_a: $\sigma^2_B > 1.5^2$

$\alpha = 0.05$ n = 44   df = 44 – 1 = 43

$$\chi^2 = \frac{(n-1)s^2}{\sigma^2} = \frac{(44-1)1.5353^2}{1.5^2} = 45.0477$$

Since the table in the book does not contain df = 43, use Excel's CHIINV function to find the critical value. If $\chi^2 > 59.3035$, reject the null hypothesis

Since 45.0477 < 59.3035, do not reject the null hypothesis and conclude that the variability in computer lab usage as measured by the standard deviation is not more than 1.5 minutes.

b. H_o: $\sigma^2_{AS} \le \sigma^2_E$
    H_a: $\sigma^2_{AS} > \sigma^2_E$

$\alpha = 0.05$ $\qquad$ $n_E = 57$ $\qquad$ $s_E = 1.2589$ $\qquad$ $n_{AS} = 54$ $\qquad$ $s_{AS} = 1.3806$

$$F = = \frac{1.3806^2}{1.2589^2} = 1.2027$$

If $F > 1.5653$, reject the null hypothesis

Since $1.2027 < 1.5653$, do not reject the null hypothesis and conclude that that the variability in usage for Arts and Sciences is not greater than that for Engineering students.

CHAPTER 11

ANALYSIS OF VARIANCE

11.1.

a. $df_B + df_W = df_T$ ➔ $df_B = df_T - df_W = 246 - 240 = 6 = k - 1$ ➔ $k = 7 =$ number of populations.

b.

Source	SS	df	MS	F
Between Samples	1,745	6	290.833	14.667
Within Samples	4,759	240	19.829	
Total	6,504	246		

c. H_0: $\mu_1 = \mu_2 = \mu_3 = \mu_4 = \mu_5 = \mu_6 = \mu_7$
H_A: At least two population means are different

d. F critical = 2.8778 (Minitab); from text table use $F_{6,200} = 2.893$

Since $14.667 > 2.8778$ reject H_o and conclude that at least two populations means are different.

11.3.

a. H_0: $\mu_1 = \mu_2 = \mu_3$
H_A: At least two population means are different

b. Using Equation 11-4, SSB = 53.444.
c. Using Equation 11-6, SSW = 33.592.
d.

ANOVA					
Source of Variation	SS	df	MS	F	P-value
Between Groups	53.44444	2	26.72222	11.93252	0.000792
Within Groups	33.59167	15	2.239444		
Total	87.03611	17			

F critical = 3.682

Since $11.93 > 3.682$ reject H_0 and conclude that at least two populations means are different.

11.5.

a.

ANOVA

Source of Variation	SS	df	MS	F
Between Groups	55.6	2	27.8	7.419635
Within Groups	101.164	27	3.746815	
Total	156.764	29		

F-critical = 3.3541; since 7.4196 > 3.3541 reject H_0 and conclude that at least two populations means are different.

b.   F-critical = 5.4881; since 7.4196 > 5.4881 reject H_0 and conclude that at least two populations means are different.

11.7.

The overall mean is $(111 + 126 + 100 + 105)/4 = 110.5$
$SSB = 20(111 - 110.5)^2 + 20(126 - 110.5)^2 + 20(100 - 110.5)^2 + 20(105 - 110.5)^2 = 7620$

ANOVA

Source of Variation	SS	df	MS	F
Between Groups	7620	3	2540	16.08667
Within Groups	12000	76	157.8947	
Total	19620	79		

Decision Rule:

If F > 2.7249 reject H_0, otherwise do not reject H_0
Since 16.08667 > 2.7249 reject H_o and conclude that at least two populations means are different

11.9.

a. H_0: $\mu_1 = \mu_2 = \mu_3$
     H_A: At least two population means are different

Anova: Single Factor

SUMMARY

Groups	Count	Sum	Average	Variance
Car 1	8	111	13.8750	0.3821
Car 2	6	77.6	12.9333	0.1347
Car 3	7	105.1	15.0143	0.3881

ANOVA

Source of Variation	SS	df	MS	F	P-value	F crit
Between Groups	14.1488	2	7.0744	22.4311	0.00001	3.5546
Within Groups	5.6769	18	0.3154			
Total	19.82571	20				

Since $0.00001 < 0.05$ reject H_0 and conclude that at least two populations means are different.

b.

	Absolute Differences	Critical Range	Significant?
Car 1 - Car 2	0.9417	0.774203544	yes
Car 1 - Car 3	1.1393	0.741930751	yes
Car 2 - Car 3	2.0810	0.797551593	yes

Student reports will vary but they should recommend Car 2.

c. $(15.0143 - 12.9333) \pm 1.7341(0.5616)\sqrt{(1/6)+(1/7)}$; 1.5392 ----- 2.6228 range for cents per mile so the maximum and minimum difference in average savings per year would be ($0.015392)(30,000) ----- ($0.026228)(30,000); $461.76 ----- $786.84

11.11.

In the first printing of this text, the data listed in this problem were incorrect. The data should have been:

Display Type	Sample Mean	Sample Variance
A	98	100.75
B	77	83.00
C	84	64.75
D	103	144.25
E	91	101.00

The following solutions were developed using these data.

a. $SSB = 5(98 - 90.6)^2 + 5(77 - 90.6)^2 + 5(84 - 90.6)^2 + 5(103 - 90.6)^2 + 5(91 - 90.6)^2 = 2186.00$
   $SSW = (5-1)(100.75 + 83.00 + 64.75 + 144.25 + 101.00) = 1975.00$
   $SST = 2186 - 1975 = 4161$

H_o: $\mu_1 = \mu_2 = \mu_3 = \mu_4 = \mu_5$
H_A: At least two population means are different

ANOVA

Source of Variation	SS	df	MS	F
Between Groups	2186	4	546.5	5.5342
Within Groups	1975	20	98.75	
Total	4161	24		

Decision Rule:

If F > 2.8661 reject H_o, otherwise do not reject H_o

Since 5.5342 > 2.8661 reject H_o and conclude that at least two populations means are different.

b. The assumptions are (i) All populations are normally distributed, (ii) the observations are independent. The answers will vary but should include issues like possible differences in store location.

c.

	Absolute Difference	Critical Range	Significant?
A – B	21	18.7985	Yes
A – C	14	18.7985	No
A – D	5	18.7985	No
A – E	7	18.7985	No
B – C	7	18.7985	No
B – D	26	18.7985	Yes
B – E	14	18.7985	No
C – D	19	18.7985	Yes
C – E	7	18.7985	No
D – E	12	18.7985	No

Recommendation: Display Type A or Display Type C

11.13.

a.

Analysis of Variance

Source	DF	SS	MS	F	p-value
Blocks	9	8346.3	927.4	10.56	0.000
Groups	2	248.3	124.1	1.41	0.269
Error	18	1580.4	87.8		
Total	29	10175.0			

b. H_0: $\mu_{b1} = \mu_{b2} = \mu_{b3} = \mu_{b4} = \mu_{b5} = \mu_{b6} = \mu_{b7} = \mu_{b8} = \mu_{b9} = \mu_{b10}$
H_A: Not all block means are equal
Since $10.56 > 2.456$ reject H_0 and conclude that there is an indication that blocking was necessary.

c. Since p-value $0.269 > 0.05$ do not reject H_0 and conclude that the means are not different.

d. Given the results in c., the LSD approach to multiple comparisons is not necessary.

11.15.

a. $df_B = k - 1 = 6 \rightarrow k = 7$

b. $df_{BL} = b - 1 = 14 \rightarrow b = 15$

c.

ANOVA

Source of Variation	SS	df	MS	F
Between Blocks	34,500	14	2,464.2857	3.6380
Between Samples	41,700	6	6,950.0000	10.2601
Within Samples	56,900	84	677.3810	
Total	133,100	104		

d. H_0: $\mu_{b1} = \mu_{b2} = \mu_{b3} \ldots = \mu_{b15}$
    H_A: Not all block means are equal

If F > 1.8113 reject H_0, otherwise do not reject H_0

Since 3.638> 1.8113 reject H_0 and conclude that there is an indication that blocking was necessary.

e. F for testing the main hypothesis $= \dfrac{MSB}{MSW} = \dfrac{6950.0000}{677.3810} = 10.2601$

f. H_0: $\mu_1 = \mu_2 = \mu_3 = \mu_4 = \mu_5 = \mu_6 = \mu_7$
    H_A: At least two population means are different

Decision Rule:
If F > 2.2086 reject H_o, otherwise do not reject H_o

Since 10.2601 > 2.2086 reject H_o and conclude that at least two populations means are different.

11.17.

a. H_0: $\mu_1 = \mu_2 = \mu_3 = \mu_4$
    H_A: At least two population means are different

Anova: Single Factor

SUMMARY

Groups	Count	Sum	Average	Variance
1	6	8310	1385	243710
2	6	6730	1121.667	98816.67
3	6	11640	1940	333960
4	6	13320	2220	114720

ANOVA

Source of Variation	SS	df	MS	F	P-value	F crit
Between Groups	4543500	3	1514500	7.656659	0.00134	3.098393
Within Groups	3956033	20	197801.7			
Total	8499533	23				

Since 7.656659 > 3.098393 reject H_0 and conclude that at least 2 means are different

b. There may be a difference in cash sales depending on which week the data were observed. In this case, a randomized block ANOVA is a more appropriate technique. The data were not sampled randomly over the period of he test, but were taken for six specific weeks.

c. H_0: $\mu_1 = \mu_2 = \mu_3 = \mu_4$
  H_A: At least two population means are different

ANOVA

Source of Variation	SS	df	MS	F	P-value	F crit
Weeks (Blocks)	3105033	5	621006.7	10.94606	0.00014	2.901295
Drive-in	4543500	3	1514500	26.69506	2.9E-06	3.287383
Error	851000	15	56733.33			
Total	8499533	23				

Since 26.6951 > 3.2874 reject H_o and conclude that at least 2 means are different

d. The results of the primary hypothesis are the same but in this case the MSE is significantly
    smaller than in the one-way ANOVA.

e. It would cause the mean square within to be significantly larger which decreases the value of the
    calculated F.

f. $LSD = t_{.025} \sqrt{MSW} \sqrt{\dfrac{2}{b}}$

  $LSD = 2.1315\sqrt{56,733.33}\sqrt{\dfrac{2}{6}} = 293.11$

    Least Significant Difference (LSD) 293.112167

	Mean Difference	Absolute Mean Difference	Significant?
D1 - D2	263.333333	263.3333333	NO
D1 - D3	-555	555	YES
D1 - D4	-835	835	YES
D2 - D3	-818.33333	818.3333333	YES
D2 - D4	-1098.3333	1098.333333	YES
D3 - D4	-280	280	NO

11.19.
  a. The local news station is interested in determining which store has the lowest prices. They
      designed the experiment the way they did because they wanted to use a variety of items rather
      than letting specific items affect the outcome of the experiment. If someone designed a specific
      list they could inadvertently select items that were in fact lower priced at one store or higher
      priced at another store. It was attempting to remove the effect of items selected.

b.

H_0: $\mu_1 = \mu_2 = \mu_3 \ldots = \mu_8$

H_A: At least two blocks have different means

ANOVA

Source of Variation	SS	df	MS	F	P-value	F crit
Shopper (Blocks)	86099.68	19	4531.562	952.6155	4.92E-45	1.867331
Stores	395.8113	2	197.9056	41.60331	2.68E-10	3.244821
Error	180.7648	38	4.756969			
Total	86676.26	59				

Since 952.6155 > 1.8673 reject H_0 and conclude that there is an indication that blocking was effective.

c. H_0: $\mu_1 = \mu_2 = \mu_3$

H_A: At least two population means are different

Using the ANOVA table shown in part b

Since the p-value of 2.68E-10 < 0.05 reject H_0 and conclude that at least two means are different

d. $LSD = t_{.025}\sqrt{MSW}\sqrt{\dfrac{2}{b}}$

$LSD = 2.024\sqrt{4.75}\sqrt{\dfrac{2}{20}} = 1.396$

Least Significant Difference (LSD)	1.3962405

	Mean Difference	Absolute Mean Difference	Significant?
D1 - D2	-6.29	6.29	YES
D1 - D3	-3.032	3.032	YES
D2 - D3	3.258	3.258	YES

Store 2 has the highest average prices.

11.21.

The randomized complete block design is used whenever we are testing situations where an additional factor affects the observed responses in a one-way design. In this respect, the randomized complete block design is analogous to the paired samples hypothesis testing procedure. Whenever an additional factor could potentially introduce a source of variation on the observed responses the results could be affected. In cases such as this we can control for the additional source of variability by blocking. By blocking we have an additional source of variation to account for called the block variation. The effect of blocking is to reduce the sum of squares within. If the variation in the blocks is significant, the variation within the factor levels will be reduced. This makes it easier to detect a difference in the population means if such a difference actually exists. If we do not block when it is needed we may not be able to detect a difference when in fact it exists.

11.23.

Student answers will vary but some examples might include variability in performing audits of for profit versus not for profit organizations. Finance students might be interested in the difference in the variability between bond and stock portfolios. Operations management students might be interested in testing variances across different manufacturing plant outputs, or testing whether there are differences in production variances between the day and night shift. Marketing students might be interested in knowing if there are different population variances in consumer non-durable spending between urban and rural shoppers.

11.25.

If the null hypothesis is not rejected we conclude that there is no difference in population means. In this case we would expect that the Tukey-Kramer procedure for multiple comparisons would show no significant difference in any pairwise comparison.

11.27.

In the two-sample t-test for a difference between any two means, the estimate of the population variances only includes data from the two specific samples under consideration. For ANOVA situations where there are three or more groups, we would be disregarding some of the information available to estimate the common population variance. To overcome this problem we base our confidence intervals using as our estimate of the pooled standard deviation the square root of the mean square within (MSW) value. The MSW is the weighted average of all sample variances in the problem under consideration. This is preferred to the two-sample t-test procedure because we are assuming that each of the sample variances is an estimate of the common population variance. Using the MSW enables us to incorporate all the information related to the estimate of the common population variance not just some of it as would be the case with the two-sample t-test approach.

11.29.

H_0: all golf balls have the same mean driving distance
H_A: not all golf balls have the same mean driving distance

Anova: Single Factor

SUMMARY

Groups	Count	Sum	Average	Variance
New Gordon	36	9389	260.8056	246.6754
Competitor 1	36	9608	266.8889	316.3873
Competitor 2	36	9509	264.1389	283.4944
Competitor 3	36	9607	266.8611	232.9802

ANOVA

Source of Variation	SS	df	MS	F	P-value	F crit
Between Groups	897.8542	3	299.2847	1.108937	0.347701	2.669253
Within Groups	37783.81	140	269.8843			
Total	38681.66	143				

Since p-value = .3477 > alpha = .05, to don't reject the null hypothesis

11.31.

a. H_0: $\mu_1 = \mu_2 = \mu_3 = \mu_4$
    H_A: At least two population means are different

Anova: Single Factor

SUMMARY

Groups	Count	Sum	Average	Variance
Little Rock	33	3873389	117375.4189	4894622
Wichita	33	3682859	111601.7744	6368664
Tulsa	33	3911588	118532.9843	5019125
Memphis	33	3970136	120307.1513	6399072

ANOVA

Source of Variation	SS	df	MS	F	P-value	F crit
Between Groups	1404504005	3	468168001.8	82.56392	8.74E-30	2.675385
Within Groups	725807427.5	128	5670370.528			
Total	2130311433	131				

Since the p-value = 8.74E-30 < 0.05 reject H_0 and conclude that at least two of the means are different.

b.   The Tukey-Kramer critical range is computed using:

$$CR = q_{.01}\sqrt{\frac{MSW}{2}(\frac{1}{n_i}+\frac{1}{n_j})}$$

$$CR = 3.63\sqrt{\frac{5,670,370.5}{2}(\frac{1}{33}+\frac{1}{33})} = 1,504.72$$

	Absolute Difference	Critical Range	Significant?
Wichita - Little Rock	5773.644529	1504.72	yes
Little Rock - Tulsa	1157.565324	1504.72	no
Tulsa - Memphis	1774.167074	1504.72	yes

c. $n = 1.96^2(6368664)/500^2 = 97.8634$ or 98

11.33.

a. H_0: $\mu_{\alpha 1} = \mu_{\alpha 2} = \mu_{\alpha 3}$
H_A: At least two population means are different

b.   The company blocks on days.
H_0: $\mu_{b1} = \mu_{b2} = \mu_{b3} = \mu_{b4} = \mu_{b5} = \mu_{b6} = \mu_{b7} = \mu_{b8} = \ldots = \mu_{b50}$
H_A: Not all block means are equal

ANOVA

Source of Variation	SS	df	MS	F	P-value	F crit
Days (Blocks)	502.1862	49	10.2487	1.542025	0.035303	1.482944
Call Centers	377.3375	2	188.6687	28.38721	1.88E-10	3.089198
Error	651.3332	98	6.646258			
Total	1530.857	149				

Since $1.542 > 1.4829$ reject H_0 and conclude that there is an indication that blocking was effective.

c.   Since $28.38721 > 3.0892$ reject H_0 and conclude that at least two populations means are different.

d. The Least Significant Difference is computed using:

$$LSD = t_{\alpha/2}\sqrt{MSW}\sqrt{\frac{2}{b}}$$

$$LSD = t_{.05,2,98}\sqrt{MSW}\sqrt{\frac{2}{b}}$$

$$LSD = 1.984\sqrt{6.646}\sqrt{\frac{2}{50}} = 1.023$$

Least Significant Difference (LSD)		1.023	
	Mean Difference	Absolute Mean Difference	Significant?
Center 1 – Center 2	-0.8062	0.8062	NO
Center 1 – Center 3	-3.6944	3.6944	YES
Center 2 – Center 3	-2.8882	2.8882	YES

Center 3 takes the greatest amount of time to handle calls.

e. Student answers will vary but they might mention such things as determining if harder to solve calls are going to Center 3 or whether they need additional training at Center 3.

11.35.

Students using Excel will need to rearrange the data in order to run an ANOVA. The data for each major will need to be placed in a separate column.

a. H_0: $\mu_1 = \mu_2 = \mu_3$
    H_A: Not all means are equal

b.

Anova: Single Factor

SUMMARY

Groups	Count	Sum	Average	Variance
Engineering	57	586.0531	10.28163	1.584783
Arts & Sciences	54	553.0176	10.24107	1.905996
Business	44	442.1425	10.04869	2.35726

ANOVA

Source of Variation	SS	df	MS	F	P-value	F crit
Between Groups	1.477949	2	0.738975	0.385824	0.680554	4.747562
Within Groups	291.1279	152	1.915315			
Total	292.6058	154				

Since $0.3858 < 4.7476$ do not reject H_0 and conclude that there is no difference in the average hours of weekly laboratory use by major.

c. 0.680554

d. $P(\bar{x}_1 - \bar{x}_2 \geq 10.2816 - 10.0487) = P(\bar{x}_1 - \bar{x}_3 \geq 0.2329) =$

$t = (0.2329 - 0)/[1.9153\sqrt{(1/57) + (1/44)}]$

$t = .61$

Students can use Excel's TDIST function to calculate $P(t > .61) = .2727$

CHAPTERS 7–11

SPECIAL REVIEW

SR.1.

Conditions: (1) Parameter of concern: average, (2) sample size = 50 > 30 ==> Use a large sample hypothesis test for the mean of a population. Research hypothesis: average of new starter units is greater than 1000 ==>

H_0: $\mu \leq 1000$

H_A: $\mu > 1000$

$\alpha = 0.05$

$$z = \frac{\bar{x} - \mu}{\frac{s}{\sqrt{n}}} = \frac{1010 - 1000}{\frac{48}{\sqrt{50}}} = 1.4731$$

Rejection region: z > 1.645

Decision: z =1.4731 < 1645 = z_α ==> do not reject H_0

Conclusion: The average cycles for the new starter unit is not greater than that of the old starter unit. Do not recommend changing suppliers.

SR.3.

Conditions: (1) Parameter of concern: difference between two proportions, (2)

$n_1 \bar{p}_1 = 800(.05) = 40 > 5$; $n_1(1 - \bar{p}_1) = 800(.95) = 760 > 5$;

$n_2 \bar{p}_2 = 900(.09) = 81 > 5$; $n_2(1 - \bar{p}_2) = 900(.91) = 819 > 5$ ==> use a normal approximation ==> Use a large sample hypothesis test for the difference between two proportions. Research hypothesis: There is a difference in the turnover rates for the two trial policies.

==>

H_0: $p_1 - p_2 = 0$

H_A: $p_1 - p_2 \neq 0$

$\alpha = 0.05$ $\qquad \bar{p} = \dfrac{\bar{p}_1 n_1 + \bar{p}_2 n_2}{n_1 + n_2} = \dfrac{40 + 81}{800 + 900} = .0712$

$$z = \frac{\bar{p}_1 - \bar{p}_2 - (p_1 - p_2)}{\sqrt{\bar{p}(1 - \bar{p})\left(\dfrac{1}{n_1} + \dfrac{1}{n_2}\right)}} = \frac{.05 - (.09) - 0}{\sqrt{.0712(.9288)\left(\dfrac{1}{800} + \dfrac{1}{900}\right)}} = -3.2011$$

Rejection region: z < -1.96 or z > 1.96

Decision: z =-3.2011 < -1.96 = $-z_{\alpha/2}$ ==> reject H_0

Conclusion: There is a difference in the turnover rates for the two trial policies.

SR.5.

Conditions: (1) Parameter of concern: population variances, (2) assume population is normally distributed ==> Use a hypothesis test for the equality of two variances. Research hypothesis: There is no difference in variability of attendance between downtown and suburban theaters.

$H_0: \sigma_1^2 = \sigma_2^2$

$H_A: \sigma_1^2 \neq \sigma_2^2$

$\alpha = 0.05$

$$F = \frac{s_1^2}{s_2^2} = \frac{1684}{1439} = 1.1703$$

Rejection region: $F > 3.137$

Decision: $F_\alpha = 3.137 > 1.1703 = F$ ==> do not reject H_0

Conclusion: There is no difference in variability of attendance between downtown and suburban theaters.

Conditions: (1) Parameter of concern: population means, (2) sample sizes < 30, (3) population variances unknown, (4) population variances equal, and (5) assume population is normally distributed ==> Use a hypothesis test for the equality of two means. Research hypothesis: There is no difference in mean attendance between downtown and suburban theaters.

$H_0: \mu_1 = \mu_2$

$H_A: \mu_1 \neq \mu_2$

$\alpha = 0.05$ $\qquad s_p = \sqrt{\dfrac{(11-1)1684 + (10-1)(1439)}{11+10-2}} = 39.5973$

$$t = \frac{\bar{x}_1 - \bar{x}_2 - (\mu_1 - \mu_2)}{s_p\sqrt{\dfrac{1}{n_1} + \dfrac{1}{n_2}}} = \frac{855 - 750}{39.5973\sqrt{\dfrac{1}{11} + \dfrac{1}{10}}} = 6.0689$$

Rejection region: $t < -2.0930$ or $t > 2.0930$

Decision: $t_{\alpha/2} = 2.0930 < 6.0689 = t$ ==> reject H_0

Conclusion: There is a difference in the average attendance between downtown and suburban theaters.

SR.7.

Conditions: (1) Parameter of concern: differences among three population means, (2) population variances unknown, (3) samples are independent, and (4) assume population is normally distributed ==> Use an analysis of variance for the difference between population means. Research hypothesis: There is no difference in mean strength of the three types of shocks after 20,000 miles.

The equality of the populations' variances must be verified first.

Conditions: (1) Parameter of concern: population variances, (2) assume population is normally distributed ==> Use a hypothesis test for the equality of population variances. Research hypothesis: There is no difference in variability among the strength of the three types of shocks after 20,000 miles.

$H_0: \sigma_1^2 = \sigma_2^2 = \sigma_3^2$

H_A: at least two σ_i^2 differ

$\alpha = 0.05$

$$F = \frac{s_{max}^2}{s_{min}^2} = \frac{4.0280}{3.0695} = 1.3123$$

Rejection region: $F_H > 10.8$

Decision: $F_H = 10.8 > 1.3123 = F$ ==> do not reject H_0

Conclusion: There is no difference in variability of the strength of the three types of shocks after 20,000 miles.

$H_0: \mu_1 = \mu_2 = \mu_3$

H_A: at least two μ_i differ

$\alpha = 0.05$

Anova: Single Factor						
SUMMARY						
Groups	Count	Sum	Average	Variance		
Manufacturer	6	64.3	10.71667	3.069667		
Competitor 1	6	61.8	10.3	3.304		
Competitor 2	6	64.3	10.71667	4.029667		
ANOVA						
Source of Variation	SS	df	MS	F	P-value	F crit
Between Groups	0.694444	2	0.347222	0.100128	0.905321	3.682317
Within Groups	52.01667	15	3.467778			
Total	52.71111	17				

Rejection region: $F > 3.682$

Decision: $F_\alpha = 3.682 > 0.10 = F$ ==> do not reject H_0

Conclusion: There is no difference in average strength of the three types of shocks after 20,000 miles.

SR.9.

Conditions: (1) Parameter of concern: differences among three population means, (2) treatment effects for Phosphor type are different for different levels of the glass type ➔ interaction, (3) samples are independent, and (4) assume population is normally distributed ==> Use a two factor analysis of variance for the difference between population means. Research hypothesis: There is no difference in brightness of the monitors for the three Phosphor types. There is no difference in brightness of the monitors for glass types. There is no interaction between the glass type and relationship between the Phosphor type and the brightness of the monitor types.

Two-way ANOVA: Brightness versus GlassType, PhosType

```
Analysis of Variance for Brightne
Source          DF       SS       MS        F       P
GlassTyp        1      7896     7896     33.11    0.000
PhosType        2       181       90      0.38    0.692
Interaction     2      1650      825      3.46    0.065
Error          12      2861      238
Total          17     12588
```

Test for Interaction: p-value = 0.692 > 0.05 = α. Therefore, do not reject the null hypothesis that interaction does not exist.
Test for Factor 1: Glass type
p-value = 0.065 > 0.05 = α. Therefore, do not reject the null hypothesis that the average brightness of the monitors is not different between the glass types.
Test for Factor 2: Phosphor type
p-value = 0.000 < 0.05 = α. Therefore, reject the null hypothesis that the average brightness of the monitors is not different among the Phosphor types

SR.11.

Conditions: (1) Parameter of concern: difference between two proportions, (2)

$$n_1 \bar{p}_1 = 250\left(\frac{9}{250}\right) = 9 > 5; \; n_1(1 - \bar{p}_1) = 250\left(\frac{241}{250}\right) = 241 > 5;$$

$$n_2 \bar{p}_2 = 250\left(\frac{16}{250}\right) = 16 > 5; \; n_2(1 - \bar{p}_2) = 250\left(\frac{234}{250}\right) = 234 > 5 \text{==> use a normal approximation.}$$

Requires range of possible values ==> Use a large sample confidence interval for the difference between two proportions.
==>

$$p_1 - p_2 \pm z_{\alpha/2}\sqrt{\frac{p_1(1 - p_1)}{n_1} + \frac{p_2(1 - p_2)}{n_2}} = \frac{16}{250} - \frac{9}{250} \pm 1.96\sqrt{\frac{0.064(0.936)}{250} + \frac{0.036(0.964)}{250}} =$$

$$0.028 \pm 0.0381 =$$
$$(0.0019, 0.0781)$$

Using a 95% confidence level, it is estimated that the percentage of the blenders returned with the old switch is somewhere between 0% and 7% greater than the percentage of blenders returned with the new switch. Therefore the claim that the difference is somewhere between 3% and 6% seems quite plausible.

CHAPTER 12

INTRODUCTION TO LINEAR REGRESSION AND CORRELATION ANALYSIS

12.1.

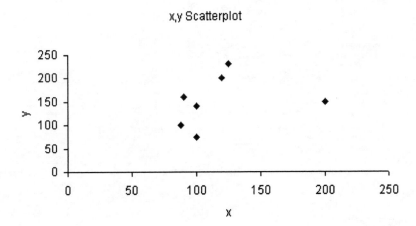

x,y Scatterplot

There appears to be a very weak curvilinear relationship.

12.3.
Because the two variables have a negative linear relationship as x increases y will decrease. However, without further information the student cannot determine whether the decrease will be large or small. The scatterplot of x_1, y for Exercise 12.2 shows a negative, linear relationship.

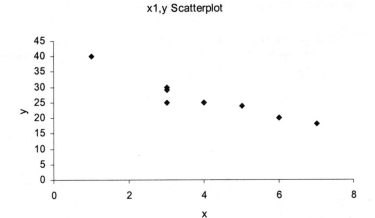

x1,y Scatterplot

12.5.

The following figure shows the curvilinear relationship. This relationship describes what economists would call decreasing returns to scale. An example of such a relationship might be the relationship between advertising expenditure and sales. As advertising expense increases sales may increase rapidly. However, after a saturation point is reached the increase in sales might taper off.

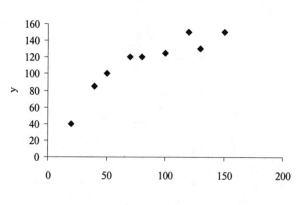

x.y Scatterplot

12.7

a.

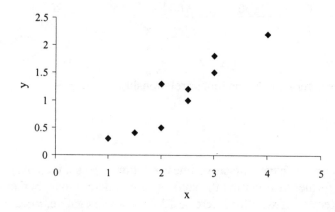

x,y Scatterplot

There appears to be a fairly strong positive relationship.

b. Using Excel's CORREL function, the sample correlation coefficient is 0.847065. The correlation coefficient indicates the strength of the linear relationship between two variables. In this case the relationship is a positive one.

c. H_0: $\rho = 0$
H_A: $\rho \neq 0$
d.f. = 7-2 = 5

Decision Rule:
    If t > 2.5706 or t < -2.5706, Reject H_0, otherwise do not reject H_0

$$t = 0.847065/\sqrt{(1-0.847065^2)/(7-2)} = 3.5638$$

Since 3.5638 > 2.5706 reject H_0 and conclude that the correlation coefficient is not 0.

d. Because we rejected the null hypothesis we could have committed a Type I Error.

12.9.

a. The correlation coefficient equal to 0.8 suggest that there is a fairly strong positive linear relationship between height and weight. This suggests that as height increases weight will also increase. These are randomly selected variables because you randomly selected individuals and measured both height and weight. To be fixed you would need to pick specific heights and then find individuals who met this height and then determine their weight.

b. H_0: $\rho = 0$
H_A: $\rho \neq 0$
d.f. = 32 - 2 = 30
Decision Rule:

    If t > 1.6973 or t < -1.6973, Reject H_0, otherwise do not reject H_0
$$t = 0.8/\sqrt{(1-0.8^2)/(32-2)} = 7.303$$
Since 7.303 > 1.673, reject the null hypothesis or since p-value is essentially = 0 < 0.1 reject H_0 and conclude that there is a correlation between height and weight.

12.11.

a. No you cannot assume this because correlation does not assume cause and effect. Two unconnected variables could be highly correlated.

b. In this case you can probably assume that an increase in the common dividends will cause an increase in the stock price. Stock prices are based on expected future value. Individuals will assume that if a company is raising their dividends they must expect future growth. Companies do not raise dividends in one year if they expect to have to decrease dividends in the next year.

12.13.

a. The scatter plot shows almost no linear relationship between the two variables. Since both the EPS and the common dividends are random variables, a correlation model would be more appropriate.

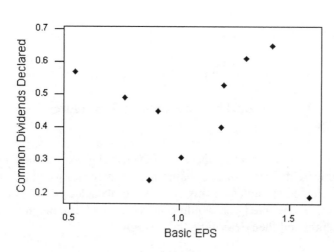

b. The correlation coefficient is –0.1087. This correlation indicates that there is a slight tendency for dividends to decrease as EPS increases.

c. H_0: $\rho \geq 0$
    H_A: $\rho < 0$
    d.f. = 10 - 2 = 8

    Decision Rule
           If t < -2.306, Reject H_0, otherwise do not reject H_0

$$t = -0.1087/\sqrt{(1-(-0.1087^2)/(10-2))} = -0.3092$$

To find the p-value use Excel's TDIST function. Since p-value = 0.3825 > 0.025 do not reject the null hypothesis that the correlation coefficient is greater than or equal to 0.

12.15.

a. $R^2 = 0.568498$

b. (1) $\hat{y} = 58.7246 + 12.9410(0) = 58.7246$

    (2) The y-intercept

12.17.

a. $\hat{y} = 19.75 - .08346(10) = 18.9154$

b.   (1) $\hat{y} = 19.75 - .08346(117.22) = 9.9668$
  (2) Note that the data set used to construct the regression equation does not have any x values any where near a value of 10. Since no such values exist it is almost impossible to determine the relationship between x and y for such x values. Attempting to predict a y value in such cases is called extrapolation and should be avoided. Since x = 117.22 is in the center of the x values, the prediction error is as small as it can be. This prediction is quite valid whereas the prediction when x = 10 is of questionable validity.

12.19.

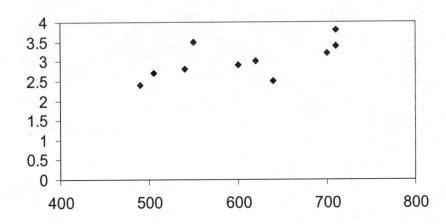

Scatterplot

a.

There appears to be a weak positive linear relationships.

b.   (1)   r = 0.6239

  (2) H_0: $\rho = 0$
    H_A: $\rho \neq 0$
    d.f. = 10-2 = 8
    Decision Rule:
    If t > 3.3554 or t < -3.3554, Reject H_0, otherwise do not reject H_0

$$t = 0.6239 / \sqrt{(1 - 0.6239)^2) / (10 - 2)} = 2.2581$$

Since 2.2580 < 3.3554 do not reject H_0 and conclude that there is not a correlation between SAT scores and final GPA.

c.   (1). $\hat{y} = 0.9772 + 0.0034(x)$
  (2). The y-intercept would indicate the average university GPA of all students who received an SAT score of 0. Such a situation seems highly unlikely. Therefore, the y-intercept has no interpretation in this case. The slope indicates that the average university GPA increases by 0.0034 for each increase of 1 unit in the SAT score.

12.21.

r = 0.9963

H_0: $\rho = 0$

H_A: $\rho \neq 0$

d.f. = 11-2 = 9

$\alpha = 0.05$ (Note, alpha was not specified so students may choose a different level which will affect the critical value.)

Decision Rule:

    If t > 2.2622 or t < -2.2622, Reject H_0, otherwise do not reject H_0

$$t = 0.9963/\sqrt{(1 - 0.9963^2)/(11 - 2)} = 34.7774$$

Since 34.7774 > 2.2622 reject H_0 and conclude there is a correlation between the computer inventory record and the actual level of inventory

12.23.

a. $\hat{y} = 1{,}096.7502 + 4.6585(x)$

b. H_0: $\beta_1 = 0$
    H_A: $\beta_1 \neq 0$

SUMMARY OUTPUT

Regression Statistics	
Multiple R	0.267295482
R Square	0.071446875
Adjusted R Square	-0.044622266
Standard Error	268.565155
Observations	10

ANOVA

	df	SS	MS	F
Regression	1	44398.24429	44398.24429	0.615554439
Residual	8	577017.9397	72127.24246	
Total	9	621416.184		

	Coefficients	Standard Error	t Stat	P-value
Intercept	1096.750239	412.0098904	2.661951241	0.02871844
Capital Expenditures	4.658464817	5.937581529	0.784572775	0.455306376

$\alpha = 0.05$ (Note, alpha was not specified so students may choose a different level which will affect the critical value.)

Decision Rule:
    If t < -2.3060 or t > 2.3060 reject H_0, otherwise do not reject H_0

Since $-2.3060 < 0.7846 < 2.3060$ do not reject H_0 and conclude that McCormick's net sales will not necessarily increase if it increases its capital expenditures.

c. Since you accepted the null hypothesis a Type II error could have occurred.

d. If the model was significant you would say that for every $1,000,000 increase in capital expenditures you would expect revenues to increase $4.6585 million dollars. Since the model is not significant you can only say there is no relationship between capital expenditures and revenues.

12.25.

   a.

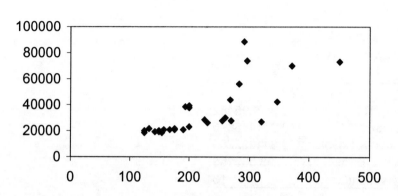

There appears to be a positive linear relationship.

   b. r = 0.7658

   c. $\hat{y}$ = -7203.81 +185.3649(x)

   d. $\hat{y}$ = -7203.81 +185.3649(133) = \$17,449.7217
      residual = 20278 – 17,449.7217 = 2,828.2783

e. $R^2 = 0.5864$ This indicates the strength of the linear relationship between price and horse power.
H$_0$: $\beta_1 = 0$
H$_A$: $\beta_1 \neq 0$

SUMMARY OUTPUT

Regression Statistics	
Multiple R	0.76576633
R Square	0.586398072
Adjusted R Square	0.571626575
Standard Error	12726.08287
Observations	30

ANOVA

	df	SS	MS	F
Regression	1	6429208430	6.43E+09	39.69794
Residual	28	4534689189	1.62E+08	
Total	29	10963897619		

	Coefficients	Standard Error	t Stat	P-value
Intercept	-7203.806176	6923.908015	-1.04042	0.307044
Horse Power	185.3649354	29.42006165	6.30063	8.18E-07

Decision Rule:
        If F > 7.6357 reject H$_0$, otherwise do not reject H$_0$
Students can find the F-critical using Excel's FINV function or can approximate it using the F table as a value of F for degrees of freedom between 1 and 24 and 1 and 30. FINV gives 7.6357.

Since 39.6979 > 7.6357 reject H$_0$ and conclude that the overall model is significant.

12.27.

  a.

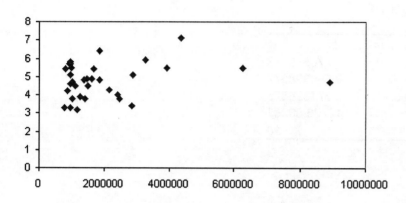

  There appears to be a weak positive linear relationship.

b.   r = 0.2283

c. $\hat{y} = 4.5225 + 0.0000001239(x)$

$H_0: \beta_1 \leq 0$
$H_A: \beta_1 > 0$

SUMMARY OUTPUT

Regression Statistics	
Multiple R	0.228273058
R Square	0.052108589
Adjusted R Square	0.021531447
Standard Error	0.931307973
Observations	33

ANOVA

	df	SS	MS	F
Regression	1	1.47808381	1.478084	1.704168
Residual	31	26.88737074	0.867335	
Total	32	28.36545455		

	Coefficients	Standard Error	t Stat	P-value
Intercept	4.522490178	0.251052281	18.01414	5.61E-18
1995 Population	0.0000001239	9.49161E-08	1.305438	0.20135

$\alpha = 0.05$ (Students may select a different alpha.)
Decision Rule:
     If p-value $< \alpha$ reject H_0, otherwise do not reject H_0

Since .20135 $>$ .05 do not reject H_0 and conclude that cities with a larger population in 1995 do not have higher unemployment rates in 1985.

12.29.

a.

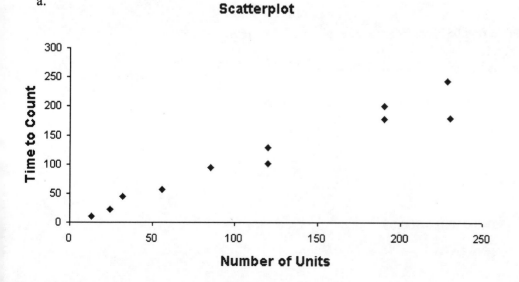

b. H_0: $\beta_1 = 0$
     H_A: $\beta_1 \neq 0$

	Coefficients	Standard Error	t Stat	P-value
Intercept	6.25799191	10.16786653	0.615468	0.553489
x	0.924892926	0.072224407	12.80582	4.42E-07

The regression equation is $6.258 + 0.925(x)$
Decision Rule:
     If $\alpha < .1$; reject H_0, otherwise do not reject.

Since p-value = 0.0000 < α < .1 do not reject the hypothesis and conclude that the number of units is not linearly related to the time required.

c.   The 90% confidence interval is $0.92489 \pm 1.8331(0.0722) = 0.7925$ ----- 1.0573; it does contain the hypothesized value (= 1). Therefore, you could conclude the accountant takes an additional minute to count each additional unit.

12.31.

a. $\hat{y} = 9,784 - 345.5(80) = -17,856$

$$s = \sqrt{\frac{SSE}{n-2}} = \sqrt{\frac{800.25}{18}} = 6.6677$$

$$-17,856 \pm 1.7341(6.6677)\sqrt{\frac{1}{20} + \frac{(80-67.2)^2}{145,789}} ; \quad -17858.6143 ------ -17853.3857$$

b. $1.7341(6.6677)\sqrt{\dfrac{1}{20} + \dfrac{(80-67.2)^2}{145,789}} = 2.614339$

12.33.

a.   For every mile the distance from headquarters increases, the total volume of business decreases by $10.12.

b.   We first need to find 95% confidence interval for the true regression slope
     $10.12 \pm 1.96(3.12)$;   4.0048 ----- 16.2352
     Multiplying this by 100 we find: 400.48 ------ 1623.52

c.   Finding a 90% confidence interval for the true regression slope
     $10.12 \pm 1.645(3.12)$;   4.9876 ----- 15.2542
     Multiplying this by 50 we find: 249.38 ------ 762.71

12.35.

a. $\hat{y} = -4.7933 + 1.0488x$

b. $\hat{y} = -4.7933 + 1.0488(100) = 100.09$

c. $100.09 \pm 1.8331(9.333)\sqrt{1 + \dfrac{1}{12} + \dfrac{(100 - 115.0909)^2}{116936.3}}$;   82.2671 ------ 117.9129

d. $100.09 \pm 1.8331(9.333)\sqrt{\dfrac{1}{12} + \dfrac{(100 - 115.0909)^2}{116936.3}}$;   95.0939 ------ 105.0861

12.37.

a. $\hat{y} = 46.3298 + (-0.0060)(4012 + 570) = 18.8378$

b.   Using PHStat Excel Add-in the 95% confidence interval is

For Average Predicted Y (YHat)	
Interval Half Width	2.420934464
Confidence Interval Lower Limit	**16.25832354**
Confidence Interval Upper Limit	**21.10019247**

c.   Using PHStat Excel Add-in the 95% confidence interval is

For Individual Response Y	
Interval Half Width	6.346362472
Prediction Interval Lower Limit	**12.33289554**
Prediction Interval Upper Limit	**25.02562048**

d.   Looking at the confidence interval equation, 13-22 and 13-23, we see that as the value of x_p moves farther from the average of x, the value under the square root becomes larger and the interval becomes wider.

e.   The largest curb weight in the sample was 4,860. The conclusions and inferences made from a regression line are statistically valid only over the range of the data contained in the sample used to develop the regression line. The 6,000 pounds is outside of the range of the sample.

f.   The confidence interval is found by finding the confidence interval of the slope coefficient and multiplying it by the difference in weight. The interval for the slope coefficient can be found in the regression output.

	Coefficients	Standard Error	t Stat	P-value	Lower 95%	Upper 95%	Lower 90.0%	Upper 90.0%
Intercept	-7203.81	6923.908015	-1.04042	0.307044	-21386.8	6979.1924	-18982.276	4574.66326
Horse Power	185.3649	29.42006165	6.30063	8.18E-07	125.1006	245.62927	135.317578	235.412292

The lower 90% = 13.3 x 135.318 = 1799.73, the upper 90% = 13.3 x 235.412 = 3130.98

12.39.

A negative linear relationship exists whenever increases in one variable are associated with decreases in the other variable. When two variables are negatively linearly related, they tend to move in opposite directions at a constant rate. For example, the two variables, beer consumption and disposable income may be negatively correlated such that decreased amount of beer consumption are associated with higher levels of income.

12.41.

The student is correct. If the correlation coefficient between the two variables is 0.45 we expect to see a slope of the simple linear regression model that is positive. There is a relationship in the simple linear regression model between the correlation coefficient and the slope of the regression line. The two statistics would have the same sign. Someone has made a mistake in his or her calculations if one statistic is positive and the other is negative.

12.43.

The prediction interval for a specific value of the dependent variable will always be less precise or wider than the confidence interval for predicting the average value of the dependent variable. This is shown by equations 13-24 and 13-25. Intuitively, we would expect to be more precise in predicting an average value than we would be in predicting a specific, particular value.

12.45.

a.

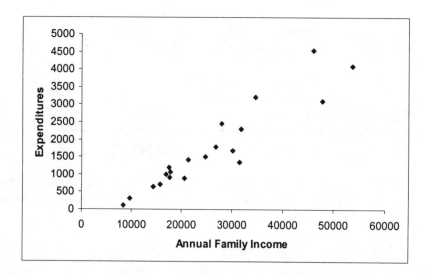

There appears to be a positive linear relationship between the annual family income and recreational expenditures.

b. The correlation coefficient is 0.9389

c. H_0: $\rho \leq 0$
   H_A: $\rho > 0$
   $\alpha = .025$.   d.f. = 20-2 = 18.

If t > 2.1009 reject H_0, otherwise do not reject H_0.

$$t = 0.9389/\sqrt{(1 - 0.9389^2)/(20 - 2)} = 11.57$$

Since 11.57 > 2.1009 reject H_0 and conclude there is a positive correlation between income levels and expenditures on recreation. As family income increases there is an increase in recreational expenditures.

12.47.

$H_0: \rho \leq 0$

$H_A: \rho > 0$

d.f. = 335-2 = 333.

Students can use Excel's TINV to get the critical value for alpha = .01 and 333 degrees of freedom which gives t = 2.3376.

If t > 2.3376 reject H_0, otherwise do not reject H_0.

$$t = 0.104/\sqrt{(1-0.104^2)/(335-2)} = 1.9082$$

Since 1.9082 < 2.3376 do not reject H_0 and conclude there is not a positive correlation between the amount of supplement feed and the daily weight gain.

12.49.

Students can use TINV to get critical t for 90% confidence and 98 degrees of freedom

a. $0.015 \pm 1.661(0.0000122)$; 0.0148 ----- 0.0152

b.   It would be unwise to extrapolate the results of the study beyond the range of the survey data. You cannot interpret the intercept if the sample did not include individuals with no income.

c. $H_o: \beta_1 = 0$

   $H_a: \beta_1 \neq 0$

   Decision Rule:
   Using TINV t value is approximately 1.98
   If t > 1.98 or t < -1.96, reject H_0, otherwise do not reject H_0.

$$t = \frac{b_1 - \beta_1}{s_{b_1}} = \frac{0.015}{0.000122} = 122.95$$

Since 122.95 > 1.98 reject H_0 and conclude that the overall model is significant.

12.51.

a.

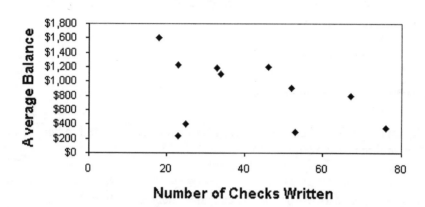

b.

SUMMARY OUTPUT						
Regression Statistics						
Multiple R	0.378864769					
R Square	0.143538513					
Adjusted R Square	0.048376126					
Standard Error	453.9233193					
Observations	11					
ANOVA						
	df	*SS*	*MS*	*F*	*Significance F*	
Regression	1	310790.7635	310790.8	1.508353	0.250539111	
Residual	9	1854417.418	206046.4			
Total	10	2165208.182				
	Coefficients	*Standard Error*	*t Stat*	*P-value*	*Lower 95%*	*Upper 95%*
Intercept	1219.803532	333.178933	3.661106	0.005227	466.0998481	1973.507
Number of Checks Written	-9.119641901	7.425508984	-1.22815	0.250539	-25.91732304	7.678039

The regression model is $\hat{y} = 1219.8035 + (-9.1196)(x)$

To find the confidence interval for the change in the number of checks, we need to find the confidence interval for the slope coefficient and then multiply it by 25. The interval is found in the output.

c.   Lower 90%: 25 x –22.7314 = -568.285; Upper 90%: 25 x 4.4922 = 112.305

d. $H_0: \beta_1 = 0$
   $H_A: \beta_1 \neq 0$

SUMMARY OUTPUT

Regression Statistics	
Multiple R	0.378864769
R Square	0.143538513
Adjusted R Square	0.048376126
Standard Error	453.9233193
Observations	11

ANOVA

	df	SS	MS	F
Regression	1	310790.7635	310790.8	1.508353
Residual	9	1854417.418	206046.4	
Total	10	2165208.182		

Decision Rule:
   If F > 5.117 reject H_0, otherwise do not reject H_0.

Since 1.5 < 5.117 do not reject H_0 and conclude that the overall model is not significant so that an increase in the number of checks written by an individual cannot be used to predict the checking account balance of that individual.

12.53.
   a.

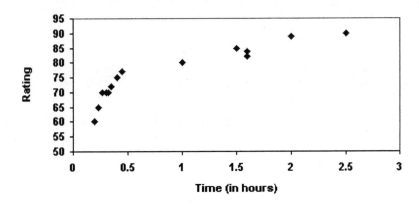

There appears to be a possible positive linear relationship between time (in hours) and rating.

b.

SUMMARY OUTPUT

Regression Statistics	
Multiple R	0.915504887
R Square	0.838149199
Adjusted R Square	0.824661632
Standard Error	3.786842178
Observations	14

ANOVA

	df	SS	MS	F
Regression	1	891.1322016	891.1322	62.14236
Residual	12	172.0820842	14.34017	
Total	13	1063.214286		

	Coefficients	Standard Error	t Stat	P-value
Intercept	66.71114789	1.587951365	42.01083	2.15E-14
Time (x)	10.61666113	1.346772042	7.883042	4.37E-06

$\hat{y} = 66.7111 + 10.6167(x)$

Student reports will vary but they should include a test to determine if the model is significant. Since F=62.14236 students should conclude that the overall model is significant at the .10 level. They should also comment on what the R^2 is and what this means to the model.

12.55.

a. The correlation coefficient is equal to 0.7059.

b. H_0: $\rho \leq 0$
    H_A: $\rho > 0$
    d.f. = 17-2 = 15.

If t > 1.3406 reject H_0, otherwise do not reject H_0.

$$t = 0.7059/\sqrt{(1-0.7059^2)/(17-2)} = 3.8598$$

Since 3.8598 > 1.3406 reject H_0 and conclude there is a positive correlation between house price and weeks on the market. As house price increases there is an increase in weeks on the market.

12.57.

The interval is found by finding the 95% confidence interval estimate for the slope coefficient and multiplying that by 10,000.

$.000528 \pm (2.1315)(.0001368);$ $.0002385$ ---- $.0008175$

Multiplying by 10,000 gives an interval estimate of: 2.385 - - - 8.175

12.59.

a.

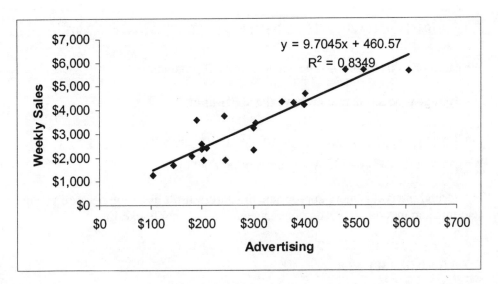

b. The 95% confidence interval for the increase in sales if found by finding the 95% confidence interval for the slope coefficient in the regression model and multiplying it by 50. The interval can be found in the shown output.

	Coefficients	Standard Error	t Stat	P-value	Lower 95%	Upper 95%
Intercept	460.567578	330.389599	1.394014	0.180285	-233.55575	1154.69091
Advertising	9.70447122	1.017240888	9.539993	1.83E-08	7.5673258	11.8416167

Lower 95%: 50 x 7.5673 = 378.365   Upper 95%: 50 x 11.8416 = 592.08

A $50 increase in advertising will result in an increase in sales of $378.365 to $592.08.

c. No it is not appropriate in this case. It is appropriate if the value 0 is in the range of x values in the sample.

d.

For Average Predicted Y (YHat)	
Interval Half Width	286.0036653
Confidence Interval Lower Limit	**2115.458156**
Confidence Interval Upper Limit	**2687.465486**

e. The conclusions and inferences made from a regression line are statistically valid only over the range of the data contained in the sample used to develop the regression line. The $100 is outside of the range of the sample.

12.61.

a. $\hat{y} = 88.5 + 1.5(15) = 110.8$ which can be rounded to 111 whole units of production

$$111 \pm 2.101(11)\sqrt{(1/20)+(15-13.5)^2/1,245}\; ;\; 105.7397 \text{ ----- } 116.2603$$

We can round this to 106 ----- 116 whole units of production

His average production rate is above the upper limit.

b. $111 \pm 2.101(11)\sqrt{1+(1/20)+(15-13.5)^2/1,245}\; ;\; 87.2979 \text{ ----- } 134.7021$

We can round to 87 ---- 135 whole units of production

The second interval is more appropriate to address Jim's assertion because you are trying to determine an individual person not an average of all people like Jim.

12.63.

$$\hat{y} = 1.0 + 0.028(88) = 3.464$$

$$3.464 \pm 1.96(0.2)\sqrt{(1/400)+(88-68)^2/148885.73}\; ;\; 3.4358 \text{ ----- } 3.4922$$

A 95% confidence interval means that if many random samples were taken from this population, and regression models determined, 95% of the calculated average values of the dependent variable would have values in the above interval. So, while the company is not sure what the actual average value would be, it expects it to be in the range shown above.

CHAPTER 13

MULTIPLE REGRESSION ANALYSIS
AND MODEL BUILDING

13.1.

a. $b_1 = 4.14$. This implies that, holding x_2 constant and increasing x_1 by one unit, the average y is estimated to increase by 4.14 units. $b_2 = 8.72$. This implies that, holding x_1 constant and increasing x_2 by one unit, the average y is estimated to increase by 4.14 units.

b. $\hat{y} = 12.67 + 4.14(4) + 8.72(9) = 107.71$

13.3.

a. $b_1 = \dfrac{1981 - \dfrac{72(157)}{6}}{938 - \dfrac{72^2}{6}} = 1.3108$; $b_0 = \dfrac{157}{6} - 1.3108\left(\dfrac{72}{6}\right) = 10.437$

$\hat{y} = 10.437 + 1.3108x_1$

b. $b_1 = \dfrac{2554 - \dfrac{96(157)}{6}}{1548 - \dfrac{96^2}{6}} = 3.500$; $b_0 = \dfrac{157}{6} - 3.500\left(\dfrac{96}{6}\right) = -29.83$

$\hat{y} = -29.83 + 3.500x_2$

c. $\hat{y} = -21.82 + 0.7513\, x_1 + 2.4357\, x_2$

13.5.

The largest correlation that exists among these independent variables is 0.503749. There does not exist highly correlated independent variables in this set. Therefore, no potential multicollinearity problems are indicated.

13.7.

a.

	Calls Received	Ads Place Previous Week	Calls Received the Previous Week	Airline Bookings
Calls Received	1			
Ads Place Previous Week	0.5843589	1		
Calls Received the Previous Week	0.654483	0.709017466	1	
Airline Bookings	0.5339732	0.360694798	0.219988054	1

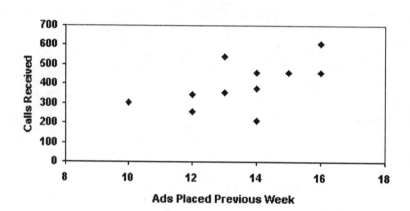

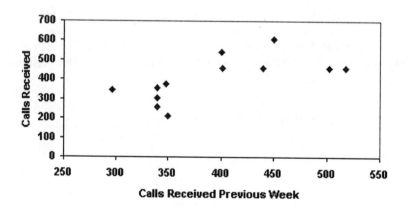

b.

Calls Received – Ads Placed Previous Week – indicates a weak positive linear relationship
Calls Received – Calls Received Previous Week – indicates a weak positive linear relationship
Calls Received – Airline Bookings – indicates a weak positive linear relationship.
A multiple regression model is possible, but the relations are not strong.

c.

SUMMARY OUTPUT

Regression Statistics	
Multiple R	0.58435892
R Square	0.341475348
Adjusted R Square	0.275622883
Standard Error	97.82751928
Observations	12

ANOVA

	df	SS	MS	F
Regression	1	49626.01471	49626.01471	5.185460356
Residual	10	95702.23529	9570.223529	
Total	11	145328.25		

	Coefficients	Standard Error	t Stat	P-value
Intercept	-93.01960784	219.3201303	-0.424127086	0.680452322
Ads Place Previous Week	36.01960784	15.81777236	2.277160591	0.046007257

$$\hat{y} = -93.0196 + 36.0196(x)$$

SUMMARY OUTPUT

Regression Statistics	
Multiple R	0.654482969
R Square	0.428347957
Adjusted R Square	0.371182753
Standard Error	91.14669001
Observations	12

ANOVA

	df	SS	MS	F
Regression	1	62251.059	62251.059	7.493158862
Residual	10	83077.191	8307.7191	
Total	11	145328.25		

	Coefficients	Standard Error	t Stat	P-value
Intercept	**-18.32798293**	155.8801498	-0.117577401	0.908730578
Calls Received the Previous Week	**1.067908547**	0.390123033	2.737363487	0.020927236

$$\hat{y} = -18.3280 + 1.0679(x)$$

SUMMARY OUTPUT

Regression Statistics	
Multiple R	0.533973192
R Square	0.28512737
Adjusted R Square	0.213640107
Standard Error	101.927027
Observations	12

ANOVA

	df	SS	MS	F
Regression	1	41437.06165	41437.06165	3.988505888
Residual	10	103891.1884	10389.11884	
Total	11	145328.25		

	Coefficients	Standard Error	t Stat	P-value
Intercept	**27.47299419**	189.951057	0.144631963	0.88787488
Airline Bookings	**0.120610493**	0.060392078	1.997124405	0.073740491

$$\hat{y} = 27.4730 + 0.1206(x)$$

d. The second model, calls received the previous week as the independent variable, appears to be the best model. It has the largest F-value, the highest R^2 and the smallest s^2.

13.9.

  a.

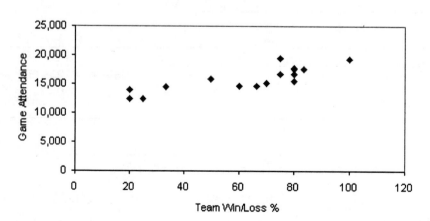

There appears to be a positive linear relationship between team win/loss percentage and game attendance.

Scatterplot

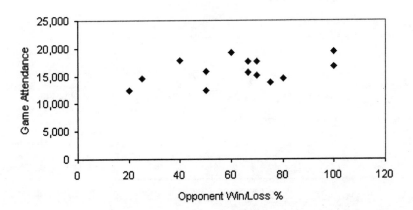

There appears to be a positive linear relationship between opponent win/loss percentage and game attendance.

Scatterplot

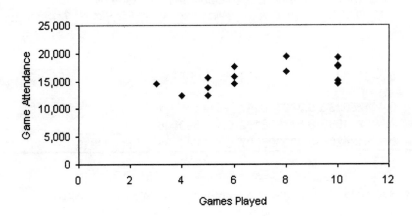

There appears to be a positive linear relationship between games played and game attendance.

Scatterplot

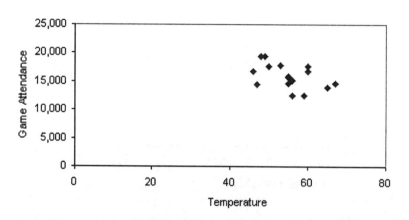

There does not appear to be any relationship between temperature and game attendance.

b.

	Game Attendance	Team Win/Loss %	Opponent Win/Loss %	Games Played	Temperature
Game Attendance	1				
Team Win/Loss %	0.848748849	1			
Opponent Win/Loss %	0.414250332	0.286749997	1		
Games Played	0.599214835	0.577958172	0.403593506	1	
Temperature	-0.476186226	-0.330096097	-0.446949168	-0.550083219	1

No alpha level was specified. Students will select their own. We have selected .05.

Critical $t = \pm 2.1448$

t for game attendance and team win/loss % = $0.8487/\sqrt{(1-0.8487^2)/(16-2)} = 6.0043$

t for game attendance and opponent win/loss % = $0.4143/\sqrt{(1-0.4143^2)/(16-2)} = 1.7032$

t for game attendance and games played = $0.5992/\sqrt{(1-0.5992^2)/(16-2)} = 2.8004$

t for game attendance and temperature = $-0.4762/\sqrt{(1-(-0.4762)^2)/(16-2)} = -2.0263$

There is a significant relationship between game attendance and team win/loss % and games played. Therefore a multiple regression model could be effective.

c. Multiple regression equation using x_1, x_2, x_3, x_4 as independent variables to predict y

Regression Analysis

Regression Statistics	
Multiple R	0.880534596
R Square	0.775341175
Adjusted R Square	0.693647057
Standard Error	1184.124723
Observations	16

ANOVA

	df	SS	MS	F	Significance F
Regression	4	53230058.97	13307514.74	9.490783318	0.001427993
Residual	11	15423664.97	1402151.361		
Total	15	68653723.94			

	Coefficients	Standard Error	t Stat	P-value	Lower 95%
Intercept	14122.24086	4335.791765	3.25713079	0.007637823	4579.222699
Team Win/Loss %	63.15325348	14.93880137	4.227464568	0.001418453	30.27315672
Opponent Win/Loss %	10.09582009	14.31396102	0.705312811	0.495280282	-21.40901163
Games Played	31.50621796	177.129782	0.177870811	0.862057676	-358.3540008
Temperature	-55.4609057	62.09372861	-0.89318047	0.390882768	-192.12835

d. $R^2 = 0.7753$ so 77.53% is explained.

e. H_0: $\beta_1 = \beta_2 = \beta_3 = \beta_4 = 0$
    H_A: at least one β_i does not equal 0

    Decision Rule:
    If p-value < α, , reject H_o, otherwise do not reject H_o

    Since p-value (Significance F) = .00143 reject H_o and conclude that the overall model is significant.

f. For team win/loss % the p-value = 0.0014 < 0.08 so this variable is significant
    For opponent win/loss % the p-value = 0.4953 > 0.08 so this variable is not significant
    For games played the p-value = 0.8621 > 0.08 so this variable is not significant
    For temperature the p-value = 0.3909 > 0.08 so this variable is not significant

g. The standard error of the estimate is 1184.1274. Practical significance is a decision made based on whether an interval of $\pm 3(1184.1274)$ is small enough to add value to the value being estimated.

h. Multicollinearity is present when the independent variables are correlated with one another. In this case many of the pairs of variables have a correlation of 0.5 or greater.

	VIF
Team Win/Loss Percentage and all other X	1.569962033
Temperature and all other X	1.963520336
Games Played and all other X	1.31428258
Opponent Win/Loss Percentage and all other X	1.50934547

The low VIF values indicate multicollinearity is not a problem since no VIF is greater than 5.

i.

	Coefficients	Standard Error	t Stat	P-value	Lower 95%	Upper 95%
Intercept	14122.24086	4335.791765	3.25713079	0.007637823	4579.222699	23665.25902
Team Win/Loss %	63.15325348	14.93880137	4.227464568	0.001418453	30.27315672	96.03335024
Opponent Win/Loss %	10.09582009	14.31396102	0.705312811	0.49528028	-21.40901163	41.6006518
Games Played	31.50621796	177.129782	0.177870811	0.862057676	-358.3540008	421.3664367
Temperature	-55.46090576	62.09372861	-0.89318047	0.390882768	-192.128358	81.20653863

Because the confidence intervals for Opponent win/loss %, games played, and temperature all include the value 0 it is indicating the same thing as the t-tests in that these variables are not significantly different from 0.

13.11.

a. The number of dummy variables = number of levels $-1 = 4 - 1 = 3$.

b. $y = \beta_0 + \beta_1 x_1 + \beta_2 x_2 + \beta_3 x_3 + \beta_4 x_4 + \varepsilon$; $x_1 = \{1$ for level 1, 0 otherwise$\}$,
    $x_2 = \{1$ for level 2, 0 otherwise$\}$, $x_3 = \{1$ for level 3, 0 otherwise$\}$

c. β_0 = the average value of y for the fourth level of the categorical variable and when $x_4 = 0$.

    β_i = the difference in the average value of y when the categorical variable at level i is changed from level i to level four while holding x_4 constant, $i = 1, 2,$ and 3.

    β_4 = the amount of change in the average value of y when x_4 is increased by one unit while holding all other x_i constant.

13.13.

$x_4 = 1$ if gas water heater, 0 otherwise
$x_5 = 1$ if constructed before 1974, 0 otherwise

The model would be: $y = \beta_0 + \beta_1 x_1 + \beta_2 x_2 + \beta_3 x_3 + \beta_4 x_4 + \beta_5 x_5 + \varepsilon$

13.15.

a. If the number of acres farmed increases by 1, the average farm income will increase by 4.2 holding the other independent variables constant.

b. If the farm is row-irrigated the average farm income will increase by 2,345 holding the other independent variables constant.

c. If the land is sprinkler-irrigated the average farm income will increase by 4,670 holding the other independent variables constant.

d. $\hat{y} = -23{,}200 + 4.2(1{,}000) + 4{,}670(1) = \$-14{,}330$

13.17.

a. You will need two dummy variables for the type of client

$x_2 = 1$ if manufacturing, 0 otherwise
$x_3 = 1$ if service, 0 otherwise

Regression Analysis

Regression Statistics	
Multiple R	0.835474124
R Square	0.698017012
Adjusted R Square	0.568595732
Standard Error	975.3064045
Observations	11

ANOVA

	df	SS	MS	F
Regression	3	15390889.56	5130296.519	5.393371239
Residual	7	6658558.078	951222.5826	
Total	10	22049447.64		

	Coefficients	Standard Error	t Stat	P-value
Intercept	-586.2555597	974.2029083	-0.601779727	0.566292865
Hours (x1)	22.86106295	29.33445824	0.779324532	0.461318736
Manufacturing (x2)	2302.267018	895.0615733	2.572188425	0.036889988
Service (x3)	1869.813042	764.538844	2.445674352	0.044387958

$\hat{y} = -586.2556 + 22.8611(x_1) + 2302.2670(x_2) + 1869.8130(x_3)$

b. F critical at the 5% significance level would be 4.347. Since F = 5.3934 > 4.347 conclude that the overall model is significant and the model would be useful in predicting the net profit earned by the client.

c. The p-value for hours is 0.4613 so you would conclude that the hours spent working with a client is not useful in this model in predicting the net profit.

d.

Regression Analysis

Regression Statistics	
Multiple R	0.819643712
R Square	0.671815815
Adjusted R Square	0.589769769
Standard Error	951.0704495
Observations	11

ANOVA

	df	SS	MS	F
Regression	2	14813167.64	7406583.818	8.188277754
Residual	8	7236280	904535	
Total	10	22049447.64		

	Coefficients	Standard Error	t Stat	P-value
Intercept	71	475.5352248	0.149305448	0.885007898
Manufacturing (x2)	2689	726.3920544	3.701857673	0.006026483
Service (x3)	2127	672.5083643	3.162785941	0.013338842

$$\hat{y} = 71 + 2689(x_2) + 2127(x_3)$$

e. Manufacturing: 2760
Government: 71
$(2760 - 71) \pm 2.3060(951.07)$; 495.8326 ----- 4882.1674

13.19.

a.

Plot

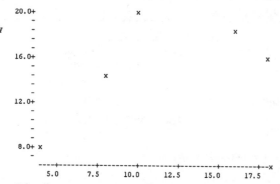

The data seems to suggest a nonlinear relationship.

b.

$$\hat{y} = 9.398 + 0.5181x$$

Predictor	Coef	SE Coef	T	P
Constant	9.398	4.331	2.17	0.118
x	0.5181	0.3513	1.47	0.237

S = 4.048   R-Sq = 42.0%   R-Sq(adj) = 22.7%

Analysis of Variance

Source	DF	SS	MS	F	P
Regression	1	35.64	35.64	2.18	0.237
Residual Error	3	49.16	16.39		
Total	4	84.80			

The p-value = 0.237 > α = 0.05. Therefore, do not reject H_0 and conclude that there is not a linear relationship between the dependent and independent variables.

c. $\hat{y} = -5.445 + 3.8509x - 0.14793x^2$

Predictor	Coef	SE Coef	T	P
Constant	-5.445	4.660	-1.17	0.363
x	3.8509	0.9609	4.01	0.057
x2	-0.14793	0.04205	-3.52	0.072

S = 1.849   R-Sq = 91.9%   R-Sq(adj) = 83.9%

Analysis of Variance

Source	DF	SS	MS	F	P
Regression	2	77.961	38.981	11.40	0.081
Residual Error	2	6.839	3.419		
Total	4	84.800			

The adjusted R^2 (.839) for the curvilinear model exceeds the R^2 of the simple linear model. The model's variance estimate is smaller for the curvilinear model and the F-test for the simple linear model is not significant. It appears that the curvilinear model provides a better fit of the data.

13.21.

a.

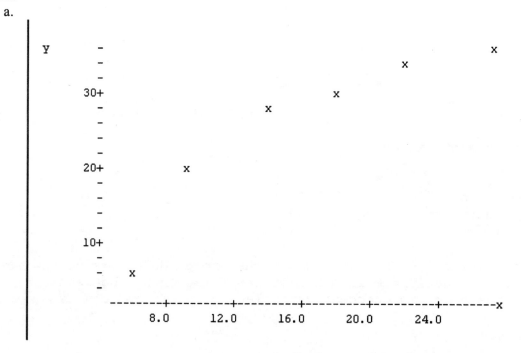

b. $\hat{y} = 4.937 + 1.2643x$

Predictor	Coef	SE Coef	T	P
Constant	4.937	5.448	0.91	0.416
x	1.2643	0.3102	4.08	0.015

S = 5.498   R-Sq = 80.6%   R-Sq(adj) = 75.7%

Analysis of Variance

Source	DF	SS	MS	F	P
Regression	1	501.94	501.94	16.61	0.015
Residual Error	4	120.89	30.22		
Total	5	622.83			

The p-value = 0.015 < α = 0.05. Therefore, reject H_0 and conclude that there is a linear relationship between the dependent and independent variables.

c. $\hat{y} = -25.155 + 18.983 \ln x$

```
Predictor              Coef       SE Coef            T           P
Constant            -25.155         6.917        -3.64       0.022
lnx                  18.983         2.561         7.41       0.002


S = 3.251          R-Sq = 93.2%      R-Sq(adj) = 91.5%

Analysis of Variance

Source                DF            SS            MS          F          P
Regression             1        580.57        580.57      54.95      0.002
Residual Error         4         42.27         10.57
Total                  5        622.83
```

The adjusted R^2 (91.5%) for the curvilinear model exceeds the R^2 of the simple linear model. The model's variance estimate is smaller for the curvilinear model and the F-test has a smaller p-value. It appears that the logarithmic model provides a better fit of the data.

13.23.

a.

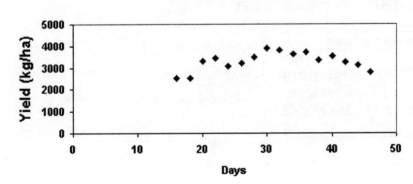

SUMMARY OUTPUT SIMPLE LINEAR REGRESSION

Regression Statistics	
Multiple R	0.279123232
R Square	0.077909779
Adjusted R Square	0.012046191
Standard Error	415.8160232
Observations	16

ANOVA

	df	SS	MS	F
Regression	1	204526.2382	204526.2382	1.182896072
Residual	14	2420641.512	172902.9651	
Total	15	2625167.75		

	Coefficients	Standard Error	t Stat	P-value
Intercept	2902.964706	364.6679609	7.960569661	1.45046E-06
Days	12.26323529	11.27539503	1.087610257	0.295137486

SUMMARY OUTPUT – 2ND ORDER MODEL

Regression Statistics	
Multiple R	0.891151457
R Square	0.794150919
Adjusted R Square	0.76248183
Standard Error	203.883143
Observations	16

ANOVA

	df	SS	MS	F
Regression	2	2084779.382	1042389.691	25.07653158
Residual	13	540388.3682	41568.33602	
Total	15	2625167.75		

	Coefficients	Standard Error	t Stat	P-value
Intercept	-1070.397689	617.2526804	-1.734132104	0.106527339
Days	293.4829482	42.17763668	6.958259668	9.94294E-06
Days2	-4.535801821	0.674415013	-6.725535071	1.41423E-05

b.   For the simple linear model $F = 1.1829 < 4.6001$ so conclude that the simple linear model is not a significant model.

For the 2nd Order Model $F = 25.0765 > 3.8056$ so conclude that the 2nd order model is a significant model.

c. The 2nd Order model with a squared term would be preferred to the simple linear model. As stated in part b the simple linear model is not significant and has an R^2 of 0.0779. The 2nd order model is significant and has an R^2 of 0.7942.

d. Charles should use the 2nd order model with days squared for the reasons stated in parts b and c above.

13.25.

a.

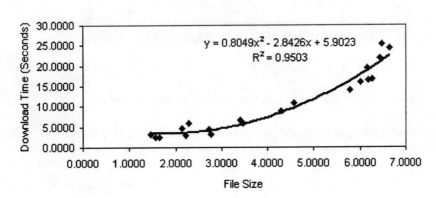

b. Correlation Coefficient between file size and download time = 0.9477

H_0: $\rho = 0$
H_A: $\rho \neq 0$
d.f. = 20-2 = 18

Decision Rule:

If p-value < .05, Reject H_0, otherwise do not reject H_0.

$t = 0.9477 / \sqrt{(1 - 0.9477^2)/(20 - 2)} = 12.5978$

Since $t_{\alpha/2} = 2.445$ and t = 12.5987, we know the p-value < .05. we can reject H_0 and conclude there is a relationship between file size and download time.

c.   The linear model can be found using the Chart Wizard option in Excel.

Linear Model

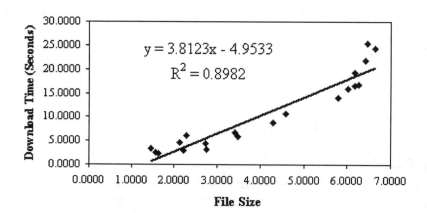

Because we have a curve in the data a nonlinear model would fit better.

d.   The nonlinear model was shown in part a. Comparing the R Square value of the linear model (.8982) with the R Square value for the nonlinear model (.9503) we see the nonlinear model provides a better fit.

13.27.

a. $y = \beta_o + \beta_1 x + \beta_2 x^2 + \varepsilon$
      The model is found from the following output.

SUMMARY OUTPUT

Regression Statistics	
Multiple R	0.48629779
R Square	0.23648554
Adjusted R Square	0.23165317
Standard Error	55460.6381
Observations	319

ANOVA

	df	SS	MS	F	Significance F
Regression	2	3.01054E+11	1.51E+11	48.9377965	3.05582E-19
Residual	316	9.71979E+11	3.08E+09		
Total	318	1.27303E+12			

	Coefficients	Standard Error	t Stat	P-value	Lower 95%	Upper 95%
Intercept	207311.77	4806.438152	43.1321	1.88E-134	197855.0992	216768.44
Age	-2192.3367	543.7555979	-4.03184	6.9424E-05	-3262.176232	-1122.497
Age Sq	6.83853883	10.39694787	0.657745	0.51118094	-13.61746434	27.29454

price = 207311.77 − 2192.3367(age) + 6.8385(age sq)

b.

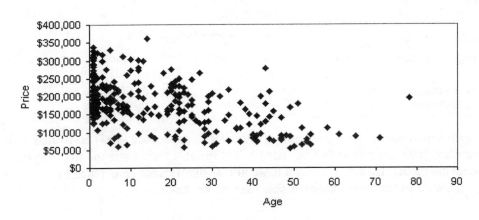

c.

SUMMARY OUTPUT

Regression Statistics	
Multiple R	0.485221836
R Square	0.23544023
Adjusted R Square	0.233028369
Standard Error	55410.98371
Observations	319

ANOVA

	df	SS	MS	F
Regression	1	2.99723E+11	2.99723E+11	97.61768237
Residual	317	9.7331E+11	3070377116	
Total	318	1.27303E+12		

	Coefficients	Standard Error	t Stat	P-value
Intercept	205722.9719	4151.648878	49.55211241	2.5246E-151
Age	-1856.764476	187.9284676	-9.88016611	3.03059E-20

The estimate of the model is price = 205722.97 − 1856.76(age)

13.29.

a.

```
                 y        x1       x2
x1           -0.088
              0.765

x2            0.062    -0.366
              0.834     0.198

x3            0.383    -0.128    0.129
              0.176     0.664    0.660

Cell Contents: Pearson correlation
               P-Value
```

None of the independent variables are significantly (at the 0.05 significance level) correlated with the dependent variable. It would appear that no independent variables will enter the first step of the stepwise regression model. However, using a more liberal significance level (such as Minitab's 0.25), x_3 would be the most likely variable to enter the model.

b.

```
Forward selection.  Alpha-to-Enter: 0.25

Response is    y    on  3 predictors, with N =    14


       Step         1
Constant        26.19

x3               0.42
T-Value          1.44
P-Value          0.176

S                4.46
R-Sq            14.68
R-Sq(adj)        7.57
C-p              0.0
```

c.

The regression equation is
y = 27.9 - 0.035 x1 - 0.002 x2 + 0.412 x3

Predictor	Coef	SE Coef	T	P
Constant	27.92	22.47	1.24	0.243
x1	-0.0346	0.2699	-0.13	0.901
x2	-0.0017	0.2608	-0.01	0.995
x3	0.4120	0.3217	1.28	0.229

S = 4.886   R-Sq = 14.8%   R-Sq(adj) = 0.0%

Analysis of Variance

Source	DF	SS	MS	F	P
Regression	3	41.60	13.87	0.58	0.641
Residual Error	10	238.76	23.88		
Total	13	280.36			

Of course, the difference between the two models is that the full model has more independent variables. However, each of the variables and the entire model are not significant. The adjusted R^2 is 0% for the full model and 7.57% for the forward selection model. Neither model offers a good approach to fitting this data.

13.31.

a.

Backward elimination. Alpha-to-Remove: 0.05

Response is Calls Re on 3 predictors, with N =   12

Step	1	2	3
Constant	-269.84	-248.04	-18.33
Ads Plac	5		
T-Value	0.24		
P-Value	0.817		
Calls Re	0.83	0.92	1.07
T-Value	1.59	2.57	2.74
P-Value	0.150	0.030	0.021
Airline	0.089	0.093	
T-Value	1.62	1.87	
P-Value	0.145	0.094	
S	86.2	81.5	91.1
R-Sq	59.11	58.82	42.83
R-Sq(adj)	43.78	49.67	37.12
C-p	4.0	2.1	3.2

$\hat{y} = -18.33 + 1.07x_2$

b. There is one independent variables (x_2) and one dependent variable (y).

c. x_1 was the first variable removed. It was removed because the p-value associated with it (0.817) was larger than the specified significance level (0. 05). x_3 was the last variable removed. It was removed because the p-value associated with it (0.094) was larger than the specified significance level (0. 05).

13.33.

State University Football
Table of Results for General Stepwise

Team Win/Loss Percentage entered.

	df	SS	MS	F	Significance F
Regression	1	49456399.47	49456399.47	36.0669839	3.22371E-05
Residual	14	19197324.47	1371237.462		
Total	15	68653723.94			

	Coefficients	Standard Error	t Stat	P-value
Intercept	11392.04318	805.2977978	14.1463732	1.10211E-09
Team Win/Loss Percentage	72.2162984	12.02486781	6.005579398	3.22371E-05

No other variables could be entered into the model. Stepwise ends.

a.   Team Win/Loss Percentage entered at Step 1 because it had the highest correlation with the dependent variable, Game Attendance.

b.   Only one step occurred in this model. The R^2 = 49456399.47/68653723.94 = 0.7204; the standard error of the estimate is $\sqrt{1371237.462}$ = 1,170.9985

c.   The final model is significant with a p-value of 3.2237E-05. The model stopped at this step because no other variables could be entered or removed based on the requirements established in the model.

d.   Again, the overall model is significant with a p-value of 3.2237E-05. The Team Win/Loss Percentage is significant with a p-value of 3.2237E-05.

13.35.

a. The regression equation is
$$\hat{y} = 5.494 + 1.2213 \, x$$

b.

$H_0 : \beta_1 = 0.0$

$H_A : \beta_1 \neq 0.0$

Predictor	Coef	SE Coef	T	P
Constant	5.494	4.274	1.29	0.255
x	1.2213	0.2086	5.85	0.002

S = 4.944   R-Sq = 87.3%   R-Sq(adj) = 84.7%

Analysis of Variance

Source	DF	SS	MS	F	P
Regression	1	837.79	837.79	34.28	0.002
Residual Error	5	122.21	24.44		
Total	6	960.00			

The p-value equals 0.002 which is smaller than the significance level = 0.05. Thus, the regression equation is found to be significant.

c.

Note, the solution was done using Minitab. The Minitab standardized residuals will be slightly different than those computed in Excel (Minitab uses Studentized Standardized Residuals) . The plots will still provide the same general conclusions.

RESI1	SRES1
-7.82146	-2.07346
3.51475	0.85039
5.40844	1.20642
2.52340	0.55140
0.63835	0.14135
-3.46796	-0.82305
-0.79552	-0.23246

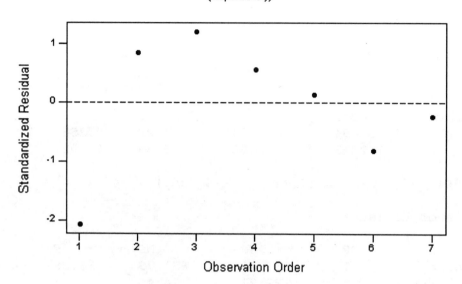

Residuals Versus the Order of the Data

(response is y)

This graph indicates that the error terms are not independent of each other. Some "time" related factor is influencing the randomness of the residuals.

No evidence is available to refute the assumption that the standardized residuals have equal variances at each value of the independent variable.

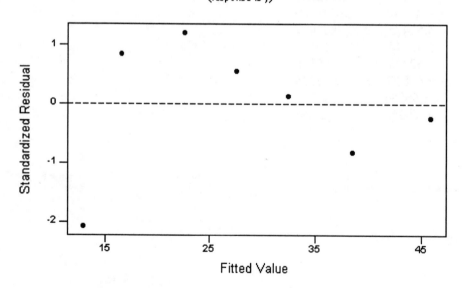

Residuals Versus the Fitted Values

(response is y)

The standardized residuals are negative for small values, positive for the intermediate values, and negative again for the large values of the fitted values. This indicates that, perhaps, a 2nd order term be placed into the model.

Normal Probability Plot for SRES1
ML Estimates - 95% CI

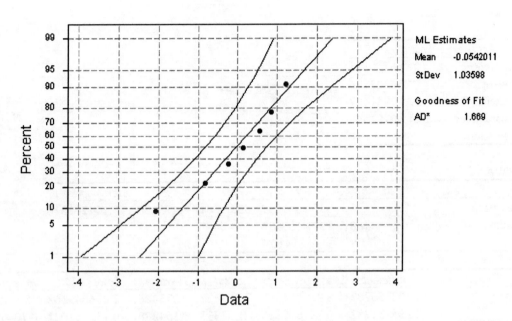

The normal probability plot indicates that the assumption that the standardized residuals possess a normal distribution cannot be rejected.

13.37.

Note, the first printing of the text contained a typographical error in the data list for this problem. The value 132 should have been 32. The solution given is for the correct data.

a. The regression equation is

$\hat{y} = 16.928 + .286x$

b.

SUMMARY OUTPUT						
Regression Statistics						
Multiple R	0.486110611					
R Square	0.236303526					
Adjusted R Square	0.140841467					
Standard Error	11.60384568					
Observations	10					
ANOVA						
	df	SS	MS	F	Significance F	
Regression	1	333.3061237	333.3061	2.475366	0.154288216	
Residual	8	1077.193876	134.6492			
Total	9	1410.5				
	Coefficients	Standard Error	t Stat	P-value	Lower 95%	Upper 95%
Intercept	16.92786283	8.219716367	2.059422	0.073426	-2.026849362	35.882575
x	0.285731782	0.181609619	1.57333	0.154288	-0.133061022	0.7045246

The p-value equals 0.154 which is larger than the significance level = 0.05. Thus, the regression equation is not found to be significant.

c.

RESIDUAL OUTPUT			
Observation	Predicted y	Residuals	Standard Residuals
1	21.49957134	-6.499571341	-0.594099288
2	22.35676669	-2.356766687	-0.215422424
3	23.7854256	4.214574403	0.385237044
4	24.92835273	-9.928352725	-0.907510199
5	26.07127985	8.928720147	0.816137866
6	27.49993876	-7.499938763	-0.685538791
7	29.21432945	25.78567055	2.356962899
8	34.07176975	-9.071769749	-0.829213446
9	37.21481935	-5.214819351	-0.476665352
10	38.35774648	1.642253521	0.150111691

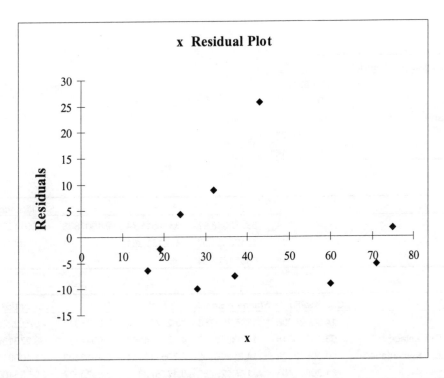

This graph indicates the residuals are randomly scattered around 0. However, there appears to be an increase in the variance as a function of time.

13.39.

No, the residuals should not be plotted against each x individually. This is satisfactory in simple linear regression where the fitted value of the dependent variable is determined solely by the one dependent variable. However, in multiple regression more than one independent variable determines the fitted value of the dependent variable and correspondingly determines the residual. So to determine the validity of the assumptions about the entire model, the statistic that incorporates all components of the model must be used. This statistic is the predicted value of y.

13.41.

a.

SUMMARY OUTPUT

Regression Statistics	
Multiple R	0.880534596
R Square	0.775341175
Adjusted R Square	0.693647057
Standard Error	1184.124723
Observations	16

ANOVA

	df	SS	MS	F	Significance F
Regression	4	53230058.97	13307514.74	9.4907833	0.001427993
Residual	11	15423664.97	1402151.361		
Total	15	68653723.94			

	Coefficients	Standard Error	t Stat	P-value	Lower 95%
Intercept	14122.24086	4335.791765	3.25713079	0.0076378	4579.222699
Team Win/Loss Percentage	63.15325348	14.93880137	4.227464568	0.0014185	30.27315672
Opponent Win/Loss Percentage	10.09582009	14.31396102	0.705312811	0.4952803	-21.40901163
Games Played	31.50621796	177.129782	0.177870811	0.8620577	-358.3540008
Temperature	-55.4609057	62.09372861	-0.89318047	0.3908828	-192.12835

Students should recognize that the overall model is significant by looking at the F and Significance F and should recognize that only team win/loss percentage variable is significant. Students can determine this by looking at the p-values of all the independent variables.

b.

RESIDUAL OUTPUT

Observation	Predicted Game Attendance	Residuals	Standard Residuals
1	14615.28455	-113.2845461	-0.111717834
2	13226.07735	-767.0773523	-0.756468762
3	16954.06403	-1354.064031	-1.335337483
4	16792.71228	-12.71227981	-0.01253647
5	15983.81404	-1383.81404	-1.364676053
6	18640.79321	659.2067879	0.650090035
7	14959.28101	-356.2810143	-0.351353689
8	14923.38203	865.617969	0.853646573
9	16953.96812	846.0318821	0.83433136
10	17458.24315	1991.756852	1.964211086
11	12695.06465	1194.935346	1.178409529
12	16458.92747	-1361.927469	-1.34309217
13	16916.67146	749.3285431	0.738965417
14	12472.55998	27.44001682	0.027060525
15	17884.93123	-1104.931227	-1.089650157
16	17423.22544	119.7745624	0.118118094
	Average Residuals		0.00

The residuals are the difference between the actual values and the predicted values from the model. The mean of this is 0 so you would expect the average of the residuals to be 0.

c.

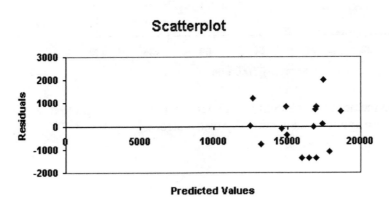

Scatterplot

The plot of residuals does not appear to have a pattern, therefore the constant variance assumption has apparently not been violated.

d.

Scatterplot

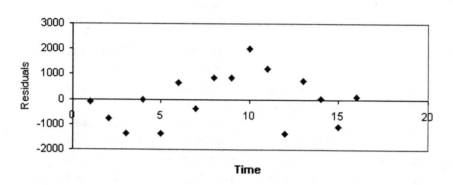

The plot of the residuals against time shows a systematic variation about zero, indicating that the residuals are dependent.   However, this plot assumes that the observations are collected in time-series order. If not, then this check for independence should not be performed.

e.

Normal Probability Plot

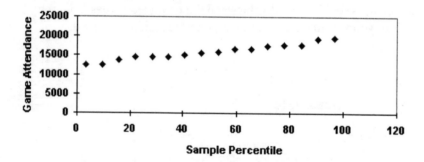

Based upon the normal probability plot which is almost a straight line we can assume the model error terms are approximately normally distributed.

13.43.

  a.

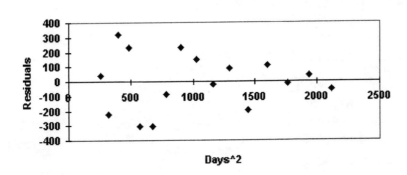

The residuals do not exhibit a constant variance. When Days^2 is small the variance of the residuals is large and decreases as Days^2 increases.

  b.

The residuals seem to possess a normal distribution.

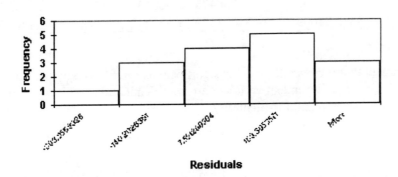

  c. within 1 standard deviation $= 9/16 = 56.25\%$
within 2 standard deviations $= 16/16 = 100\%$
within 3 standard deviations $= 16/16 = 100\%$

Since there are 56.25% within one standard deviation and 100% within two standard deviations, the residuals appear to be normally distributed.

13.45.

The least squares objective is the same for both simple linear and multiple linear regression. We wish to minimize the sum of the squared differences between the observed y values and the expected y values.

13.47.

A model is apt if it satisfies the regression assumptions.

13.49.

Student answers will vary depending upon the company selected.

13.51.

Regression Statistics	
Multiple R	0.905486545
R Square	0.819905883
Adjusted R Square	0.770789305
Standard Error	1.849512571
Observations	15

ANOVA

	df	SS	MS	F	Significance F
Regression	3	171.3056691	57.10189	16.69306	0.000208868
Residual	11	37.62766427	3.420697		
Total	14	208.9333333			

	Coefficients	Standard Error	t Stat	P-value	Lower 95%
Intercept	21.48048774	10.53116151	2.039707	0.066137	-1.698454194
Case Analysis Score	2.363993584	1.183937188	1.996722	0.071203	-0.241835915
Written Presentation Score	1.531347982	1.773536135	0.863443	0.406327	-2.372180707
Oral Presentation Score	3.807380091	2.493027189	1.527212	0.154937	-1.67973853

Students should comment that the overall model is significant as can be seen by the significance F but that none of the individual independent variables are significant at the .05 level. This should lead the students to a discussion on multicolleniarity.

13.53.

a. This relationship is measured using the F-statistic from the ANOVA portion of the multiple regression printout shown in problem 51. The critical F would be 3.5874. The calculated F is $16.6931 > 3.5874$ so conclude that the overall regression model is significant. However, none of the three independent variables are individually significant in the presence of the others.

b. Based strictly on the model developed and the correlation matrix from problem 52, a student should respond with improve oral presentation skills because this is the most highly correlated of the three independent variables so this would have the biggest impact on job rating.

SUMMARY OUTPUT

Regression Statistics	
Multiple R	0.86237169
R Square	0.74368494
Adjusted R Square	0.7239684
Standard Error	2.02964112
Observations	15

ANOVA

	df	SS	MS	F	Significance F
Regression	1	155.3805732	155.3806	37.71883	3.53539E-05
Residual	13	53.55276014	4.119443		
Total	14	208.9333333			

	Coefficients	Standard Error	t Stat	P-value	Lower 90.0%	Upper 90.0%
Intercept	21.518808	11.28202776	1.907353	0.078812	1.539107371	41.49850865
Oral Presentation Score	7.54518808	1.228544704	6.141566	3.54E-05	5.369519315	9.720856845

13.55.

a. The R^2 is 0.8199. This factor is measured by SSR/TSS.

b. Job Rating $= 21.4805 + 2.3640(9.1) + 1.5313(9.4) + 3.8074(9.3) = 92.7959$

c. Using the Excel printout this interval would be -2.3722 ----- 5.4349; this indicates that the effect could be 0 since this interval contains the value 0.

13.57.

Regression Statistics	
Multiple R	0.919126442
R Square	0.844793416
Adjusted R Square	0.782710783
Standard Error	23849.68125
Observations	15

ANOVA

	df	SS	MS	F	Significance F
Regression	4	30960327043	7740081761	13.60756414	0.000470491
Residual	10	5688072957	568807295.7		
Total	14	36648400000			

	Coefficients	Standard Error	t Stat	P-value	Lower 95%	Upper 95%
Intercept	-125307.8062	31082.09519	-4.031510921	0.002393684	-194563.0421	-56052.6
Pages X1	175.8963214	39.76976966	4.422864977	0.001288354	87.28373715	264.5089
Competing Books X2	-1573.777885	1995.851361	-0.788524595	0.448679286	-6020.812614	2873.257
Advertising Budget X3	1.591706487	0.444463005	3.581190042	0.005001797	0.601381026	2.582032
Age of Author X4	1613.747496	625.0234231	2.581899232	0.027327123	221.1082826	3006.387

a. $R^2 = 0.8448$; F critical would be 3.4780; since F = 13.6076 > 3.4780 conclude that the overall model is significant.

b.

	Coefficients	Lower 95%	Upper 95%
Intercept	-125307.8062	-194563.0421	-56052.6
Pages X1	175.8963214	87.28373715	264.5089
Competing Books X2	-1573.777885	-6020.812614	2873.257
Advertising Budget X3	1.591706487	0.601381026	2.582032
Age of Author X4	1613.747496	221.1082826	3006.387

c.   The critical t-value would be ± 2.2281

	Coefficients	Standard Error	t Stat	P-value
Intercept	-125307.8062	31082.09519	-4.031510921	0.002393684
Pages X1	175.8963214	39.76976966	4.422864977	0.001288354
Competing Books X2	-1573.777885	1995.851361	-0.788524595	0.448679286
Advertising Budget X3	1.591706487	0.444463005	3.581190042	0.005001797
Age of Author X4	1613.747496	625.0234231	2.581899232	0.027327123

Pages – t = 4.4229 > 2.2281 conclude pages is significant

Competing Books – t = -0.7885 > -2.2281 conclude competing books is insignificant.

Advertising Budget - t = 3.5812 > 2.2281 conclude advertising budget is significant

Age of Author – t = 2.5819 > 2.2281 conclude age of author is significant.

d. The interval is found as follows: $175.8963 \pm 2.2281(39.7698)$

        87.2852 ------ 264.5074

e.

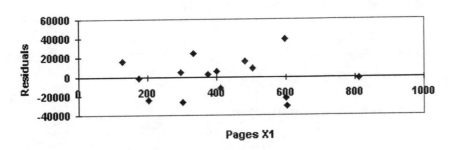

The plot appears to be linear since the model bands around 0

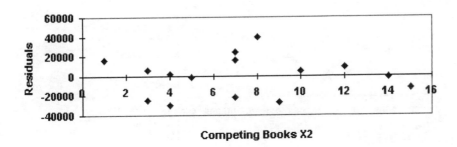

The plot appears to have a non-linear trend.

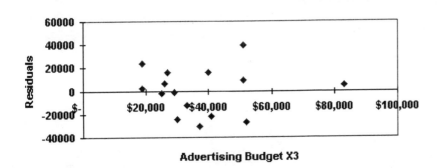

The plot appears to be linear since the model bands around 0

Age of Author X4 Residual Plot

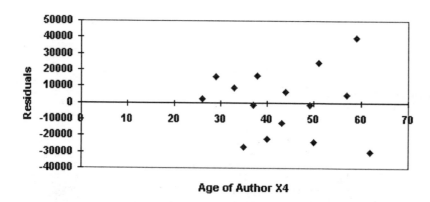

The plot appears to have a non-uniform (funnel) appearance.

Scatterplot

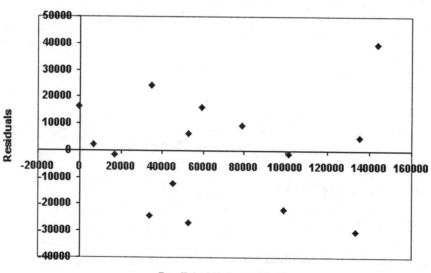

It appears the assumption of constant variance might have been violated.

Scatterplot

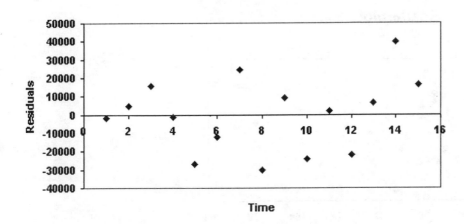

The alternating up and down pattern suggests the residuals are not independent.

Normal Probability Plot

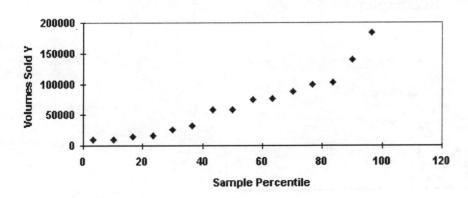

It appears the residuals are normally distributed.

Based upon the previous plots it appears that the model is not apt.

13.59.

Scatterplot

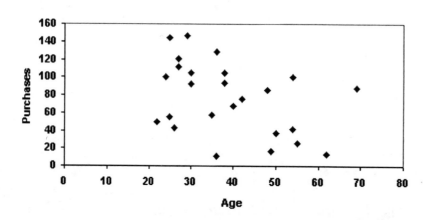

There appears to be a negative linear relationship between age and purchases.

Scatterplot

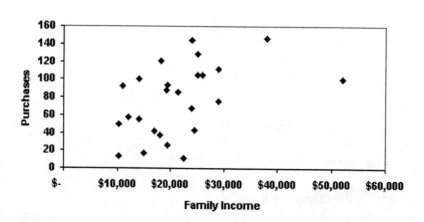

There appears to be a slight positive linear relationship between purchases and family income.

Scatterplot

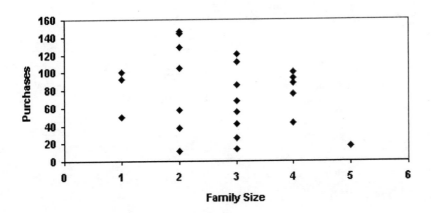

Based on the scatter plot it is difficult to detect any pattern of relationship between family size and purchases.

Scatterplot

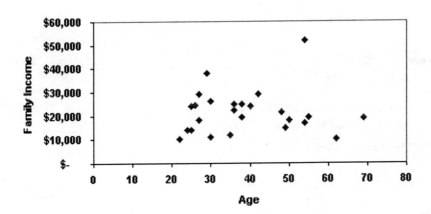

There does not appear to be any relationship between age and family income.

Scatterplot

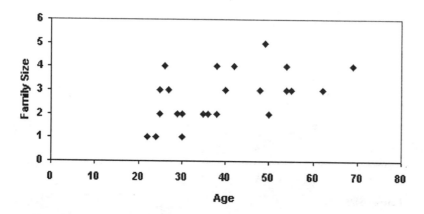

There appears to be a slightly positive linear relationship between age and family size.

Scatterplot

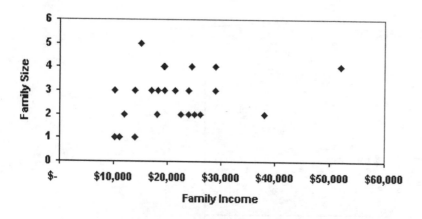

There seems to be little correlation between income and family size.

13.61.

Family income was brought into the model because it had the highest correlation with average monthly purchases.

   Using PHStat:
J.J. McCracken
Table of Results for Forward Selection

Family Income X2 entered.

	df	SS	MS	F	Significance F
Regression	1	8118.480548	8118.480548	6.14241706	0.020968538
Residual	23	30399.27945	1321.707802		
Total	24	38517.76			

	Coefficients	Standard Error	t Stat	P-value	Lower 95%	Upper 95%
Intercept	33.7553515	18.76904387	1.798458765	0.08524316	-5.071321127	72.5820241
Family Income X2	0.0019913	0.000803465	2.478390013	0.02096854	0.000329208	0.00365339

13.63.

Using the Excel printout from problem 13.61 the interval is: $0.000329 – 0.003653$. This interval indicates that as income increases, families spend more money at McCracken, and the average per dollar increase in purchasing is in the range indicated.

13.65.

There are several issues to address when deciding whether to add a new variable to the regression model. Among these are:

1. Did the adjusted R^2 increase? In this case, the answer is yes, from 0.1763 to 0.3905.

2. Did the standard error decrease? Yes, from 36.3553 to 32.5313. Note that when the adjusted R^2 increases, the SEE will also decrease.

3. For a model that will be used for forecasting purposes, is the added variable significant? In this case the critical t value is equal to ± 2.074. Since the calculated $t = -2.593 < -2.074$ we conclude the variable is significant.

4. Does the introduction of the new variable into the model introduce a high level of multicollinearity? In this case, age, is negatively correlated with the dependent variable. This is consistent with the resulting sign on the regression coefficient when age is entered. The low correlation between x_1 and x_2 is an indication that the addition of x_1 will not introduce much multicollinearity problem.

13.67.

For reasonable levels of alpha, only two variables will enter the model. In order for the variable, Family Size, to enter, the significance level would have to be larger than .25. Thus, the model will be cut-off at two variables.

Possible points to consider in the report are:

Relatively low R^2 compared to 1.0

The relatively large standard error given the size of the dependent variable.

The fact that there are many other variables that could have been included in the model but no data were collected.

13.69.

To deal with the categorical variables, we will recode the data, using dummy variables, as follows:

Driver Sex: Male = 1   Female = 0

Seat belt status:	D1	D2	D3
Not observed	0	0	0
Wearing	1	0	0
Not wearing	0	1	0
Not required	0	0	1

Knowledge of seat belt law	D4	D5	D6
No response	0	0	0
Aware	1	0	0
Not aware	0	1	0
Uncertain	0	0	1

Employment Status	D7	D8	D9
No response	0	0	0
Employed	1	0	0
Unemployed	0	1	0
Retired	0	0	1

Insurance Certificate	D10	D11	D12
Not observed	0	0	0
In vehicle	1	0	0
Not in vehicle	0	1	0
Other	0	0	1

Because D9 and D12 have no entries, they must be eliminated before the correlation matrix is determined. The correlation matrix becomes:

	Driv Citat	Vehil Year	Sex	Age	D1	D2	D3	D4	D5	D6	D7	D8	Year In State	Regis Vehic	Years Ed	D10	D11	Ins Status
Driv Citat	1																	
Vehic Year	0.030071	1																
Sex	0.257473	-0.25833	1															
Year	0.290971	0.116277	-0.04182	1														
D1	0.017898	0.155711	-0.12042	0.064997	1													
D2	0.012496	-0.06634	0.052132	-0.08079	-0.907	1												
D3	0.016939	-0.24442	0.129048	-0.01959	-0.107	-0.262	1											
D4	0.103341	0.189027	0.045194	-0.06644	0.1669	-0.099	-0.182	1										
D5	-0.08893	0.073879	-0.11676	-0.00231	-0.107	0.118	-0.031	-0.641	1									
D6	-0.00774	-0.22917	0.104828	0.181912	-0.087	-0.059	0.3936	-0.521	-0.0251	1								
D7	0.134696	-0.09875	0.192186	-0.30686	-0.107	0.083	0.0098	0.0392	0.0098	-0.1905	1							
D8	0.134696	0.098752	-0.19219	0.306856	0.107	-0.083	-0.01	-0.039	-0.0098	0.1905	-1	1						
Year in State	0.174276	0.12232	0.088115	0.610012	-0.113	0.092	-0.05	0.0234	-0.0856	0.0744	-0.039	0.0391	1					
No. Veh	0.176535	-0.04777	0.136736	0.330033	0.1512	-0.129	0.0028	0.0265	-0.0433	0.0584	-0.012	0.0118	0.285945	1				
Years Edu	0.005358	0.247238	-0.13712	0.048782	0.2284	-0.206	-0.116	0.1549	0.0024	-0.287	-0.059	0.0593	0.055306	0.108400	1			
D10	0.067598	0.070845	-0.02452	0.034299	-0.004	0.035	-0.001	0.2242	-0.0012	-0.2036	0.1382	-0.138	0.103962	0.189502	-0.1026	1		
D11	0.067597	-0.07084	0.024523	-0.0343	0.0043	-0.035	0.0012	-0.224	0.0012	0.2036	-0.138	0.1382	-0.10396	0.189502	0.1026	-1	1	
Ins Stat	0.002831	0.060221	0.127365	0.046721	-0.098	0.07	0.0482	0.0783	-0.1815	0.0392	-0.042	0.0425	0.166711	0.149672	-0.0169	0.1409	-0.141	1

Because of the large number of independent variables neither Excel or the PHStat programs will handle this problem. Using the stepwise option in Minitab we find:

(Note, in the first printing of the text, the problem asks for the dependent variable to be *Vehicle Year*. The correct dependent variable should be *Driving Citations*. The following solution uses Driving Citations as the dependent variable.)

Stepwise Regression

```
F-to-Enter:        4.00    F-to-Remove:       4.00

Response is Driving  on 17 predictors, with N =  100

        Step         1         2
Constant        1.3364    0.9381

Driver A     -0.0190   -0.0183
T-Value        -3.01     -2.99

Driver S                  0.57
T-Value                   2.62

S               1.07      1.04
R-Sq            8.47     14.49
```

So only the drives sex (male or female) and the drivers age are significant in the model. However, only 14.49% of the variation in the number of driving citations can be explained by the available data.

13.71.

Students should recognize the data problem associated with the SAT or ACT column. The tests use different scales and so should not be treated as one variable. This can be dealt with several ways:

1. The individual scores could be standardized. That is the average and standard deviation for both SAT and ACT scores could be found and the individual scores converted to z scores.

2. The data could be separated into two sets and two regression models determined.

3. The variable could be dropped from analysis.

Students will likely choose option 3, so we will present that solution.

a.

	1995 Population	Percentage Growth	1998 Unemployment	1998 Average manufacturing Income	1998 Average White Color Income	Labor Stress Index
1995 Population	1					
Percentage Growth	0.071670365	1				
1998 Unemployment	0.228273058	-0.0978607	1			
1998 Average manufacturing Income	0.272177498	-0.3529804	0.116154188	1		
1998 Average White Color Income	0.643103107	0.07982032	0.082136823	0.190613085	1	
Labor Stress Index	0.099448738	-0.1327263	-0.528255909	0.187802093	0.19275602	1

Looking at the correlations between labor stress index and the independent variables, 1998 unemployment looks most promising followed by the two 1998 income levels.

b.

SUMMARY OUTPUT

Regression Statistics	
Multiple R	0.63646464
R Square	0.40508723
Adjusted R Square	0.2949182
Standard Error	9.49777541
Observations	33

ANOVA

	df	SS	MS.	F	Significance F
Regression	5	1658.451685	331.6903	3.676961	0.011477833
Residual	27	2435.608921	90.20774		
Total	32	4094.060606			

	Coefficients	Standard Error	t Stat	P-value
Intercept	106.867926	24.87495665	4.296206	0.000201
1995 Population	6.9663E-07	1.33212E-06	0.522951	0.605274
Percentage Growth	-0.3883299	0.38970631	-0.99647	0.32787
1998 Unemployment	-7.1832151	1.850992849	-3.88074	0.000606
1998 Average manufacturing Incom	0.00047643	0.000567569	0.839418	0.408606
1998 Average White Color Income	0.00065578	0.00080226	0.817412	0.420848

The signs for the regression coefficients agree with the signs in the correlation matrix.

c.   The overall model is significant at the 5% significance level because the significance F = 0.01148 is less than 0.05.

d. $R^2 = 0.4051$;

e.   Looking at the p-values for the independent variables given in the printout, only 1998 unemployment is significant at the 0.05 level.

13.73.

Need to create two dummy variables for the stock exchange.

$X_7 = 1$ if NYSE, 0 otherwise
$X_8 = 1$ if NASDAQ, 0 otherwise
If both are 0, the designation is OTC.

Also need to eliminate observations with no data for some variables (-99 in the data set).

	Growth %	Sales	EPS	Profits	Last Yr Price	P/E ratio	X7	X8	Stk-Price
Growth %	1								
Sales	-0.09866	1							
EPS	0.358471	-0.15644	1						
Profits	-0.1172	0.744225	-0.01751	1					
Last Yr Price	-0.16851	0.505016	0.214602	0.668754	1				
P/E ratio	-0.00722	-0.27566	0.150827	-0.1032	-0.0857454	1			
X7	0.006398	0.209664	-0.03129	0.143019	0.2176906	-0.10315	1		
X8	-0.09525	-0.09168	-0.22298	-0.07548	0.00200916	0.09867	-0.16479	1	
Stk-Price	-0.07017	0.201503	0.447163	0.507966	0.65544737	0.306452	0.024908	-0.07927	1

The best predictors would be the ones most highly correlated with the stock price so the best variables would probably be profits, last year price and PE ratio. Sales and profits appear to be fairly highly correlated so you should probably not use both of those in the model.

13.75.

Since we have 8 independent variables in the model, we need to use Minitab to do the stepwise regression.

Stepwise Regression

F-to-Enter: 4.00   F-to-Remove: 4.00

Response is Stk-Pric on 8 predictors, with N =   61

Step	1	2	3	4
Constant	4.541	-6.394	-8.735	-6.528
Last Yr	1.19	1.24	1.13	0.83
T-Value	6.67	7.87	7.50	4.12
P/E rati		0.427	0.375	0.380
T-Value		4.19	3.88	4.07
EPS			0.076	0.087
T-Value			3.14	3.66
Profits				0.046
T-Value				2.24
S	11.5	10.2	9.47	9.15
R-Sq	42.96	56.21	62.68	65.75

As can be seen in the Minitab printout last years price entered at step 1, followed by P/E Ratio, EPS and Profits. While the model has four significant variables, its final R-squared value is 65.75%. Students will have to decide if this is a high enough value to be useful.

INTRODUCTION TO DECISION ANALYSIS

14.1.

A good outcome occurs whenever the "best" outcome results, or at the very least, the worst outcome does not occur. There is, however, an important distinction between a good outcome and a good decision. In decision analysis if we have properly used all the information available in making the decision, it was a good decision. It is important, however, that decision makers realize that in an uncertain environment, where they do not have control over the outcomes of their decisions, bad outcomes can, and will, occur. However, in the long run, by making good decisions there should be an increase in the number of good outcomes.

14.3.

The decision environment described here is one of certainty. In such an environment the results of selecting each alternative are known before the decision is made. In this problem, Varsity Contracting knows what outcomes will occur in terms of the time required and the costs involved. The following table provides a breakdown of the revenues and expenses for the decision facing Varsity.

Annual Revenues & Costs	Accept Contract	Reject Contract
Annual Revenues	$0.10 * 100,000 * 12 months = $120,000	$0.00
Costs:		
Labor	2 workers @ $8.00 per hour for 8 hours per night for 5 nights per week for 52 weeks = $33,280	$0.00
Supplies	$200 per week for 52 weeks = $10,400	$0.00
Overhead	20% of Labor Cost (0.2*$33,280) = $6,656	$0.00
Total Annual Costs	$50,336	$0.00
Profit	**$69,664**	**$0.00**

Given that Varsity will realize an annual profit of $69,664, Varsity should sign the contract.

14.5.

Multiplying each state of nature outcome by the appropriate probabilities, we find the following table:

		States of Nature			Expected Values
		S_1	S_2	S_3	
	A_1	150	80	-20	51
Alternatives	A_2	60	40	45	48.5
	A_3	240	70	-10	81
Probabilities		0.3	0.2	0.5	

Select the alternative with the largest expected value, A_3.

14.7.

Multiplying each state of nature outcome by the appropriate probabilities, we find the following table:

		States of Nature				Expected Values
		S_1	S_2	S_3	S_4	
	A_1	170	45	-60	100	32.0
Alternatives	A_2	30	190	175	-65	91.5
	A_3	145	-50	120	110	85.5
	A_4	-40	80	10	70	37.0
Probabilities		0.1	0.2	0.4	0.3	

Select the alternative with the largest expected value, A_2.

14.9.

a.

	Demand			
Purchase	10,000	15,000	20,000	25,000
10,000	8,500	8,500	8,500	8,500
15,000	5,250	12,750	12,750	12,750
20,000	2,000	9,500	17,000	17,000
25,000	(1,250)	6,250	13,750	21,250

b. 1. The maximum values are 8500, 12750, 17000 and 21250, in order, so purchase 25,000 hotdogs and buns.

2. The minimum values are 8500, 5250, 2000 and –1250, in order, so purchase 10,000 hotdogs and buns.

3.

Opportunity Loss Table				
	Demand			
Purchase	10,000	15,000	20,000	25,000
10,000	-	4,250	8,500	12,750
15,000	3,250	-	4,250	8,500
20,000	6,500	3,250	-	4,250
25,000	9,750	6,500	3,250	-

The maximum regret values are 12750, 8500, 6500, 9750, so purchase 20,000 hotdogs and buns.

14.11.

a.

Production	Demand			
	20000	40000	60000	80000
20000	$ 2,800,000.00	$ 2,600,000.00	$ 2,400,000.00	$ 2,200,000.00
40000	$ 1,800,000.00	$ 5,800,000.00	$ 5,600,000.00	$ 5,400,000.00
60000	$ 800,000.00	$ 4,800,000.00	$ 8,800,000.00	$ 8,600,000.00
80000	$ (200,000.00)	$ 3,800,000.00	$ 7,800,000.00	$ 11,800,000.00

Acquisition Cost	$ 200,000.00
Selling Price	$ 250.00
Discount Price	$ 50.00
Coupon (Demand Exceeds Supply)	$ 10.00
Variable Production Cost	$ 100.00

b.   Maximin: Max(2200000, 1800000, 800000, -200000) so produce 20,000.
     Maximax: Max(2800000, 5800000, 8800000, 11800000) so produce 80,000.

14.13.

Purchases	Demand				
	100,000	150,000	200,000	225,000	250,000
100,000	1000000	1000000	1000000	1000000	1000000
150,000	675000	1575000	1575000	1575000	1575000
200,000	350000	1250000	2150000	2150000	2150000
225,000	187500	1087500	1987500	2437500	2437500
250,000	25000	925000	1825000	2275000	2725000

Fixed Cost	150,000
Variable Cost	5
Shipping	1.5
Sales Price	18

Probabilities	0.1	0.4	0.2	0.2	0.1

Purchases	Expected Value
100,000	1,000,000
150,000	1,485,000
200,000	1,610,000
225,000	1,582,500
250,000	1,465,000

Using the expected value criterion, 200,000 dozen roses should be purchased. The expected profit of purchasing this amount is $1,610,000.

14.15.

Probability of Demand	0.15	0.2	0.2	0.3	0.15
			Demand		
Supply	500	1000	2000	4000	7000
500	$ (7,000.00)	$ (7,000.00)	$ (7,000.00)	$ (7,000.00)	$ (7,000.00)
1000	$ (8,500.00)	$ (4,000.00)	$ (4,000.00)	$ (4,000.00)	$ (4,000.00)
2000	$(11,100.00)	$ (6,600.00)	$ 2,400.00	$ 2,400.00	$ 2,400.00
4000	$(16,700.00)	$(12,200.00)	$ (3,200.00)	$ 14,800.00	$14,800.00
7000	$(23,000.00)	$(18,500.00)	$ (9,500.00)	$ 8,500.00	$35,500.00

Supply	Expected Value
500	-7000
1000	-4675
2000	-1425
4000	1075
7000	-1175

Best Expected Value Decision

Supply 4,000 for EV of 1,075

14.17.

a.

Revenue per unit $ 600,000
Variable Cost per unit $350,000
Salvage Cost per unit $150,000

States of Nature (possible successful restaurants)

Purchase	0	1	2	3	4	5
0	-	-	-	-	-	-
1	(200,000)	250,000	250,000	250,000	250,000	250,000
2	(400,000)	50,000	500,000	500,000	500,000	500,000
3	(600,000)	(150,000)	300,000	750,000	750,000	750,000
4	(800,000)	(350,000)	100,000	550,000	1,000,000	1,000,000
5	(1,000,000)	(550,000)	(100,000)	350,000	800,000	1,250,000

The maximum values for each alternative are 0; 250,000; 500,000; 750,000; 1,000,000; and 1,250,000, so purchase 5 restaurants for a maximum profit of $1,250,000.

b. The minimum values for each alternative are 0; -200,000; -400,000; -600,000; -800,000; and -1,000,000, so purchase no restaurants for a profit of $0.

c.

Mall Option:

Revenue per unit	$ 500,000
Variable Cost per unit	$250,000 (includes franchise cost)
Salvage Cost per unit	$100,000

Purchase	States of Nature (possible successful restaurants)					
	0	**1**	**2**	**3**	**4**	**5**
0	-	-	-	-	-	-
1	(150,000)	250,000	250,000	250,000	250,000	250,000
2	(300,000)	100,000	500,000	500,000	500,000	500,000
3	(450,000)	(50,000)	350,000	750,000	750,000	750,000
4	(600,000)	(200,000)	200,000	600,000	1,000,000	1,000,000
5	(750,000)	(350,000)	50,000	450,000	850,000	1,250,000

Larger Buildings:

Revenue per unit	$ 1,000,000
Variable Cost per unit	$500,000 (includes franchise cost)
Salvage Cost per unit	$200,000

Purchase	States of Nature (possible successful restaurants)					
	0	**1**	**2**	**3**	**4**	**5**
0	-	-	-	-	-	-
1	(300,000)	500,000	500,000	500,000	500,000	500,000
2	(600,000)	200,000	1,000,000	1,000,000	1,000,000	1,000,000
3	(900,000)	(100,000)	700,000	1,500,000	1,500,000	1,500,000
4	(1,200,000)	(400,000)	400,000	1,200,000	2,000,000	2,000,000
5	(1,500,000)	(700,000)	100,000	900,000	1,700,000	2,500,000

d. Mall Option:

Maximax: The maximum values for each alternative are 0, 250,000; 500,000; 750,000; 1,000,000; 1,250,000, so purchase 5 franchises for a maximum profit of 1,250,000
Maximin: The minimum values for each alternative are 0; -150,000; -300,000; -450,000; -600,000; - 750,000, so purchase 0 franchises for a profit of $0.

Larger Building Option:

Maximax: The maximum values for each alternative are 0, 500,000; 1,000,000; 1,500,000; 2,000,000; 2,500,000, so purchase 5 franchises for a maximum profit of 2,500,000
Maximin: The minimum values for each alternative are 0, -300,000; -600,000; -900,000; -1,200,000; -1,500,000, so purchase 0 franchises for a profit of $0

e.

Purchase Expected Profit

Purchase	Expected Profit	
0	-	
1	223,000	
2	401,000	
3	489,000	Optimal
4	397,000	
5	251,000	

Mall Option:

Purchase Expected Profit

Purchase	Expected Profit	
0	-	
1	230,000	
2	420,000	
3	550,000	
4	580,000	Optimal
5	490,000	

Larger Building Option:

Purchase Expected Profit

Purchase	Expected Profit	
0	-	
1	428,000	
2	736,000	Optimal
3	844,000	
4	632,000	
5	364,000	

Based on the expected value criteria they should purchase 3 franchises with the larger building option for an expected profit of $844,000.

14.19.

a.

	Opportunity Loss Table		
	States of Nature		
Probabilities	0.5	0.2	0.3
Alternative	S_1	S_2	S_3
A_1	0	25	40
A_2	15	15	20
A_3	35	0	0

b.

		States of Nature		Expected Values
		S_1	S_2	S_3	
	A_1	145	55	80	107.5
Alternatives	A_2	130	65	100	108.0
	A_3	110	80	120	107.0
Probabilities		0.5	0.2	0.3	

$$\text{EVUC} = .5(145) + .2(80) + .3(120) = 124.5$$
$$\text{EVPI} = 124.5 - 108.0 = 16.5$$

14.21.

	Demand			
Production	**20000**	**40000**	**60000**	**80000**
20000	$ 2,800,000	$ 2,600,000	$ 2,400,000	$ 2,200,000
40000	$ 1,800,000	$ 5,800,000	$ 5,600,000	$ 5,400,000
60000	$ 800,000	$ 4,800,000	$ 8,800,000	$ 8,600,000
80000	$ (200,000)	$ 3,800,000	$ 7,800,000	$ 11,800,000
Prob.	0.1	0.3	0.4	0.2	**EVUC**
EVUC	$ 280,000	$ 1,740,000	$ 3,520,000	$ 2,360,000	**$7,900,000**

Production	**Expected Value**
20000	$ 2,460,000.00
40000	$ 5,240,000.00
60000	$ 6,760,000.00
80000	$ 6,600,000.00

$$\text{EVPI} = \$7,900,000 - \$6,760,000 = \$1,140,000$$

14.23.

Probability of Demand	0.15	0.2	0.2	0.3	0.15		
	Demand						
Supply	**500**	**1000**	**2000**	**4000**	**7000**		
500	$ (7,000.00)	$ (7,000.00)	$ (7,000.00)	$ (7,000.00)	$ (7,000.00)		
1000	$ (8,500.00)	$ (4,000.00)	$ (4,000.00)	$ (4,000.00)	$ (4,000.00)		
2000	$(11,100.00)	$ (6,600.00)	$ 2,400.00	$ 2,400.00	$ 2,400.00		
4000	$(16,700.00)	$(12,200.00)	$ (3,200.00)	$ 14,800.00	$14,800.00		
7000	$(23,000.00)	$(18,500.00)	$ (9,500.00)	$ 8,500.00	$35,500.00	**EVUC**	
EVUC	$ (1,050.00)	$ (800.00)	$ 480.00	$ 4,440.00	$ 5,325.00	**$8,395.00**	

Supply	Expected Value
500	-7000
1000	-4675
2000	-1425
4000	1075
7000	-1175

EVPI = $8,395 - $1,075 = $7,320

14.25.

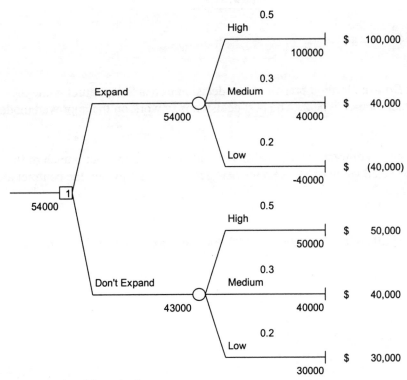

The owners should expand.

14.27.

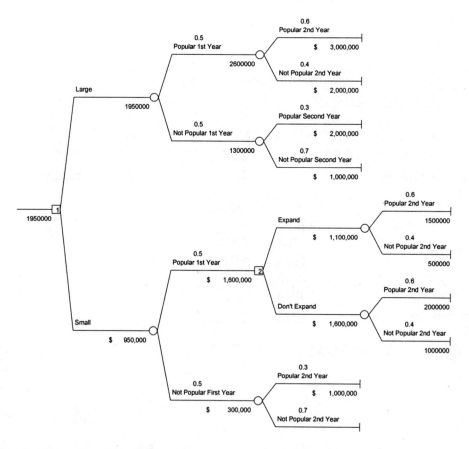

The developer should build the large resort.

14.29.

The expected value of the *Do Not Develop* branch on the decision tree is $78 per unit while the expected value of the develop branch is $82. The best decision is to work on the improved model.

14.31.

The expected value of the don't contract branch is $82. By evaluating the contract branch of the decision tree we find an expected value of $81. So the best decision is not to sign the contract and develop the improved model.

14.33.

Max (-400,000; -800,000; -1,200,000; -1,600,000; -2,000,000) so Max = -400,000 which is associated with build 10

14.35.

Variable Land Cost (per block)	200,000
Fixed Construction Cost (per block)	250,000
Variable Construction Cost (Per Unit)	70,000
Selling Price(per unit)	200,000
Auction Value	75,000

Demand

Build	0	10	20	30	40	50	EV
10	(400,000)	850,000	850,000	850,000	850,000	850,000	787,500
20	(800,000)	450,000	1,700,000	1,700,000	1,700,000	1,700,000	1,450,000
30	(1,200,000)	50,000	1,300,000	2,550,000	2,550,000	2,550,000	1,800,000
40	(1,600,000)	(350,000)	900,000	2,150,000	3,400,000	3,400,000	1,837,500
50	(2,000,000)	(750,000)	500,000	1,750,000	3,000,000	4,250,000	1,625,000
Probabilities	0.05	0.10	0.25	0.25	0.20	0.15	

Optimal decision based on expected value would be build 40 at an expected profit of $1,837,500

14.37.

Decision	Failure	Successful	EV
Don't Market	-	-	-
Market	(20,000,000)	50,000,000	22,000,000
Probabilities	0.4	0.6	

Based on the expected value the company should market the product.

14.39.

Decision	Exellent	Good	Fair	Poor	EV
Don't Market	-	-	-	-	0
Market	70,000,000	50,000,000	10,000,000	(20,000,000)	31,000,000
Probabilities	0.3	0.3	0.1	0.3	

Based on the expected value the company should market the product.

14.41.

Prepare	Demand						EV
	3	4	5	6	7	8	
3	10.5	7	3.5	0	-3.5	-7	3.325
4	8.5	14	10.5	7	3.5	0	9.425
5	6.5	12	17.5	14	10.5	7	12.825
6	4.5	10	15.5	21	17.5	14	13.975
7	2.5	8	13.5	19	24.5	21	13.325
8	0.5	6	11.5	17	22.5	28	11.775
Probabilities	0.1	0.3	0.25	0.2	0.1	0.05	

Based on the expected value they should prepare 6 orders for an expected value of $13.975

14.43.

Opportunity Loss
Table:

Build	Demand						EOL
	0	10	20	30	40	50	
10	-	-	850,000	1,700,000	2,550,000	3,400,000	1,657,500
20	400,000	400,000	-	850,000	1,700,000	2,550,000	995,000
30	800,000	800,000	400,000	-	850,000	1,700,000	645,000
40	1,200,000	1,200,000	800,000	400,000	-	850,000	607,500
50	1,600,000	1,600,000	1,200,000	800,000	400,000	-	820,000
Probabilities	0.05	0.10	0.25	0.25	0.20	0.15	

To minimize the EOL you would build 40 units for an expected opportunity loss of $607,500. This is the EVPI. The $607,500 is the most you would pay for perfect information so if someone is willing to sell it to you for $10,000 you would definitely purchase it.

14.45.

The following decision tree represents the decision faced by Graciela Grimm and the Grimm Group.

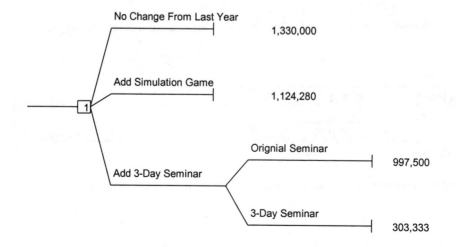

14.47.

If the original margins can be maintained, then the revenues and costs become (use new demand values in calculating revenues):

Seminar	Revenues	Costs	Profits
Quality	$1,320,000	$792,000	$528,000
Material	$1,035,000	$621,000	$414,000
JIT	$1,609,800	$1,046,370	$563,430

The total profit is $1,505,430 if margins can be maintained.

The decision tree with the new information becomes:

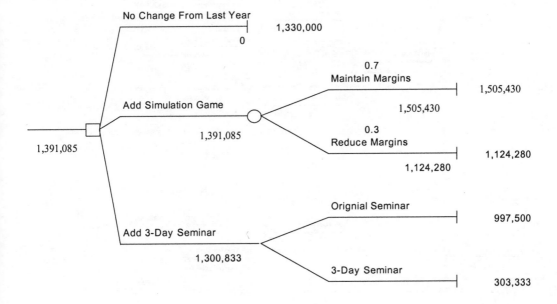

As can be seen from the tree, the best decision now is to add the simulation game.

18.49.

NOTE: The solution below is based upon a correction that needs to be made to the textbook problem. On problem 14.48, in the table entitled "League Race" the Yes/No column needs to be reversed. The table should be as follows:

League Race		
Player Strike	*Tight*	*Not Tight*
No	$5.00	$2.50
	p = 0.42	p = 0.28
Yes	$4.00	$2.00
	p = 0.18	p = 0.12

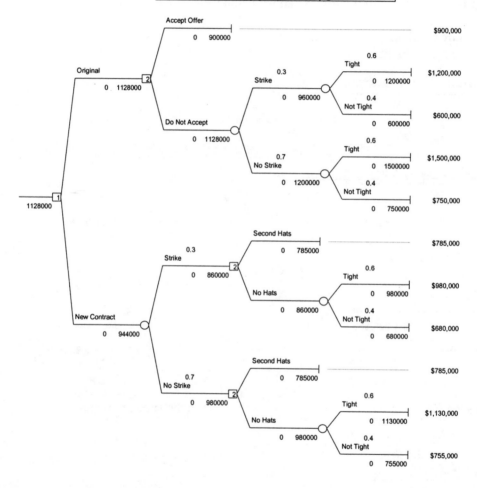

14.51.

The expected cost to you for the above proposal is $944,000. The expected cost of buying them on the open market is $1,128,000. In this case since we are discussing cost you would accept the proposal if you were the purchasing manager.

14.53.

The decision tree for the Gregston Corporation is shown below. By folding back the decision tree the expected values for the various alternatives are determined. Based on expected profits, Gregston should Not Test and Drill.

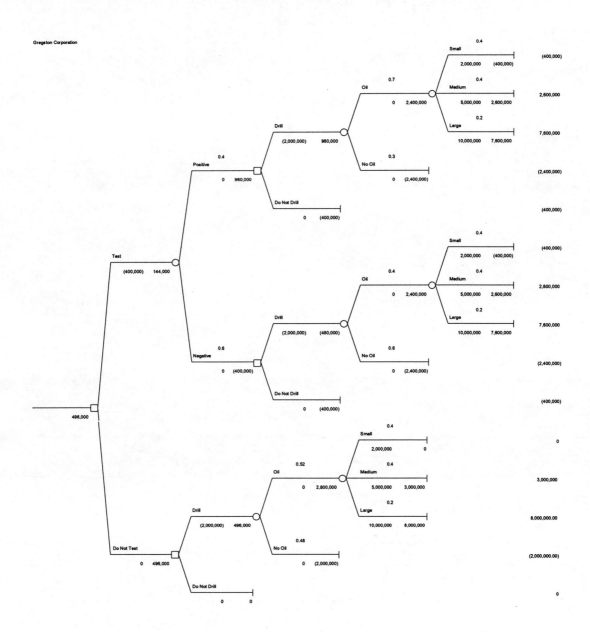

Note: the probabilities associated with the branches No Test –Drill are based on the probability the test has been positive in this area and the probabilities of finding oil when the test is both positive and when the test is negative as follows:

$(0.7*0.4) + (0.6*0.4) = 0.52$ = probability of Oil. $1-0.52 = 0.48$ = probability of No Oil.

14.55.

For the decision to change, the expected value of the Test branch will have to be greater than the expected value of the Do Not Test branch.

$$(x)(960,000) + (1-x)(-400,000) \geq 496,000; \; x \geq 0.66$$

CD-ROM CHAPTER 15

ANALYZING AND FORECASTING
TIME SERIES DATA

15.1

Planning is the process of determining how to deal with the future. Forecasting is the process of predicting the timing and magnitude of future events, predicting what the future will be like.

Manufacturing firms must plan their production: an exercise known as aggregate production planning in which the firm states how many units to produce on a period by period basis and what level of employment to have over that time period. A forecast of the firm's demand is a necessary input to the production planning process.

Likewise, service organizations will use a forecast in their budgeting and planning activities. Short term demand forecasts may be used as one input to determine the number of workers to schedule for a particular shift.

Electric utility companies will use a demand forecast to plan their long-term capacity requirements, as well as plan and prepare for short-term needs.

15.3.

a. An example of a short-term forecast would be a prediction made of the demand requirements for the next few weeks. This demand forecast could then be used in constructing the anticipated build schedule (i.e., master production schedule) for a manufacturing firm. The firm would use the production schedule to determine workforce levels, manage capacity at critical work centers, and ensure that needed parts and materials were available.

b. A medium term forecast, generally made for a period of time between 3 months to two years, is often used for staff planning decisions, purchasing and distribution decisions, and other issues related to capacity management decisions.

c. Long term forecasts, generally made for a forecast horizon of more than two years, serve to support capacity planning and facility expansion decisions. For example, an integrated circuit manufacturer forecasts the demand for dynamic random access memory chips several years into the future to determine whether the firm will have sufficient capacity at that time to meet the predicted level of demand. Due to the long lead time in constructing new fabrication facilities the firm uses the forecast to help determine whether demand will be sufficiently high to support the construction of a new plant.

15.5

Regression models may use, in addition to, or in lieu of, times series data other variables of interest. Regression models may use time-series data, so the two techniques are not necessarily exclusive. However, regression models need not use time series data (past history of the variable of interest) to produce a forecast. For example, a regression model may use dummy variables, or include some variable other than the variable of interest to generate a forecast. Furthermore, while regression models can be used for forecasting, they need not be developed explicitly for forecasting. Recall that a regression model is also used to determine to what extent variation in the a dependent variable can be explained by a set of independent variables.

15.7

A seasonal component is a pattern in the time series that repeats itself with the same period of recurrence. While we often think of seasonal effects as being associated with the seasons (spring, summer, fall, winter) of the year, the seasonal pattern may be hourly, daily, weekly, or monthly. In fact a seasonal pattern can be any repeating pattern where the period of recurrence is at most one year. An example of a seasonal component that is not associated with the seasons is the sales of tickets to a movie theater. Ticket \sales may well be higher on Friday and Saturday evenings, than they are on Tuesday and Wednesday afternoons. If this pattern repeats itself over time, the series is said to exhibit a daily seasonal effect. Likewise, phone calls coming to a switchboard may be higher at certain hours of the day (between 9:00 a.m. and 10:00 a.m.) than at other times (between 3:00 p.m. and 4:00 p.m.). If this pattern repeats itself in a predictable way then we have an hourly seasonal component.

15.9

a. This part of the exercise is done using Equation 15-1 following Example 15-1. Radio advertising has a base value of 300 and newspaper advertising has a base value of 400.

Year	Radio advertising	Index	Newspaper Ad	Index
1	300	100.00	400	100
2	310	103.33	420	105
3	330	110.00	460	115
4	346	115.33	520	130
5	362	120.67	580	145
6	380	126.67	640	160
7	496	165.33	660	165

b. The unweighted aggregate index is found using Equation 15-2 following Example 15-2.

Year	Radio advertising	Newspaper Ad	Sum	Index
1	300	400	700	100.00
2	310	420	730	104.29
3	330	460	790	112.86
4	346	520	866	123.71
5	362	580	942	134.57
6	380	640	1020	145.71
7	496	660	1156	165.14

c. The Laspreyres Index is found using Equation 15-4 following Example 15-4.

Year	Radio Ads	Percent Radio	Newspape	Laspeyres
1	300	30	400	100
2	310	35	420	104.59
3	330	35	460	113.78
4	346	38	520	126.43
5	362	40	580	139.08
6	380	42	640	151.89
7	496	45	660	165.08

d. The Paasche Index is constructed using Equation 15-3 following Example 15-3.

Year	Radio Ads	Percent Radio	Newspape	Paasche
1	300	30	400	100
2	310	35	420	104.52
3	330	35	460	113.56
4	346	38	520	125.28
5	362	40	580	136.89
6	380	42	640	148.27
7	496	45	660	165.13

15.11.

From the time series plot we see that there is a positive, linear trend. We can also see that there are movements that are not attributed to the trend. In other words, the time series exhibits random components. No seasonal or cyclical components are present.

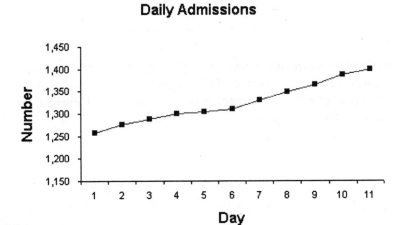

15.13.

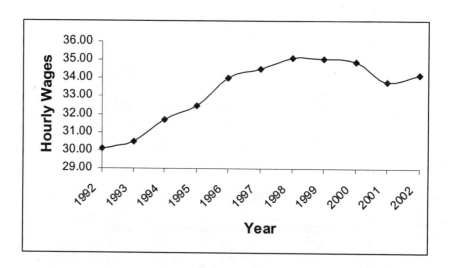

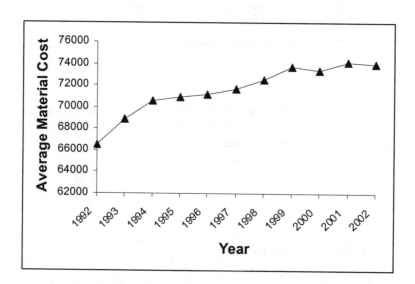

Both graphs show an upward trend with random components. The average material cost time series exhibits a cyclical component with a recurrence period of five years. The hourly wages time series may be indicating a cyclical component with a recurrence period of nine years. However, there is not enough data to determine if this pattern will repeat.

15.15.

This exercise should be done using Equation 15-4 following Exercise 15-4. However, first we must convert hourly wages to reflect their impact on the cost of a house. So, in 1992:

$$.6(\text{cost of a house}) = \$66500$$
$$\text{Cost of a house} = \$110833$$
$$\text{Labor cost} = \$110833 - 66500 = \$44333$$

Year	Labor Cost	Material Cost	% Material Cost	% Labor	Laspeyres Index
1992	44333	66500	60	40	100.00
1993	49893	68900	58	42	106.36
1994	57764	70600	55	45	113.59
1995	58009	70900	55	45	114.07
1996	55943	71200	56	44	112.95
1997	61078	71700	54	46	117.04
1998	66923	72500	52	48	121.92
1999	73700	73700	50	50	127.88
2000	67754	73400	52	48	123.44
2001	74100	74100	50	50	128.57
2002	83447	74000	47	53	134.96

15.17.

This exercise follows the procedure outlined in Figures 15-20 and 15-21.

Month	Sales	12-Period Moving Average	Centered Moving Average	Ratio to MA
1	23500			
2	21700			
3	18750			
4	22000			
5	23000			
6	26200	28337.500		
7	27300	28337.500	28337.500	0.963
8	29300	28479.167	28408.333	1.031
9	31200	28700.000	28589.583	1.091
10	34200	28883.333	28791.667	1.188
11	39500	29208.333	29045.833	1.360
12	43400	29500.000	29354.167	1.478
13	23500	29816.667	29658.333	0.792
14	23400	30075.000	29945.833	0.781
15	21400	30350.000	30212.500	0.708
16	24200	30475.000	30412.500	0.796
17	26900	30683.333	30579.167	0.880
18	29700	30616.667	30650.000	0.969
19	31100	31241.667	30929.167	1.006
20	32400	31825.000	31533.333	1.027
21	34500	32525.000	32175.000	1.072
22	35700	33216.667	32870.833	1.086
23	42000	33850.000	33533.333	1.252
24	42600	34191.667	34020.833	1.252
25	31000	34450.000	34320.833	0.903
26	30400	34808.333	34629.167	0.878
27	29800	35241.667	35025.000	0.851
28	32500	35800.000	35520.833	0.915
29	34500	35933.333	35866.667	0.962
30	33800	36333.333	36133.333	0.935
31	34200	36450.000	36391.667	0.940
32	36700	36883.333	36666.667	1.001
33	39700	37000.000	36941.667	1.075
34	42400	37175.000	37087.500	1.143
35	43600	37366.667	37270.833	1.170
36	47400	37525.000	37445.833	1.266
37	32400	37800.000	37662.500	0.860
38	35600	38075.000	37937.500	0.938
39	31200	38366.667	38220.833	0.816
40	34600	38725.000	38545.833	0.898
41	36800	39266.667	38995.833	0.944
42	35700	39658.333	39462.500	0.905
43	37500			
44	40000			
45	43200			
46	46700			
47	50100			
48	52100			

15.19.

The individual ratio to moving average values are shown below, along with the normalized values.

	Ratio to MA Values			Total	Seasonal Index	Normalized Index
January	0.792	0.903	0.860	2.556	0.852	0.849
February	0.781	0.878	0.938	2.598	0.866	0.863
March	0.708	0.851	0.816	2.375	0.792	0.789
April	0.796	0.915	0.898	2.608	0.869	0.866
May	0.880	0.962	0.944	2.785	0.928	0.925
June	0.969	0.935	0.905	2.809	0.936	0.933
July	0.963	1.006	0.940	2.909	0.970	0.966
August	1.031	1.027	1.001	3.060	1.020	1.016
September	1.091	1.072	1.075	3.238	1.079	1.075
October	1.188	1.086	1.143	3.417	1.139	1.135
November	1.360	1.252	1.170	3.782	1.261	1.256
December	1.478	1.252	1.266	3.996	1.332	1.327
				Sum =	12.045	

The normalized index for January, .849, compared to July, .966, indicates that both months have sales below the average trend value for the year, but January's are lower than July's.

15.21.

As seen in the graph, the sales data show a slight upward trend with a likely seasonal component with lower sales during July and November of each year. The Durbin-Watson Statistic is less than 1.21, the value of d_L for an $\alpha = .01$, indicating autocorrelation is present.

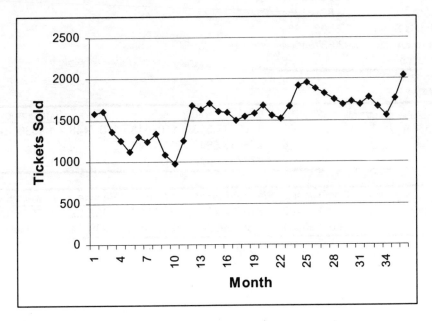

Durbin-Watson Calculations

Sum of Squared Difference of Residuals	771319.4741
Sum of Squared Residuals	1095250.271
Durbin-Watson Statistic	0.704240387

15.23.

The output for both models is shown as follows. The seasonally adjusted model provides a better fit. It is more significant, has a higher multiple R value and a lower standard error.

SUMMARY OUTPUT   UNADJUSTED DATA

Regression Statistics	
Multiple R	0.698345044
R Square	0.487685801
Adjusted R Square	0.472617736
Standard Error	179.4804815
Observations	36

ANOVA

	df	SS	MS	F	Significance F
Regression	1	1042598.479	1042598	32.36552	2.18351E-06
Residual	34	1095250.271	32213.24		
Total	35	2137848.75			

	Coefficients	Standard Error	t Stat	P-value	Lower 95%	Upper 95%
Intercept	1271.019048	61.09538155	20.80385	6.43E-21	1146.858376	1395.17972
Month	16.38185328	2.879530709	5.689071	2.18E-06	10.52994665	22.2337599

SUMMARY OUTPUT   SEASONALLY ADJUSTED DATA

Regression Statistics	
Multiple R	0.908522157
R Square	0.82541251
Adjusted R Square	0.820277584
Standard Error	93.63784504
Observations	36

ANOVA

	df	SS	MS	F	Significance F
Regression	1	1409417.513	1409418	160.7448	1.93365E-14
Residual	34	298113.5648	8768.046		
Total	35	1707531.077			

	Coefficients	Standard Error	t Stat	P-value	Lower 95%	Upper 95%
Intercept	1224.627402	31.87444017	38.42036	1.35E-29	1159.850789	1289.40402
Month	19.04690081	1.502297342	12.67852	1.93E-14	15.99386729	22.0999343

15.25.

This exercise is completed using the procedures outlined in Figure 15-19 through 15-25.

a.

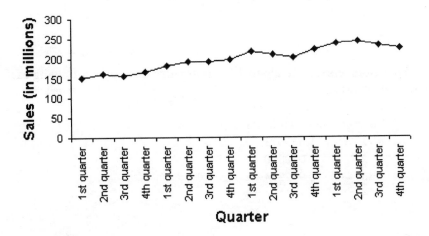

There appears to be an upward linear trend but you also see a seasonal component as a slight drop in the 3rd quarter.

Year	Quarter	Period	Actual Sales	4 Period Moving Average	Centered Moving Average	Ratio to MA	Deasonalized Sales
1997	1st quarter	1	152				146.8580
	2nd quarter	2	162	159.5			158.6838
	3rd quarter	3	157	167	163.25	0.961715	163.5528
	4th quarter	4	167	174.5	170.75	0.978038	169.6889
1998	1st quarter	5	182	183	178.75	1.018182	175.8431
	2nd quarter	6	192	190.5	186.75	1.028112	188.0697
	3rd quarter	7	191	199.25	194.875	0.980115	198.9719
	4th quarter	8	197	203.5	201.375	0.978274	200.1719
1999	1st quarter	9	217	206.25	204.875	1.059182	209.6591
	2nd quarter	10	209	212.25	209.25	0.998805	204.7217
	3rd quarter	11	202	217	214.625	0.941176	210.4311
	4th quarter	12	221	225.25	221.125	0.999435	224.5583
2000	1st quarter	13	236	232.5	228.875	1.031131	228.0164
	2nd quarter	14	242	233.25	232.875	1.039184	237.0462
	3rd quarter	15	231				240.6415
	4th quarter	16	224				227.6066

b.

Because the seasonal index numbers do not add to 4, we normalize them by multiplying each by 4/4.00445 to get the following values:

Quarter	Seasonal Index
1	1.035013
2	1.020898
3	0.959934
4	0.984154

c.

SUMMARY OUTPUT

Regression Statistics	
Multiple R	0.976793469
R Square	0.954125481
Adjusted R Square	0.950848729
Standard Error	6.498762579
Observations	16

ANOVA

	df	SS	MS	F	Significance F
Regression	1	12297.68445	12297.684	291.1803	9.14173E-11
Residual	14	591.2748109	42.233915		
Total	15	12888.95927			

	Coefficients	Standard Error	t Stat	P-value
Intercept	147.91253	3.407979848	43.401821	2.5E-16
Quarter	6.014121728	0.352444885	17.064006	9.14E-11

RESIDUAL OUTPUT

Observation	Predicted Deseasonalized Sales	Residuals	Squared Residuals	Absolute Value
1	153.9266518	-7.068650089	49.965814	7.06865
2	159.9407735	-1.256975545	1.5799875	1.256976
3	165.9548952	-2.402046206	5.769826	2.402046
4	171.9690169	-2.280136662	5.1990232	2.280137
5	177.9831387	-2.140005093	4.5796218	2.140005
6	183.9972604	4.07242605	16.584654	4.072426
7	190.0113821	8.960555203	80.29155	8.960555
8	196.0255039	4.146408811	17.192706	4.146409
9	202.0396256	7.619495222	58.056707	7.619495
10	208.0537473	-3.332057374	11.102606	3.332057
11	214.067869	-3.6368149	13.226423	3.636815
12	220.0819908	4.476347808	20.03769	4.476348
13	226.0961125	1.920258519	3.6873928	1.920259
14	232.1102342	4.935933072	24.363435	4.935933
15	238.124356	2.51709705	6.3357776	2.517097
16	244.1384777	-16.53183587	273.3016	16.53184
			MSE	MAD
			36.954676	4.831065

Values of the MSE and MAD are best used to compare two or more forecasting models. For this model the MAD, for instance indicates the average forecasting error is less than five (million). For the final period of data this is about 2%, which might be considered acceptable.

d. and e.

Quarter	Period	Seasonally Unadjusted Forecast	Seasonal Index	Seasonally Adjusted Forecast
Quarter 1 2001	17	250.1526	1.0350134	258.9113
Quarter 2 2001	18	256.1667	1.0208982	261.5201
Quarter 3 2001	19	262.1808	0.9599344	251.6764
Quarter 4 2001	20	268.1950	0.9841541	263.9452

15.27.

This exercise is completed using the procedures outlined in Figure 15-19 through 15-25.
a.

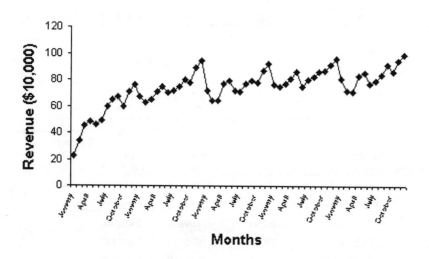

There appears to be a seasonal component and a very slight trend component.

b.

Year	Month	Period	Revenue ($10,000)	12 Period Moving Average	Centered Moving Average	Ratio to MA	Deseasonalized Data
1996	January	1	23				23.9834
	February	2	34				38.5003
	March	3	45				50.6770
	April	4	48				48.3449
	May	5	46				44.7762
	June	6	49	53.6667			53.0057
	July	7	60	57.3333	55.5	1.0811	61.3768
	August	8	65	59.75	58.5417	1.1103	63.9009
	September	9	67	61.4167	60.5833	1.1059	63.8774
	October	10	60	63.3333	62.375	0.9619	59.7616
	November	11	71	65.75	64.5417	1.1001	63.8742
	December	12	76	67.5	66.625	1.1407	65.1751
1997	January	13	67	68.5	68	0.9853	69.8648
	February	14	63	69.3333	68.9167	0.9141	71.3388
	March	15	65	70.4167	69.875	0.9302	73.2001
	April	16	71	71.9167	71.1667	0.9977	71.5102
	May	17	75	73.4167	72.6667	1.0321	73.0047
	June	18	70	74.9167	74.1667	0.9438	75.7224
	July	19	72	75.3333	75.125	0.9584	73.6521
	September	21	80	75.3333	75.375	1.0614	76.2715
	October	22	78	75.8333	75.5833	1.032	77.6900
	November	23	89	76.1667	76	1.1711	80.0677
	December	24	94	76.3333	76.25	1.2328	80.6113
1998	January	25	72	76.25	76.2917	0.9437	75.0786
	February	26	64	76.4167	76.3333	0.8384	72.4712
	March	27	64	76.3333	76.375	0.838	72.0740
	April	28	77	76.3333	76.3333	1.0087	77.5533
	May	29	79	76.1667	76.25	1.0361	76.8983
	June	30	72	76	76.0833	0.9463	77.8859
	July	31	71	76.3333	76.1667	0.9322	72.6292
	August	32	77	77.25	76.7917	1.0027	75.6980
	September	33	79	78.3333	77.7917	1.0155	75.3181
	October	34	78	78.6667	78.5	0.9936	77.6900
	November	35	87	79.25	78.9583	1.1018	78.2684
	December	36	92	79.5	79.375	1.1591	78.8961

Year	Month	Period	Revenue ($10,000)	12 Period Moving Average	Centered Moving Average	Ratio to MA	Deseasonalized Data
1999	January	37	76	80.25	79.875	0.9515	79.2496
	February	38	75	80.6667	80.4583	0.9322	84.9272
	March	39	77	81.25	80.9583	0.9511	86.7140
	April	40	81	82	81.625	0.9923	81.5821
	May	41	86	82.3333	82.1667	1.0467	83.7120
	June	42	75	82.6667	82.5	0.9091	81.1311
	July	43	80	83.0833	82.875	0.9653	81.8357
	August	44	82	82.8333	82.9583	0.9884	80.6134
	September	45	86	82.3333	82.5833	1.0414	81.9918
	October	46	87	82.5	82.4167	1.0556	86.6543
	November	47	91	82.4167	82.4583	1.1036	81.8669
	December	48	96	82.5833	82.5	1.1636	82.3264
2000	January	49	81	82.5	82.5417	0.9813	84.4634
	February	50	72	82.6667	82.5833	0.8718	81.5301
	March	51	71	83.0833	82.875	0.8567	79.9571
	April	52	83	83	83.0417	0.9995	83.5965
	May	53	85	83.25	83.125	1.0226	82.7386
	June	54	77	83.5	83.375	0.9235	83.2946
	July	55	79				80.8127
	August	56	84				82.5796
	September	57	91				86.7588
	October	58	86				85.6583
	November	59	94				84.5658
	December	60	99				84.8991

Month	January	February	March	April	May	June
	0.9853	0.9141	0.9302	0.9977	1.0321	0.9438
	0.9437	0.8384	0.8380	1.0087	1.0361	0.9463
	0.9515	0.9322	0.9511	0.9923	1.0467	0.9091
	0.9813	0.8718	0.8567	0.9995	1.0226	0.9235
Total	3.8618	3.5566	3.5760	3.9982	4.1374	3.7228
Seasonal Index	0.9655	0.8891	0.8940	0.9996	1.0343	0.9307

Month	July	August	September	October	November	December
	1.0811	1.1103	1.1059	0.9619	1.1001	1.1407
	0.9584	0.9950	1.0614	1.0320	1.1711	1.2328
	0.9322	1.0027	1.0155	0.9936	1.1018	1.1591
	0.9653	0.9884	1.0414	1.0556	1.1036	1.1636
Total	3.9370	4.0965	4.2242	4.0431	4.4766	4.6962
Seasonal Index	0.9842	1.0241	1.0560	1.0108	1.1191	1.1740

Since the seasonal index values do not add to 12, we must multiply each one by 12/12.0814 to get the following normalized values:

Month	Seasonal Index
Jan.	0.9590
Feb.	0.8831
March	0.8880
April	0.9929
May	1.0273
June	0.9244
July	0.9776
Aug.	1.0172
Sept.	1.0489
Oct.	1.0040
Nov.	1.1116
Dec.	1.1661

c.

SUMMARY OUTPUT

Regression Statistics	
Multiple R	0.814264676
R Square	0.663026962
Adjusted R Square	0.657217082
Standard Error	7.359763156
Observations	60

ANOVA

	df	SS	MS	F	Significance F
Regression	1	6181.469155	6181.4692	114.120596	2.53654E-15
Residual	58	3141.634595	54.166114		
Total	59	9323.10375			

	Coefficients	Standard Error	t Stat	P-value
Intercept	56.08801214	1.924287198	29.147423	2.4721E-36
Period	0.586097579	0.054864056	10.682724	2.5365E-15

RESIDUAL OUTPUT

Observation	Predicted Deseasonalized Data	Residuals	Squared Residuals	Absolute Residuals
1	56.67410972	-32.6906642	1068.6795	32.6906642
2	57.2602073	-18.7598886	351.93342	18.7598886
3	57.84630488	-7.16929146	51.39874	7.16929146
4	58.43240246	-10.0874645	101.75694	10.0874645
5	59.01850004	-14.2422907	202.84284	14.2422907
6	59.60459762	-6.59892089	43.545757	6.59892089
7	60.1906952	1.186057496	1.4067324	1.1860575
8	60.77679278	3.124112083	9.7600763	3.12411208
9	61.36289036	2.514461286	6.3225156	2.51446129
10	61.94898794	-2.18741295	4.7847754	2.18741295
11	62.53508551	1.339113991	1.7932263	1.33911399
12	63.12118309	2.053887888	4.2184555	2.05388789
13	63.70728067	6.157538936	37.915286	6.15753894
14	64.29337825	7.045447526	49.638331	7.04544753
15	64.87947583	8.320654667	69.233294	8.32065467
16	65.46557341	6.044647343	36.537762	6.04464734
17	66.05167099	6.953018171	48.344462	6.95301817
18	66.63776857	9.084626759	82.530443	9.08462676
19	67.22386615	6.428237081	41.322232	6.42823708
20	67.80996373	5.92184957	35.068302	5.92184957
21	68.39606131	7.875403338	62.021978	7.87540334
22	68.98215889	8.707888599	75.827324	8.7078886
23	69.56825647	10.49940207	110.23744	10.4994021
24	70.15435405	10.45691796	109.34713	10.456918
25	70.74045163	4.338160492	18.819636	4.33816049
26	71.32654921	1.144638887	1.3101982	1.14463889
27	71.91264679	0.16132786	0.0260267	0.16132786
28	72.49874436	5.054593637	25.548917	5.05459364
29	73.08484194	3.813430639	14.542253	3.81343064
30	73.67093952	4.214952815	17.765827	4.21495282
31	74.2570371	-1.62787975	2.6499925	1.62787975
32	74.84313468	0.854860305	0.7307861	0.8548603
33	75.42923226	-0.11116092	0.0123568	0.11116092
34	76.01532984	1.674717646	2.8046792	1.67471765
35	76.60142742	1.666957889	2.7787486	1.66695789
36	77.187525	1.708613557	2.9193603	1.70861356
37	77.77362258	1.476023545	2.1786455	1.47602354
38	78.35972016	6.567453387	43.131444	6.56745339
39	78.94581774	7.768183007	60.344667	7.76818301
40	79.53191532	2.050167515	4.2031868	2.05016752
41	80.1180129	3.594030675	12.917056	3.59403067

Observation	Predicted Deseasonalized Data	Residuals	Squared Residuals	Absolute Residuals
42	80.70411048	0.427027376	0.1823524	0.42702738
43	81.29020806	0.5454622	0.297529	0.5454622
44	81.87630564	-1.26285643	1.5948064	1.26285643
45	82.46240322	-0.47057872	0.2214443	0.47057872
46	83.04850079	3.605782941	13.001671	3.60578294
47	83.63459837	-1.76766661	3.1246453	1.76766661
48	84.22069595	-1.8942905	3.5883365	1.8942905
49	84.80679353	-0.3433549	0.1178926	0.3433549
50	85.39289111	-3.86280451	14.921259	3.86280451
51	85.97898869	-6.02192307	36.263557	6.02192307
52	86.56508627	-2.96863102	8.8127701	2.96863102
53	87.15118385	-4.41253613	19.470475	4.41253613
54	87.73728143	-4.44264657	19.737109	4.44264657
55	88.32337901	-7.51065463	56.409933	7.51065463
56	88.90947659	-6.32984569	40.066947	6.32984569
57	89.49557417	-2.73678313	7.4899819	2.73678313
58	90.08167175	-4.42341426	19.566594	4.42341426
59	90.66776933	-6.10192773	37.233522	6.10192773
60	91.25386691	-6.35476128	40.382991	6.35476128
			MSE*	**MAD***
			52.360577	5.1459883

H_0: Overall Model is not significant
H_A: Overall Model is significant

Since the F table does not have the appropriate values, use Excel and enter FINV(.05,1,58) to find Critical F at $\alpha = 0.05 = 4.0069$

Since $114.12 > 4.0069$ reject H_o and conclude that the overall model is significant.

While the model is highly significant, values of the MSE and MAD are best used to compare two or more forecasting models. For this model the MAD, for instance indicates the average forecasting error is just over 50,000. Manuel Guitierrez would have to decide if this is acceptable. Given how significant the model is, he would likely consider this to be a good model.

d. PHStat can be used to find a 95% confidence interval estimate of the revenues in month 120 (10 Years).

For Individual Response Y

Interval Half Width	17.81194221
Prediction Interval Lower Limit	**108.6077603**
Prediction Interval Upper Limit	**144.2316447**

This should be multiplied by 10,000 but it shows his goal is not realistic.
The standard deviation is larger because the projection is ten years in the future i.e., high leverage).

e.

Year 2002	Period	Unadjusted Forecast	Seasonal Adjustments	Adjusted Forecast
January	73	98.8731	0.9590	94.8188
February	74	99.4592	0.8831	87.8334
March	75	100.0453	0.8880	88.8379
April	76	100.6314	0.9929	99.9134
May	77	101.2175	1.0273	103.9839
June	78	101.8036	0.9244	94.1102
July	79	102.3897	0.9776	100.0930
August	80	102.9758	1.0172	104.7470
September	81	103.5619	1.0489	108.6245
October	82	104.1480	1.0040	104.5635
November	83	104.7341	1.1116	116.4182
December	84	105.3202	1.1661	122.8128

15.29.

This exercise is completed using the procedures outlined in Figure 15-19 through 15-25.

a.

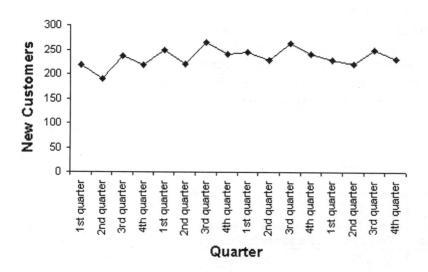

The graph indicates a seasonal component to the data.

b.

Regression analysis can be used to find the linear model needed to make forecasts for periods 13 – 16.

SUMMARY OUTPUT

Regression Statistics	
Multiple R	0.59044058
R Square	0.34862008
Adjusted R Square	0.28348208
Standard Error	17.9108678
Observations	12

ANOVA

	df	SS	MS	F	Significance F
Regression	1	1716.924825	1716.925	5.352024	0.043253006
Residual	10	3207.991841	320.7992		
Total	11	4924.916667			

	Coefficients	Standard Error	t Stat	P-value
Intercept	211.893939	11.02337709	19.22223	3.16E-09
Period	3.46503497	1.497782006	2.313444	0.043253

2001	Period	Forecast	Actual	Forecast Error	Forecast Error Squared	Absolute Error
Qtr. 1	13	256.9393939	229	27.93939394	780.6097337	27.93939394
Qtr. 2	14	260.4044289	221	-39.4044289	1552.709017	39.4044289
Qtr. 3	15	263.8694639	248	15.86946387	251.8398835	15.86946387
Qtr. 4	16	267.3344988	231	36.33449883	1320.195806	36.33449883

MSE	MAD
976.33861	29.88694639

Values of the MSE and MAD are best used to compare two or more forecasting models. For this model the MAD, for instance indicates the average forecasting error is about 30. This is better than 10% of data values. The firm might decide this level of average error is too high.

c.

Quarter		1	2	3	4
		1.0655	0.9124	1.0752	0.9593
		0.9990	0.9349	1.0894	0.9897
Total		2.0645	1.8473	2.1646	1.9490
Seasonal Index		1.0323	0.9236	1.0823	0.9745

Since the index values do not add to 4, be normalize them by multiplying each one by 4.0127.

Quarter	Index
1	1.0290
2	0.9207
3	1.0789
4	0.9714

d. Run the regression model based upon the deseasonalized sales

2001	Period	Forecast
Qtr. 1	13	256.5620033
Qtr. 2	14	260.0884382
Qtr. 3	15	263.614873
Qtr. 4	16	267.1413079

e.

Period	Forecast	Seasonal Index	Adjusted Forecast	Actual	Differences	Difference Squared	Absolute Differences
13	256.562	1.0290	264.0107	229	-35.0107	1225.7504	35.0107
14	260.0884	0.9207	239.4574	221	-18.4574	340.6745	18.4574
15	263.6149	1.0789	284.4074	248	-36.4074	1325.4997	36.4074
16	267.1413	0.9714	259.5053	231	-28.5053	812.5503	28.5053

	MSE	MAD
	926.1187	29.5952

f. The adjusted model has a lower MSE and MAD so I would recommend the deseasonalized data model.

15.31.

This exercise combines the linear model components developed in the Taft Ice Cream example with the nonlinear elements in the Harrison Equipment example.

a.

Regression Analysis

Regression Statistics	
Multiple R	0.931912269
R Square	0.868460477
Adjusted R Square	0.858342052
Standard Error	19.63573031
Observations	15

ANOVA

	df	SS	MS	F	Significance F
Regression	1	33092.62857	33092.62857	85.8296117	4.33333E-07
Residual	13	5012.304762	385.5619048		
Total	14	38104.93333			

	Coefficients	Standard Error	t Stat	P-value	Lower 95%
Intercept	36.0952381	10.66923438	3.383114176	0.004898727	13.04576299
Month	10.87142857	1.173459332	9.264427219	4.33333E-07	8.336324301

Forecast for period 16 without transformation = 36.0952 + 10.8714(16) = 210.0376

Regression Analysis

Regression Statistics	
Multiple R	0.98563659
R Square	0.971479488
Adjusted R Square	0.969285603
Standard Error	9.143186599
Observations	15

ANOVA

	df	SS	MS	F	Significance F
Regression	1	37018.16114	37018.16114	442.8122994	1.99795E-11
Residual	13	1086.772195	83.59786119		
Total	14	38104.93333			

	Coefficients	Standard Error	t Stat	P-value	Lower 95%
Intercept	65.29858233	3.620698469	18.03480265	1.39488E-10	57.47654036
Month^2	0.698807472	0.033208381	21.04310575	1.99795E-11	0.62706514

Forecast for period 16 with transformation $= 65.2986 + 0.6988(16)^2 = 244.1914$

Actual cash balance for Month 16 was 305. The transformed model had a smaller error than the model without the transformation. Based on this analysis and the analysis from problem 16 they should prefer the transformed model.

b. Model without transformation:

For Individual Response Y

Interval Half Width	48.27804189
Prediction Interval Lower Limit	**161.7600534**
Prediction Interval Upper Limit	**258.3161371**

Model with transformation:

For Individual Response Y

Interval Half Width	23.89550188
Prediction Interval Lower Limit	**220.29634337**
Prediction Interval Upper Limit	**268.08734713**

The model without the transformation has the wider interval so based on this you should select the model with the transformation.

15.33.

Equation 15-16 is used for this exercise.

a.

Year	Quarter	Actual Guests	Forecast Guests	Forecast Error	Absolute Forecast Error
Year 1	Q1	242	250.00	-8.00	8.00
	Q2	252	249.20	2.80	2.80
	Q3	257	249.48	7.52	7.52
	Q4	267	250.23	16.77	16.77
Year 2	Q1	272	251.91	20.09	20.09
	Q2	267	253.92	13.08	13.08
	Q3	276	255.23	20.77	20.77
	Q4	281	257.30	23.70	23.70
Year 3	**Q1**		**259.67**		
				Sum	112.73

Alpha	0.1
MAD	**14.091**

b.

Year	Quarter	Actual Guests	Forecast Guest	Forecast Error	Absolute Forecast Error
1999	Q1	242	250.00	-8.00	8.00
1999	Q2	252	248.00	4.00	4.00
1999	Q3	257	249.00	8.00	8.00
1999	Q4	267	251.00	16.00	16.00
2000	Q1	272	255.00	17.00	17.00
2000	Q2	267	259.25	7.75	7.75
2000	Q3	276	261.19	14.81	14.81
2000	Q4	281	264.89	16.11	16.11
2001	**Q1**		**268.92**		
				Sum	91.67

Alpha	0.25
MAD	**11.459**

c. MAD for part a was 14.091

MAD for part b was 11.459 so $\alpha = 0.25$ produced the smaller MAD

15.34.

a.

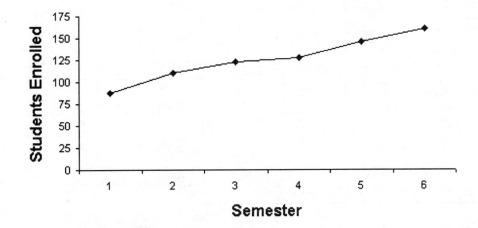

b. Yes it does appear that trend is present.

c. Equation 15-16 is used for this part of the exercise following Example 15-6.

Semester	Actual Enrollment	Forecast Enrollment	Forecast Error	Absolute Forecast Error
1	87	87.00	0.00	0.00
2	110	87.00	23.00	23.00
3	123	95.05	27.95	27.95
4	127	104.83	22.17	22.17
5	145	112.59	32.41	32.41
6	160	123.93	32.07	32.07
7		136.56		
			Sum	139.67

Alpha	0.35
MAD	**23.599**

d. Equations 15-18, 19 and 20 are used here following Example 15-7.

Semester	Actual Enrollment	Constant	Trend	Forecast Enrollment	Forecast Error	Absolute Forecast Error
Initial Values		77.93	13.54			
1	87	90.58	13.32	91.48	-4.48	4.48
2	110	105.12	13.62	103.90	6.10	6.10
3	123	119.60	13.84	118.74	4.26	4.26
4	127	132.15	13.52	133.43	-6.43	6.43
5	145	145.53	13.48	145.66	0.66	0.66
6	160	159.21	13.53	159.01	0.99	0.99
7				172.74		
					Sum	22.91

		Initial	
Alpha	0.2	Constant	13.54
Beta	0.25	77.93	10
MAD	3.819		

e. The MAD for the single exponential smoothing forecast was 23.599
    The MAD for the double exponential smoothing forecast was 3.819

    The double exponential smoothing forecast appears to be doing the better job of forecasting course enrollment.

15.35.

a. Equation 15-16 was used with an initial forecast value of 1500. Example 15-6 was then followed.

Forecast Permits

Year	Permits	$\alpha = .2$	Absolute Error	$\alpha = .5$	Absolute Error	$\alpha = .8$	Absolute Error
1	1500	1500	0	1500	0	1500	0
2	1470	1500	30	1500	30	1500	30
3	2100	1494	606	1485	615	1476	624
4	2380	1615.2	764.8	1792.5	587.5	1975.2	404.8
5	2050	1768.16	281.84	2086.25	36.25	2299.04	249.04
6	1350	1824.528	474.528	2068.125	718.125	2099.808	749.808
7	1180	1729.622	549.6224	1709.063	529.0625	1499.962	319.9616
8	1550	1619.698	69.69792	1444.531	105.4688	1243.992	306.0077
9	2000	1605.758	394.2417	1497.266	502.7344	1488.798	511.2015
10	2040	1684.607	355.3933	1748.633	291.3672	1897.76	142.2403
		MAD =	352.6123	MAD =	341.5508	MAD =	333.7059

b. For these data, $\alpha = .8$ provides the smallest MAD. The forecast would be:
    $1897.76 + .8(2040 - 1897.76) = 2011.552$

c. Equation 15-18, 19 and 20 are used. The stating values for C_O and T_O are found using linear regression and are C_O = 1711.33 and T_O = 9.21.   A series of calculations similar to that shown in Figure 15-32 should be performed. It shows the minimum MAD is found when both α and β are .2.

						Forecast Permits			Alpha = .2				
Year	Permits	C	T	Beta = .2	Absolute Error	C	T	Beta = .4	Absolute Error	C	T	Beta = .6	Absolute Error
1	1500	1676.44	0.39	1720.55	220.55	1676.44	-8.43	1720.55	220.55	1676.44	-17.25	1720.55	220.55
2	1470	1635.46	-7.88	1676.83	206.83	1628.40	-24.27	1668.00	198.01	1621.35	-39.96	1659.18	189.18
3	2100	1722.06	11.01	1627.58	472.42	1703.31	15.40	1604.13	495.87	1685.11	22.28	1581.39	518.61
4	2380	1862.46	36.89	1733.08	646.92	1850.96	68.30	1718.70	661.30	1841.91	102.99	1707.39	672.61
5	2050	1929.48	42.92	1899.35	150.65	1945.41	78.76	1919.26	130.74	1965.92	115.60	1944.90	105.10
6	1350	1847.92	18.02	1972.40	622.40	1889.34	24.83	2024.17	674.17	1935.22	27.82	2081.53	731.53
7	1180	1728.75	-9.42	1865.94	685.94	1767.33	-33.91	1914.16	734.16	1806.43	-66.15	1963.04	783.04
8	1550	1685.47	-16.19	1719.34	169.34	1696.74	-48.58	1733.42	183.42	1702.23	-88.98	1740.29	190.29
9	2000	1735.42	-2.96	1669.28	330.72	1718.53	-20.43	1648.16	351.84	1690.60	-42.57	1613.25	386.75
10	2040	1793.97	9.34	1732.46	307.54	1766.48	6.92	1698.09	341.91	1726.42	4.47	1648.03	391.97
					MAD =381				MAD = 399				MAD = 419

						Forecast Permits			Alpha = .5				
Year	Permits	C	T	Beta = .2	Absolute Error	C	T	Beta = .4	Absolute Error	C	T	Beta = .6	Absolute Error
1	1500	1610.27	-12.84	1720.55	220.55	1610.27	-34.90	1720.55	220.55	1610.27	-56.95	1720.55	220.55
2	1470	1533.72	-25.59	1597.43	127.43	1522.69	-55.97	1575.38	105.38	1511.66	-81.95	1553.32	83.32
3	2100	1804.06	33.60	1508.13	591.87	1783.36	70.69	1466.72	633.28	1764.86	119.14	1429.71	670.29
4	2380	2108.83	87.83	1837.67	542.33	2117.02	175.88	1854.04	525.96	2132.00	267.94	1883.99	496.01
5	2050	2123.33	73.17	2196.67	146.67	2171.45	127.30	2292.90	242.90	2224.97	162.96	2399.94	349.94
6	1350	1773.25	-11.48	2196.50	846.50	1824.37	-62.45	2298.75	948.75	1868.96	-148.42	2387.93	1037.93
7	1180	1470.88	-69.66	1761.77	581.77	1470.96	-178.84	1761.92	581.92	1450.27	-310.58	1720.54	540.54
8	1550	1475.61	-54.78	1401.23	148.78	1421.06	-127.26	1292.12	257.88	1344.84	-187.49	1139.69	410.31
9	2000	1710.42	3.14	1420.83	579.17	1646.90	13.98	1293.80	706.20	1578.68	65.30	1157.36	842.64
10	2040	1876.78	35.78	1713.55	326.45	1850.44	89.80	1660.88	379.12	1841.99	184.11	1643.98	396.02
					MAD =411				MAD = 460				MAD = 505

						Forecast Permits			Alpha = .8				
Year	Permits	C	T	Beta = .2	Absolute Error	C	T	Beta = .4	Absolute Error	C	T	Beta = .6	Absolute Error
1	1500	1544.11	-26.08	1720.55	220.55	1544.11	-61.36	1720.55	220.55	1544.11	-96.65	1720.55	220.55
2	1470	1479.61	-33.76	1518.03	48.03	1472.55	-65.44	1482.75	12.75	1465.49	-85.83	1447.46	22.54
3	2100	1969.17	70.90	1445.85	654.15	1961.42	156.28	1407.11	692.89	1955.93	259.93	1379.66	720.34
4	2380	2312.01	125.29	2040.07	339.93	2327.54	240.22	2117.71	262.29	2347.17	338.72	2215.86	164.14
5	2050	2127.46	63.32	2437.31	387.31	2153.55	74.54	2567.76	517.76	2177.18	33.49	2685.89	635.89
6	1350	1518.16	-71.20	2190.78	840.79	1525.62	-206.45	2228.09	878.09	1522.13	-379.63	2210.67	860.67
7	1180	1233.39	-113.92	1446.95	266.96	1207.83	-250.99	1319.16	139.17	1172.50	-361.63	1142.50	37.50
8	1550	1463.90	-45.03	1119.48	430.52	1431.37	-61.18	956.85	593.15	1402.17	-6.85	810.87	739.13
9	2000	1883.77	47.95	1418.86	581.14	1874.04	140.36	1370.19	629.81	1879.06	283.40	1395.32	604.68
10	2040	2018.34	65.28	1931.72	108.28	2034.88	148.55	2014.40	25.60	2064.49	224.61	2162.46	122.46
					MAD = 388				MAD = 397				MAD = 413

The combination of α = .2 and β = .2 gives the smallest MAD.

15.37.

Use Equation 15-16 or 15-17 and follow Example 15-6.

Month	Actual Gasoline Expenditures	Forecast Gasoline Expenditures	Forecast Error	Absolute Forecast Error
April	$ 23,586.41	$ 23,586.41	$ 86.41	$ 0.00
May	$ 23,539.22	$ 23,586.41	$ 17.62	$ 47.19
June	$ 23,442.06	$ 23,574.61	$ (83.95)	$ 132.55
July	$ 23,988.71	$ 23,541.47	$ 483.69	$ 447.24
August	$ 23,727.13	$ 23,653.28	$ 101.19	$ 73.85
September	$ 23,799.69	$ 23,671.74	$ 148.45	$ 127.95
October		$ 23,703.73		
			Sum	$ 828.77

Alpha	0.25
MAD	**138.13**

15.39.

Use Equation 15-16 or 15-17 and follow Example 15-6.

a.

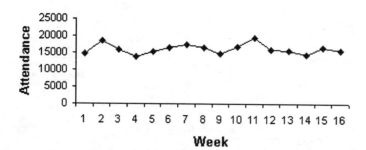

The random component is the only component clearly visible. There does not appear to be a noticeable trend or seasonal component.

b.

Week	Actual Attendance	Forecast Attendance	Forecast Error	Absolute Forecast Error
1	14560	14560.00	0.00	0.00
2	18655	14560.00	4095.00	4095.00
3	15987	15583.75	403.25	403.25
4	13689	15684.56	-1995.56	1995.56
5	15332	15185.67	146.33	146.33
6	16345	15222.25	1122.75	1122.75
7	17456	15502.94	1953.06	1953.06
8	16334	15991.21	342.79	342.79
9	14745	16076.90	-1331.90	1331.90
10	16778	15743.93	1034.07	1034.07
11	19456	16002.45	3453.55	3453.55
12	15789	16865.83	-1076.83	1076.83
13	15602	16596.63	-994.63	994.63
14	14556	16347.97	-1791.97	1791.97
15	16344	15899.98	444.02	444.02
16	15617	16010.98	-393.98	393.98
17		15912.50		MAD = 1286

Alpha	0.025

c.

Week	Actual Attendance	Forecast Attendance	Forecast Error	Absolute Forecast Error
1	14560	14560.00	0.00	0.00
2	18655	14560.00	4095.00	4095.00
3	15987	16198.00	-211.00	211.00
4	13689	16113.60	-2424.60	2424.60
5	15332	15143.80	188.24	188.24
6	16345	15219.10	1125.94	1125.94
7	17456	15669.40	1786.57	1786.57
8	16334	16384.10	-50.06	50.06
9	14745	16364.00	-1619.04	1619.04
10	16778	15716.40	1061.58	1061.58
11	19456	16141.10	3314.95	3314.95
12	15789	17467.00	-1678.03	1678.03
13	15602	16795.80	-1193.82	1193.82
14	14556	16318.30	-1762.29	1762.29
15	16344	15613.40	730.63	730.63
16	15617	15905.60	-288.62	288.62
17		15790.20		MAD = 1346

Alpha	0.4

d. Since the MAD is smaller for an alpha of 0.25 and since the time series plot reveals a relatively stable pattern, the first model is probably the one to use.

15.41.

As stated in the text there are several ways of selecting the starting values for an exponential smoothing forecasting model. One way is to use the first data value as the starting value. Another method is to use the average of the first several (or all) data values. Below, we show two approaches. One where the initial value is used and the second where the average (rounded) of the first three data values is used. Note that the forecast values are very close since the affect of the initial value is dampened. If you have enough data, any reasonable starting value can be used.

a.

Shirts Sold

There is a random component to the series. Also, it appears that sales are trending up over time with sales in the later months higher than the earlier months.

b.   Equation 15-16 or 15-17 is used following Example 15-6 (The starting method was based on the first value in the data set.)

Month	Actual Shirts Sold	Forecast Shirts Sold	Forecast Error	Absolute Forecast Error
1	37630	37630.00	0.00	0.00
2	34780	37630.00	-2850.00	4095.00
3	35150	36775.00	-1625.00	1017.50
4	45990	36287.50	9702.50	1382.25
5	36130	39198.25	-3068.25	398.97
6	47090	38277.77	8812.23	1372.08
7	37220	40921.44	-3701.44	2345.87
8	49180	39811.01	9368.99	989.28
9	40010	42621.71	-2611.71	698.65
10	50720	41838.19	8881.81	1404.22
11	63560	44502.74	19057.26	3941.80
12	48470	50219.92	-1749.92	119.38
13	64350	49694.94	14655.06	294.44
14	69590	54091.46	15498.54	1311.00
15	69000	58741.02	10258.98	608.10
16	71196	61818.71	9377.29	179.71
17		64631.90		MAD = 7576

Alpha	0.3

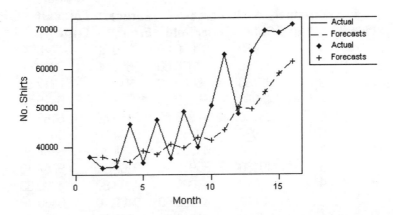

Shirts Sold: Actual vs. Forecast

The following is an alternative exponential smoothing model using 36,000 as the starting value (36,000 is the rounded average of the first three data values which was 35,853.33)

c.

Month	Actual Shirts Sold	Forecast Shirts Sold	Forecast Error	Absolute Forecast Error	MAD
1	37630	36000.00	1630.00	1630.00	1630.00
2	34780	36489.00	-1709.00	1709.00	1669.50
3	35150	35976.30	-826.30	826.30	1388.43
4	45990	35728.41	10261.59	10261.59	3606.72
5	36130	38806.89	-2676.89	2676.89	3420.76
6	47090	38003.82	9086.18	9086.18	4364.99
7	37220	40729.67	-3509.67	3509.67	4242.80
8	49180	39676.77	9503.23	9503.23	4900.36
9	40010	42527.74	-2517.74	2517.74	4635.62
10	50720	41772.42	8947.58	8947.58	5066.82
11	63560	44456.69	19103.31	19103.31	6342.86
12	48470	50187.69	-1717.69	1717.69	5957.43
13	64350	49672.38	14677.62	14677.62	6628.21
14	69590	54075.67	15514.33	15514.33	7262.94
15	69000	58729.97	10270.03	10270.03	7463.41
16	71196	61810.98	9385.02	9385.02	7583.51
17		64626.483			

Alpha	0.3

MAD   7583.51

    d.   The following value are found using the first data value as the starting value.

Month	Actual Shirts Sold	Forecast Shirts Sold	Forecast Error	Absolute Forecast Error
1	37630	37630.00	0.00	0.00
2	34780	37630.00	-2850.00	2850.00
3	35150	36062.50	-912.50	912.50
4	45990	35560.60	10429.40	10429.40
5	36130	41296.80	-5166.80	5166.80
6	47090	38455.10	8634.90	8634.90
7	37220	43204.30	-5984.30	5984.30
8	49180	39912.90	9267.10	9267.10
9	40010	45009.80	-4999.80	4999.80
10	50720	42259.90	8460.10	8460.10
11	63560	46913.00	16647.00	16647.00
12	48470	56068.80	-7598.80	7598.80
13	64350	51889.50	12460.50	12460.50
14	69590	58742.80	10847.20	10847.20
15	69000	64708.70	4291.30	4291.30
16	71196	67068.90	4127.10	4127.10
17		**69338.80**		**MAD = 7042**

Alpha	.55

Apha Value	MAD
0.05	11564
0.10	10207
0.15	9196
0.20	8435
0.25	7869
0.30	7576
0.35	7363
0.40	7214
0.45	7117
0.50	7062
0.55	7042
0.60	7053
0.65	7090
0.70	7151
0.75	7232
0.80	7333
0.85	7452
0.90	7598
0.95	7804

(1) See the data table above. The alpha value that produces the smallest MAD at the end of month 16 is 0.55. If the near term future will closely resemble the recent past, using the alpha that minimizes MAD at the end of month 16 should produce good forecasts for the short-term. (2) Using alpha = 0.55, the forecast for month 17 is 69,338.8. (3) Using alpha = 0.30, the forecast for week 17 is 64,631.90 with a MAD of 7,576 at the end of month 16. Using an alpha of 0.55, the forecast for month 17 is 69,338.8 with a MAD at the end of month 16 of 7,042.

15.43.

Regression Analysis

Regression Statistics	
Multiple R	0.887746708
R Square	0.788094217
Adjusted R Square	0.77295809
Standard Error	6360.261524
Observations	16

ANOVA

	df	SS	MS	F	Significance F
Regression	1	2106266471	2106266471	52.06709737	4.4544E-06
Residual	14	566340973.1	40452926.65		
Total	15	2672607444			

	Coefficients	Standard Error	t Stat	P-value	Lower 95%
Intercept	28848	3335.349281	8.649169117	5.45947E-07	21694.3809
Month	2488.955882	344.933611	7.215753417	4.4544E-06	1749.146207

For Individual Response Y

Interval Half Width	21378.97403
Prediction Interval Lower Limit	**49781.27597**
Prediction Interval Upper Limit	**92539.22403**

15.45.

A trend component would be illustrated if enrollments were graphed for a university with declining enrollments over the past ten years.

15.47.

Student answers will vary depending upon the state the student lives in.

15.49.

    a. This problem should be solved using the procedure developed for the Taft Ice Cream example of section 15-2.

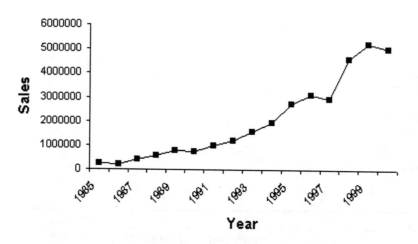

        There does appear to be an upward linear trend

    b.

Regression Analysis

Regression Statistics	
Multiple R	0.947908247
R Square	0.898530046
Adjusted R Square	0.891282192
Standard Error	567012.9456
Observations	16

ANOVA

	df	SS	MS	F	Significance F
Regression	1	3.98574E+13	3.98574E+13	123.9718762	2.43055E-08
Residual	14	4.50105E+12	3.21504E+11		
Total	15	4.43585E+13			

	Coefficients	Standard Error	t Stat	P-value	Lower 95%
Intercept	-680183698.5	61270723.46	-11.10128394	2.52359E-08	-811596447.5
Year	342385.2941	30750.59447	11.13426586	2.43055E-08	276431.7698

It is expected that as time increases by one year the sales are expected to increase by $342,385.2941. There is a fairly strong relationship since the correlation coefficient is 0.9479. Since 123.9718 > 4.6001 you would conclude that there is a significant relationship.

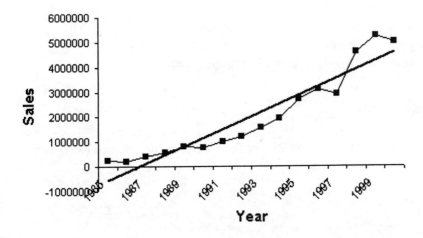

c.

Observation	Predicted Sales	Residuals	Absolute Residual
1	(548,889.7059)	788,889.7059	788,889.7059
2	(206,504.4118)	424,504.4118	424,504.4118
3	135,880.8823	269,119.1177	269,119.1177
4	478,266.1764	108,733.8236	108,733.8236
5	820,651.4706	(25,651.4706)	25,651.4706
6	1,163,036.7647	(401,036.7647)	401,036.7647
7	1,505,422.0588	(507,422.0588)	507,422.0588
8	1,847,807.3529	(630,807.3529)	630,807.3529
9	2,190,192.6471	(620,192.6471)	620,192.6471
10	2,532,577.9412	(585,577.9412)	585,577.9412
11	2,874,963.2353	(163,963.2353)	163,963.2353
12	3,217,348.5294	(113,348.5294)	113,348.5294
13	3,559,733.8236	(641,733.8236)	641,733.8236
14	3,902,119.1177	703,880.8823	703,880.8823
15	4,244,504.4118	971,495.5882	971,495.5882
16	4,586,889.7059	423,110.2941	423,110.2941
		MAD =	461,216.7279

d.

Year	Forecast
2001	4,929,275.00
2002	5,271,660.29
2003	5,614,045.59
2004	5,956,430.88
2005	6,298,816.18

e.

For Individual Response Y	
Interval Half Width	1232095.322
Prediction Interval Lower Limit	**5066720.854**
Prediction Interval Upper Limit	**7530911.499**

15.51.

Use Equations 15-18, 19, 20 and follow Example 15-7.

a.

The starting values (-891,275,11) and (342,385.29) for this model are determined using simple linear regression with the time defined as 1, 2, . . . 16.

0.2
0.4

$ (891,275.00)

$ 342,385.29

Period	Year	Sales	Constant	Trend	Forecast	Error	Absolute Error
1	1985	$240,000.00	$(391,111.76)	$405,496.47	$(548,889.71)	$788,889.71	$788,889.71
2	1986	$218,000.00	$55,107.76	$421,785.69	$14,384.71	$203,615.29	$203,615.29
3	1987	$405,000.00	$462,514.77	$416,034.22	$476,893.46	$(71,893.46)	$71,893.46
4	1988	$587,000.00	$820,239.19	$392,710.30	$878,548.98	$(291,548.98)	$291,548.98
5	1989	$795,000.00	$1,129,359.59	$359,274.34	$1,212,949.49	$(417,949.49)	$417,949.49
6	1990	$762,000.00	$1,343,307.14	$301,143.63	$1,488,633.93	$(726,633.93)	$726,633.93
7	1991	$998,000.00	$1,515,160.61	$249,427.56	$1,644,450.77	$(646,450.77)	$646,450.77
8	1992	$1,217,000.00	$1,655,070.54	$205,620.51	$1,764,588.18	$(547,588.18)	$547,588.18
9	1993	$1,570,000.00	$1,802,552.84	$182,365.23	$1,860,691.05	$(290,691.05)	$290,691.05
10	1994	$1,947,000.00	$1,977,334.45	$179,331.78	$1,984,918.07	$(37,918.07)	$37,918.07
11	1995	$2,711,000.00	$2,267,532.99	$223,678.48	$2,156,666.23	$554,333.77	$554,333.77
12	1996	$3,104,000.00	$2,613,769.17	$272,701.56	$2,491,211.47	$612,788.53	$612,788.53
13	1997	$2,918,000.00	$2,892,776.59	$275,223.90	$2,886,470.74	$31,529.26	$31,529.26
14	1998	$4,606,000.00	$3,455,600.40	$390,263.87	$3,168,000.50	$1,437,999.50	$1,437,999.50
15	1999	$5,216,000.00	$4,119,891.41	$499,874.72	$3,845,864.26	$1,370,135.74	$1,370,135.74
16	2000	$5,010,000.00	$4,697,812.91	$531,093.43	$4,619,766.13	$390,233.87	$390,233.87
17	2001				$5,228,906.34		
						MAD	**$526,262.47**

b.

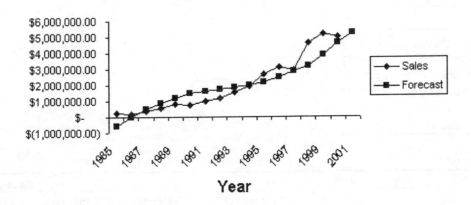

Sales vs. Forecast

c.

	Beta Values			
$ 526,262.47	0.5	0.4	0.3	0.2

Alpha Values	0.5	0.4	0.3	0.2
0.1	$568,793.54	$547,728.21	$523,915.68	$498,375.36
0.2	$538,592.87	$526,262.47	$515,577.21	$497,639.06
0.3	$481,539.18	$466,164.76	$459,595.63	$452,681.23
0.4	$454,803.56	$449,962.38	$436,850.70	$421,877.56

Different combinations of alpha and beta, including the initial values of 0.2 and 0.4, were evaluated using Excel's data table feature. Note that the combination of alpha = 0.4 and Beta = 0.2 produced the smallest MAD of the alpha/beta combinations evaluated.

15.53.

Use the procedure developed for the Taft Ice Cream example of Section 15-2.

a.

Regression Analysis

Regression Statistics	
Multiple R	0.964917946
R Square	0.931066642
Adjusted R Square	0.927619974
Standard Error	321629.8423
Observations	22

ANOVA

	df	SS	MS	F	Significance F
Regression	1	2.79443E+13	2.79443E+13	270.1352931	4.40912E-13
Residual	20	2.06892E+12	1.03446E+11		
Total	21	3.00133E+13			

	Coefficients	Standard Error	t Stat	P-value	Lower 95%
Intercept	-570875.3247	141956.932	-4.02146846	0.000669079	-866992.1583
Year	177644.8899	10808.41608	16.43579305	4.40912E-13	155098.9395

b. The data starts above the line, goes below and then above again. The residuals should go from positive to negative and then to positive again.

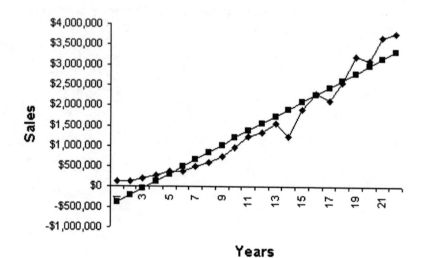

c.

Observation	Predicted Sales	Residuals	Absolute Residuals
1	-393230.4348	526230.4348	526230.4348
2	-215585.5449	343585.5449	343585.5449
3	-37940.6550	239940.6550	239940.6550
4	139704.2349	138295.7651	138295.7651
5	317349.1248	70650.8752	70650.8752
6	494994.0147	-118994.0147	118994.0147
7	672638.9046	-168638.9046	168638.9046
8	850283.7945	-237283.7945	237283.7945
9	1027928.6844	-282928.6844	282928.6844
10	1205573.5743	-230573.5743	230573.5743
11	1383218.4641	-149318.4641	149318.4641
12	1560863.3540	-225863.3540	225863.3540
13	1738508.2439	-171508.2439	171508.2439
14	1916153.1338	-682153.1338	682153.1338
15	2093798.0237	-196798.0237	196798.0237
16	2271442.9136	28557.0864	28557.0864
17	2449087.8035	-325087.8035	325087.8035
18	2626732.6934	-47732.6934	47732.6934
19	2804377.5833	395622.4167	395622.4167
20	2982022.4732	123977.5268	123977.5268
21	3159667.3631	518332.6369	518332.6369
22	3337312.2530	451687.7470	451687.7470
		MAD =	257898.2444

d. A 95% prediction interval:

For Individual Response Y

Interval Half Width	733350.1431
Prediction Interval Lower Limit	**2781607**
Prediction Interval Upper Limit	**4248307.286**

15.55.

Use the procedure developed for the Taft Ice Cream and Harrison Equipment examples of Section 15-2.

a.

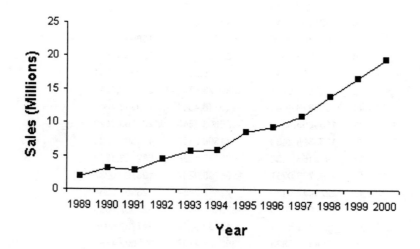

There appears to be an upward trend that may not be completely linear.

b.

Regression Analysis

Regression Statistics	
Multiple R	0.969106276
R Square	0.939166974
Adjusted R Square	0.933083671
Standard Error	1.473248634
Observations	12

ANOVA

	df	SS	MS	F	Significance F
Regression	1	335.0853846	335.0853846	154.3843918	2.1043E-07
Residual	10	21.70461538	2.170461538		
Total	11	356.79			

	Coefficients	Standard Error	t Stat	P-value	Lower 95%
Intercept	-3044.569231	245.7212521	-12.39033745	2.16079E-07	-3592.070394
Year	1.530769231	0.12319924	12.42515158	2.1043E-07	1.25626417

RESIDUAL OUTPUT

Observation	Predicted Sales (Millions)	Residuals
1	0.1308	1.7692
2	1.6615	1.4385
3	3.1923	-0.3923
4	4.7231	-0.2231
5	6.2538	-0.5538
6	7.7846	-1.9846
7	9.3154	-0.7154
8	10.8462	-1.5462
9	12.3769	-1.3769
10	13.9077	-0.0077
11	15.4385	1.1615
12	16.9692	2.4308

The $R^2 = 0.9392$ which means that 93.92% of the variation in past sales data is explained by this line. It appears from looking at the residuals that for early years and the late years the model under predicted but over predicted for all of the middle years.

c. $-3044.5692 + 1.5308(2000) = 17.031$

d. H_o: $\beta_1 = 0$
      H_a: $\beta_1 \neq 0$

Critical t = $\pm$ 2.228 using an α = 0.05, df = 10

t = (1.5308 – 0)/0.1232 = 12.4253

Since 12.4253 > 2.228 reject H_o and conclude that there is a long-term trend.

e.

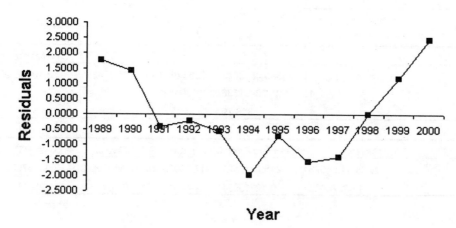

This plot suggests that we might try a curvilinear model.

Regression Analysis

Regression Statistics	
Multiple R	0.996254958
R Square	0.992523942
Adjusted R Square	0.990862596
Standard Error	0.544404124
Observations	12

ANOVA

	df	SS	MS	F	Significance F
Regression	2	354.1226173	177.0613087	597.421512	2.70101E-10
Residual	9	2.667382654	0.29637585		
Total	11	356.79			

	Coefficients	Standard Error	t Stat	P-value	Lower 95%
Intercept	472031.7193	59277.89272	7.96303137	2.29688E-05	337935.7075
Year	-474.8570089	59.44148221	-7.988646837	2.23874E-05	-609.3230861
Year2	0.119425364	0.014901345	8.014401728	2.1819E-05	0.085716154

RESIDUAL OUTPUT

Observation	Predicted Sales (Millions)	Residuals
1	2.320234132	-0.420234132
2	2.65674974	0.44325026
3	3.232116077	-0.432116077
4	4.046333142	0.453666858
5	5.099400936	0.600599064
6	6.391319458	-0.591319458
7	7.922088709	0.677911291
8	9.691708688	-0.391708688
9	11.7001794	-0.700179396
10	13.94750083	-0.047500832
11	16.433673	0.166327003
12	19.15869589	0.241304109

By developing a multiple regression model using both years and years squared the R^2 increased to 0.9925 and the residuals appear to be more random and do not have a pattern to them any longer.

The model developed is: Sales = 472031.7193 − 474.8570(years) + .1194(years^2)

15.57.

Use Equations 15-18, 19, 20 and follow Example 15-7.

a. The starting values for this model are found using simple linear regression with periods of 1, 2, … , 12 as the values of the independent variable.

Alpha	0.3
Beta	0.3
Initial Constant Value	-1.4
Initial Trend Value	1.5308

Period	Year	Sales ($ Million)	Constant	Trend	Forecast ($ Million)	Error	Absolute Error
1	1989	1.9	0.6615	1.6900	0.1308	1.7692	1.7692
2	1990	3.1	2.5761	1.7574	2.3515	0.7485	0.7485
3	1991	2.8	3.8734	1.6194	4.3334	-1.5334	1.5334
4	1992	4.5	5.1949	1.5300	5.4928	-0.9928	0.9928
5	1993	5.7	6.4175	1.4378	6.7249	-1.0249	1.0249
6	1994	5.8	7.2386	1.2528	7.8552	-2.0552	2.0552
7	1995	8.6	8.5240	1.2626	8.4914	0.1086	0.1086
8	1996	9.3	9.6406	1.2188	9.7866	-0.4866	0.4866
9	1997	11.0	10.9016	1.2314	10.8594	0.1406	0.1406
10	1998	13.9	12.6631	1.3905	12.1330	1.7670	1.7670
11	1999	16.6	14.8175	1.6196	14.0535	2.5465	2.5465
12	2000	19.4	17.3260	1.8863	16.4371	2.9629	2.9629
13	2001				19.2123		
						MAD	1.3447

b.

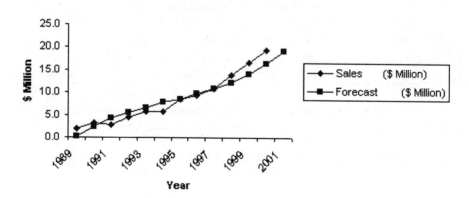

Sales vs. Forecast

c.

	Beta			
1.3447	**0.5**	**0.4**	**0.3**	**0.2**
0.1	1.4587	1.4130	1.3657	1.3176
0.2	1.4788	1.4483	1.4115	1.3623
0.3	1.4283	1.3973	1.3447	1.2900
0.4	1.3253	1.3085	1.2928	1.2537

The MAD that results from the various of combinations considered are shown in the data table above. The combination of alpha = 0.4 and beta = 0.2 produced the smallest MAD of all alpha and beta combinations considered of 1.2537.

15.59.

a. Using a linear regression model on the deseasonalized data:

	Coefficients	Standard Error	t Stat	P-value	Lower 99.0%	Upper 99.0%
Intercept	25248.99786	517.1088997	48.82724	2.79E-41	23859.52	26638.4752
Period	339.9681419	18.37273159	18.50395	6.09E-23	290.60041	389.335876

b. $60,000 = 25,248.9979 + 339.9681(x) = 102.2184$ or month number 103

15.61.

a. Use Equations 15-18, 19, 20 and follow Example 15-7.

Beta   0.2

Initial Constant
Value   23424.5567

Initial Trend
Value   420.89

	Month Number	Calls Received	Constant	Trend	Forecast Calls	Error	Absolute Error
Jan	1	23,500	23776.361	407.0759155	23845.45068	-345.45	345.45
	2	21,700	23686.749	307.7384571	24183.43646	-2,483.44	2,483.44
	3	18,750	22945.59	97.95895209	23994.48762	-5,244.49	5,244.49
	4	22,000	22834.839	56.21699001	23043.54905	-1,043.55	1,043.55
	5	23,000	22912.845	60.57474075	22891.05623	108.94	108.94
	6	26,200	23618.736	189.6379517	22973.41973	3,226.58	3,226.58
	7	27,300	24506.699	329.3030024	23808.37373	3,491.63	3,491.63
	8	29,300	25728.802	507.8629229	24836.00199	4,464.00	4,464.00
	9	31,200	27229.332	706.3963423	26236.66451	4,963.34	4,963.34
	10	34,200	29188.582	956.9672242	27935.72795	6,264.27	6,264.27
	11	39,500	32016.44	1331.145241	30145.54959	9,354.45	9,354.45
	12	43,400	35358.068	1733.241844	33347.58491	10,052.42	10,052.42
Jan	13	23,500	34373.048	1189.589453	37091.30977	-13,591.31	13,591.31
	14	23,400	33130.11	703.0839626	35562.63727	-12,162.64	12,162.64
	15	21,400	31346.555	205.7562114	33833.19378	-12,433.19	12,433.19
	16	24,200	30081.849	-88.33623802	31552.31124	-7,352.31	7,352.31
	17	26,900	29374.81	-212.076748	29993.51275	-3,093.51	3,093.51
	18	29,700	29270.187	-190.5860861	29162.73345	537.27	537.27
	19	31,100	29483.681	-109.7701131	29079.60068	2,020.40	2,020.40
	20	32,400	29979.128	11.27346978	29373.91043	3,026.09	3,026.09
	21	34,500	30892.321	191.6573973	29990.40181	4,509.60	4,509.60
	22	35,700	32007.183	376.2982435	31083.97885	4,616.02	4,616.02
	23	42,000	34306.785	760.9589906	32383.48132	9,616.52	9,616.52
	24	42,600	36574.195	1062.249229	35067.74405	7,532.26	7,532.26
Jan	25	31,000	36309.156	796.7914501	37636.44447	-6,636.44	6,636.44
	26	30,400	35764.758	528.5535691	37105.94702	-6,705.95	6,705.95
	27	29,800	34994.649	268.8211216	36293.31119	-6,493.31	6,493.31
	28	32,500	34710.776	158.2823188	35263.47007	-2,763.47	2,763.47
	29	34,500	34795.247	143.5199837	34869.05838	-369.06	369.06
	30	33,800	34711.013	97.96931632	34938.76668	-1,138.77	1,138.77
	31	34,200	34687.186	73.61000976	34808.98266	-608.98	608.98
	32	36,700	35148.637	151.1781641	34760.79614	1,939.20	1,939.20
	33	39,700	36179.852	327.185561	35299.81508	4,400.18	4,400.18
	34	42,400	37685.63	562.9040561	36507.03762	5,892.96	5,892.96
	35	43,600	39318.827	776.96269	38248.53415	5,351.47	5,351.47
	36	47,400	41556.632	1069.131089	40095.79001	7,304.21	7,304.21

	Month Number	Calls Received	Constant	Trend	Forecast Calls	Error	Absolute Error
Jan	37	32,400	40580.61	660.1005654	42625.7631	-10,225.76	10,225.76
	38	35,600	40112.569	434.4721236	41240.71105	-5,640.71	5,640.71
	39	31,200	38677.633	60.59048521	40547.04096	-9,347.04	9,347.04
	40	34,600	37910.579	-104.9384449	38738.22325	-4,138.22	4,138.22
	41	36,800	37604.512	-145.1640512	37805.64016	-1,005.64	1,005.64
	42	35,700	37107.478	-215.5379742	37459.34807	-1,759.35	1,759.35
	43	37,500	37013.552	-191.2155937	36891.94049	608.06	608.06
	44	40,000	37457.869	-64.10906545	36822.33679	3,177.66	3,177.66
	45	43,200	38555.008	168.1405197	37393.76037	5,806.24	5,806.24
	46	46,700	40318.519	487.2145671	38723.14882	7,976.85	7,976.85
	47	50,100	42664.587	858.9852223	40805.73362	9,294.27	9,294.27
	48	52,100	45238.858	1202.042338	43523.57	8,576.43	8,576.43
	49				46440.90		
						MAD	5,181.12

b.

Forecast vs. Actual

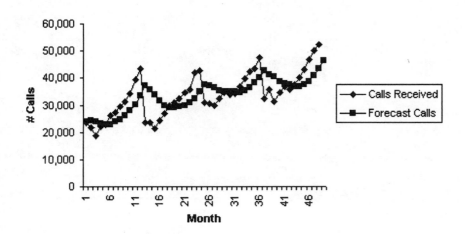

c. The double exponential explicitly models the trend effect. By developing the linear trend model on deseasonalized data you are able to adjust for both trend and seasonality. The MAD for the double exponential model is 5181.12. The MAD for the linear trend model based on deseasonalized data is 1,419.1298. I would recommend the linear trend model.

d.

		Beta		
Alpha	0.3	0.25	0.2	0.1
0.1	5190.35	5101.89	5013.90	4823.45
0.15	5397.24	5258.43	5130.99	4892.37
0.2	5538.02	5354.95	5181.12	4872.93
0.3	5374.41	5192.38	5019.96	4709.27

The data table above shows the MAD for various combinations of alpha and beta. Of the combinations considered, the values of alpha = 0.30 and beta = 0.10 provide the lowest MAD.

15.63.

Use Equation 15-16 or 15-17 and follow Example 15-6.

a. & b.

Alpha	0.2
Initial Forecast	1,375

	Month Number	Sick Days	Forecast Sick Days	Error	Absolute Error
Jan	1	1,580	1,374.83	205.17	205.17
	2	1,608	1,415.87	192.13	192.13
	3	1,370	1,454.29	-84.29	84.29
	4	1,260	1,437.43	-177.43	177.43
	5	1,125	1,401.95	-276.95	276.95
	6	1,306	1,346.56	-40.56	40.56
	7	1,240	1,338.45	-98.45	98.45
	8	1,340	1,318.76	21.24	21.24
	9	1,090	1,323.01	-233.01	233.01
	10	980	1,276.40	-296.40	296.40
	11	1,260	1,217.12	42.88	42.88
	12	1,680	1,225.70	454.30	454.30
Jan	13	1,630	1,316.56	313.44	313.44
	14	1,700	1,379.25	320.75	320.75
	15	1,610	1,443.40	166.60	166.60
	16	1,590	1,476.72	113.28	113.28
	17	1,498	1,499.37	-1.37	1.37
	18	1,540	1,499.10	40.90	40.90
	19	1,580	1,507.28	72.72	72.72
	20	1,680	1,521.82	158.18	158.18
	21	1,560	1,553.46	6.54	6.54
	22	1,520	1,554.77	-34.77	34.77
	23	1,670	1,547.81	122.19	122.19
	24	1,920	1,572.25	347.75	347.75
Jan	25	1,960	1,641.80	318.20	318.20
	26	1,880	1,705.44	174.56	174.56
	27	1,820	1,740.35	79.65	79.65
	28	1,750	1,756.28	-6.28	6.28
	29	1,690	1,755.03	-65.03	65.03
	30	1,730	1,742.02	-12.02	12.02
	31	1,690	1,739.62	-49.62	49.62
	32	1,780	1,729.69	50.31	50.31
	33	1,670	1,739.75	-69.75	69.75
	34	1,560	1,725.80	-165.80	165.80
	35	1,760	1,692.64	67.36	67.36
	36	2,040	1,706.11	333.89	333.89
	37		1,772.89		
				MAD	144.83

c.

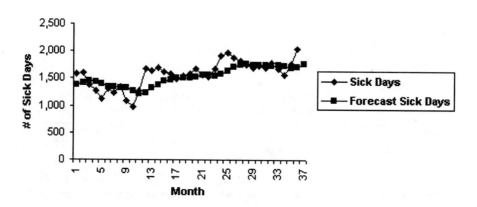

Forecast vs. Actual

d.

Alpha	MAD
0.1	172.57
0.2	144.83
0.3	138.26
0.4	134.30
0.5	131.35

The data table shows the MAD associated with each alpha value considered. The lowest MAD value of 131.35 corresponds to the alpha value of 0.5. The higher alpha value makes the single exponential smoothing model more responsive. Given that the time series has an upward trend, the higher alpha value is preferred. However, because the single exponential smoothing model is incapable of explicitly incorporating a trend effect the forecast lags behind the actual values of the time series.

15.65.

Follow the procedures outlined in Figure 15-19 through 15-25.

a.

Year	Month	Period	Inventory Level (Millions $)	12 Period Moving Average	Centered Moving Average	Ratio to MA	Deseasonalized Data
1996	January	1	5.2				6.6160
	February	2	3.3				6.3581
	March	3	2.8				6.7676
	April	4	5.3				5.5865
	May	5	9.4				7.3441
	June	6	2.6	6.9917			4.2814
	July	7	6.2	6.95	6.9708	0.8894	6.1493
	August	8	7.2	6.9167	6.9333	1.0385	7.4961
	September	9	6.8	6.9333	6.925	0.9819	7.7590
	October	10	9.7	7.0167	6.975	1.3907	8.0680
	November	11	13.6	7.0667	7.0417	1.9314	7.4520
	December	12	11.8	7.2083	7.1375	1.6532	7.5019
1997	January	13	4.7	7.3333	7.2708	0.6464	5.9799
	February	14	2.9	7.3583	7.3458	0.3948	5.5874
	March	15	3	7.275	7.3167	0.41	7.2510
	April	16	6.3	7.2667	7.2708	0.8665	6.6406
	May	17	10	7.2917	7.2792	1.3738	7.8129
	June	18	4.3	7.3	7.2958	0.5894	7.0808
	July	19	7.7	7.4583	7.3792	1.0435	7.6371
	August	20	7.5	7.55	7.5042	0.9994	7.8085
	September	21	5.8	7.6	7.575	0.7657	6.6180
	October	22	9.6	7.675	7.6375	1.257	7.9848
	November	23	13.9	7.7917	7.7333	1.7974	7.6164
	December	24	11.9	7.7667	7.7792	1.5297	7.5655
1998	January	25	6.6	7.7917	7.7792	0.8484	8.3973
	February	26	4	7.7333	7.7625	0.5153	7.7067
	March	27	3.6	7.8167	7.775	0.463	8.7012
	April	28	7.2	7.7583	7.7875	0.9246	7.5893
	May	29	11.4	7.7833	7.7708	1.467	8.9067
	June	30	4	7.85	7.8167	0.5117	6.5867
	July	31	8	7.8917	7.8708	1.0164	7.9346
	August	32	6.8	7.8917	7.8917	0.8617	7.0797
	September	33	6.8	7.8083	7.85	0.8662	7.7590
	October	34	8.9	7.875	7.8417	1.135	7.4026
	November	35	14.2	7.575	7.725	1.8382	7.7808
	December	36	12.7	7.6917	7.6333	1.6638	8.0741

Year	Month	Period	Inventory Level (Millions $)	12 Period Moving Average	Centered Moving Average	Ratio to MA	Deseasonalized Data
1999	January	37	7.1	7.8	7.7458	0.9166	9.0334
	February	38	4	7.9167	7.8583	0.509	7.7067
	March	39	2.6	8.0083	7.9625	0.3265	6.2842
	April	40	8	8.0417	8.025	0.9969	8.4325
	May	41	7.8	8.2	8.1208	0.9605	6.0941
	June	42	5.4	8.2917	8.2458	0.6549	8.8921
	July	43	9.3	8.2833	8.2875	1.1222	9.2240
	August	44	8.2	8.4667	8.375	0.9791	8.5373
	September	45	7.9	8.6083	8.5375	0.9253	9.0141
	October	46	9.3	8.7333	8.6708	1.0726	7.7353
	November	47	16.1	9.125	8.9292	1.8031	8.8219
	December	48	13.8	9.2083	9.1667	1.5055	8.7735
2000	January	49	7	9.15	9.1792	0.7626	8.9062
	February	50	6.2	9.1667	9.1583	0.677	11.9455
	March	51	4.3	9.0833	9.125	0.4712	10.3931
	April	52	9.5	9.125	9.1042	1.0435	10.0136
	May	53	12.5	9.1583	9.1417	1.3674	9.7661
	June	54	6.4	9.225	9.1917	0.6963	10.5388
	July	55	8.6				8.5297
	August	56	8.4				8.7455
	September	57	6.9				7.8731
	October	58	9.8				8.1512
	November	59	16.5				9.0410
	December	60	14.6				9.2821

Since the index values do not add to 12, we normalize them by multiplying each by 12/12.155 giving:

Month	Index
Jan.	0.7860
Feb.	0.5190
March	0.4137
April	0.9487
May	1.2799
June	0.6073
July	1.0082
Aug.	0.9605
Sept.	0.8764
Oct.	1.2023
Nov.	1.8250
Dec.	1.5729

b & c.

SUMMARY OUTPUT

Regression Statistics	
Multiple R	0.692361637
R Square	0.479364636
Adjusted R Square	0.470388164
Standard Error	0.958989957
Observations	60

ANOVA

	df	SS	MS	F	Significance F
Regression	1	49.11209264	49.1120926	53.4023441	8.91153E-10
Residual	58	53.34038083	0.91966174		
Total	59	102.4524735			

	Coefficients	Standard Error	t Stat	P-value
Intercept	6.283574533	0.250737973	25.0603227	8.366E-33
Period	0.052241819	0.007148882	7.30769075	8.9115E-10

Month	Period	Unadjusted Forecast	Seasonal Index	Adjusted Forecast
January	61	9.4703	0.7860	7.4434
February	62	9.5226	0.5190	4.9425
March	63	9.5748	0.4137	3.9614
April	64	9.6271	0.9487	9.1333
May	65	9.6793	1.2799	12.3889
June	66	9.7315	0.6073	5.9098
July	67	9.7838	1.0082	9.8644
August	68	9.8360	0.9605	9.4474
September	69	9.8883	0.8764	8.6661
October	70	9.9405	1.2023	11.9512
November	71	9.9927	1.8250	18.2369
December	72	10.0450	1.5729	15.8000

Student reports will vary but should include comments such as the unadjusted forecast only incorporates the trend. The adjusted forecast would be more reflective of what the company would expect because it all incorporates the seasonal aspect of the data.

d.   The advantage of incorporating the seasonal indexes is to give better forecasts. Because the monthly inventory levels have in the past had seasonal effects it is better to have forecasts that incorporate these seasonal effects because it is a more accurate picture of what the company expects inventory levels to look like.

CD-ROM CHAPTER 16

INTRODUCTION TO NONPARAMETRIC STATISTICS

16.1.

The hypotheses are:

$$H_O: \tilde{\mu} \le 10$$
$$H_A: \tilde{\mu} > 10$$

W is found as follows:

Values	Difference	Absolute Difference	Rank	R+	R-
10.2	0.2	0.2	1	1	
13.65	3.65	3.65	9	9	
12.3	2.3	2.3	6	6	
9.51	-0.49	0.49	2		2
11.32	1.32	1.32	3	3	
12.77	2.77	2.77	8	8	
6.16	-3.84	3.84	10		10
8.55	-1.45	1.45	4		4
11.78	1.78	1.78	5	5	
12.32	2.32	2.32	7	7	
				W = 39	

Since this is an upper tail test, and n = 10, letting α = .05, we reject if W > 45. Therefore, there is not enough evidence to reject the null hypothesis.

16.3.

The hypotheses are: H_0: $\tilde{\mu} \geq 14$

H_A: $\tilde{\mu} < 14$

W is found as follows:

Values	Difference	Absolute Differences	Rank	R+	R-
9	-5	5	10		10
15.6	1.6	1.6	4	4	
21.1	7.1	7.1	11	11	
11.1	-2.9	2.9	6		6
13.5	-0.5	0.5	2		2
9.2	-4.8	4.8	8		8
13.6	-0.4	0.4	1		1
15.8	1.8	1.8	5	5	
12.5	-1.5	1.5	3		3
18.7	4.7	4.7	7	7	
18.9	4.9	4.9	9	9	
				W = 36	

Since this is an lower tail test, and n = 11, letting α = .05, we reject if W < 13. Therefore, there is not enough evidence to reject the null hypothesis.

16.5.

a. The hypotheses are: H_0: $\tilde{\mu} \leq 4000$

H_A: $\tilde{\mu} > 4000$

b. Using the Wilcoxon Signed Rank test we find W as follows:

Life	Difference	Absolute Difference	Rank	R+	R-
1973	-2027	2027	12		12
4459	459	459	3	3	
4838	838	838	9	9	
4098	98	98	1	1	
3805	-195	195	2		2
4722	722	722	6	6	
4494	494	494	4	4	
5894	1894	1894	11	11	
4738	738	738	7	7	
3322	-678	678	5		5
5249	1249	1249	10	10	
4800	800	800	8	8	
				W = 59	

Since this is an upper tail test and n = 12, letting α = .05, sum the positive ranks and reject if W > 61. Therefore, there is not enough evidence to reject the null hypothesis and the manager can not conclude the median time is greater than 4000 hours.

16.7.

By agreeing the mean weight is 11 ounces, but also claiming that more than 50% of the tubes contain less than 11 ounces, the consumer group is stating the distribution is skewed to the right and the median is less than 11 ounces. Putting the claim in the alternative hypothesis we are testing:

$$H_O: \quad \tilde{\mu} \geq 11$$
$$H_A: \quad \tilde{\mu} < 11$$

Using the Wilcoxon Signed Rank test we find W as follows:

Ounces	Difference	Absolute Differences	Rank	R+	R-
10.9	-0.1	0.1	1.5		1.5
11.7	0.7	0.7	15	15	
10.5	-0.5	0.5	12		12
11.8	0.8	0.8	17	17	
10.2	-0.8	0.8	17		17
11.5	0.5	0.5	12	12	
10.8	-0.2	0.2	4.5		4.5
11.2	0.2	0.2	4.5	4.5	
11.8	0.8	0.8	17	17	
10.7	-0.3	0.3	8		8
10.6	-0.4	0.4	10		10
10.9	-0.1	0.1	1.5		1.5
11.6	0.6	0.6	14	14	
11.2	0.2	0.2	4.5	4.5	
11	0	0			
10.7	-0.3	0.3	8		8
10.8	-0.2	0.2	4.5		4.5
10.5	-0.5	0.5	12		12
11.3	0.3	0.3	8	8	
10.1	-0.9	0.9	19		19
				W = 92	

Since one of the differences equaled 0, we only rank 19 values. This is a lower tail test with $n = 19$ and $\alpha = .05$. We reject if $W < 53$. Therefore, there is not enough evidence to support the consumer group's claim.

16.9.

Since we are interested in differences both above and below 30, this should be a two tailed test. The appropriate hypotheses are:

$$H_O: \tilde{\mu} = 30$$
$$H_A: \tilde{\mu} \neq 30$$

Using the Wilcoxon Signed Rank test we find W as follows:

Ounces	Difference	Absolute Differences	Rank	R+	R-
25	-5	5	10.5		10.5
24	-6	6	14.5		14.5
21	-9	9	17		17
35	5	5	10.5	10.5	
25	-5	5	10.5		10.5
25	-5	5	10.5		10.5
35	5	5	10.5	10.5	
38	8	8	16	16	
32	2	2	4	4	
36	6	6	14.5	14.5	
35	5	5	10.5	10.5	
29	-1	1	1.5		1.5
30	0	0			
27	-3	3	6.5		6.5
28	-2	2	4		4
27	-3	3	6.5		6.5
31	1	1	1.5	1.5	
32	2	2	4	4	
30	0	0			
30	0	0			
				W = 71.5	W = 81.5

Because some of the differences are 0, n = 17. From Appendix P, the upper and lower values for the Wilcoxon test are 34 and 119 for $\alpha = .05$ and 23 and 130 for $\alpha = .01$. We do not reject the hypothesis in either case.

16.11.

a. The chi-square table will vary depending on how students construct the data classes, but using data classes one standard deviation wide, with the data mean of 7.6306 and a standard deviation of .2218, we find the following table and chi-square value.

e	o	$(o-e)^2/e$
14.9440	21	2.45417
32.4278	31	0.06287
32.4278	27	0.90851
14.9440	16	0.07462 sum = 3.5002

Testing at the $\alpha = .05$ level, $\chi_\alpha^2 = 5.9915$. Since the calculated $\chi^2 = 3.5002$ we do not reject the hypothesis the data come from a normal distribution.

b. Since we concluded the data come from a normal distribution we test the following:

$$H_O: \mu \geq 7.4$$
$$H_A: \mu < 7.4$$

Decision Rule: If z < -1.645, reject H_0, otherwise do not reject.

$$z = \frac{7.6306 - 7.4}{\frac{.2218}{\sqrt{95}}} = 10.13$$

Therefore, we do not reject the null hypothesis and conclude the average pH level is at least 7.4.

16.13.

a. Use U_2, reject if $U \leq 11$.

b. Use U_1, reject if $U \leq 55$.

c. Use smallest of U_1 or U_2, reject if $U \leq 64$.

d. Use z value from Equation 16-8. Reject if z < -1.645

e. Use z value from Equation 16-8. Reject if z < -1.645 or z > 1.645.

16.15

a. For this problem the claim is that $\tilde{\mu}_1 - \tilde{\mu}_2 \geq 0$. This research hypothesis must be reformulated to be $\tilde{\mu}_1 - \tilde{\mu}_2 > 0$, since the alternative hypothesis cannot contain an equal sign. The hypotheses are.

$$H_0: \tilde{\mu}_1 - \tilde{\mu}_2 \leq 0$$
$$H_A: \tilde{\mu}_1 - \tilde{\mu}_2 > 0$$

b. Constructing the table of ranks we find:

Sample 1	Rank (Sample 1)	Sample 2	Rank (Sample 2)
4.4	15.5	3.7	11
2.7	5	3.5	9.5
1	1	4	12
3.5	9.5	4.9	17
2.8	6.5	3.1	8
2.6	4	4.2	13
2.4	3	5.2	18
2	2	4.4	15.5
2.8	6.5	4.3	14
	Sum of Ranks = 53		Sum of Ranks = 118

Since the alternate hypothesis indicates population 1 has the larger median, we use U_1 as the test statistic.

$$U_1 = n_1 n_2 + \frac{n_1(n_1+1)}{2} - \sum R_1 = 9(9) + \frac{9(9+1)}{2} - 53 = 73$$

Using Appendix L with $n_1 = 9$ and $n_2 = 9$, the decision rule becomes:

Reject if $U \leq 21$

Since U = 73, we cannot reject the null hypothesis. We cannot conclude that the first population median exceeds the second population mean.

16.17.

The hypotheses to test are:

$$H_0: \ \tilde{\mu}_1 - \tilde{\mu}_2 = 0$$
$$H_A: \ \tilde{\mu}_1 - \tilde{\mu}_2 \neq 0$$

This problem can be solved using Minitab.

Mann-Whitney Test and CI: C1, C2

C1   N = 40   Median =   481.50
C2   N = 35   Median =   505.00
Point estimate for ETA1-ETA2 is   -25.00
95.1 Percent CI for ETA1-ETA2 is (-62.00,9.00)
W = 1384.0
Test of ETA1 = ETA2 vs ETA1 not = ETA2 is significant at 0.1502
The test is significant at 0.1501 (adjusted for ties)

Cannot reject at alpha = 0.05

16.19.

The hypotheses to test are:

$$H_0: \; \tilde{\mu}_1 - \tilde{\mu}_2 = 0$$
$$H_A: \; \tilde{\mu}_1 - \tilde{\mu}_2 \neq 0$$

Using Appendix N, with n = 10, the decision rule is:

Reject if $T \leq 8$

The following table is found. Note, the table shows the sum of the positive ranks because this gives a smaller sum than the sum of the negative ranks. In a two-tailed test, you always use the smallest sum to calculate T.

Item	Sample 1	Sample 2	d	Rank of d	Rank with smallest sum
1	19.6	21.3	-1.7	-7	
2	22.1	17.4	4.7	10	10
3	19.5	19	0.5	1	1
4	20	21.2	-1.2	-4.5	
5	21.5	20.1	1.4	6	6
6	20.2	23.5	-3.3	-9	
7	17.9	18.9	-1	-3	
8	23	22.4	0.6	2	2
9	12.5	14.3	-1.8	-8	
10	19	17.8	1.2	4.5	4.5
					T = 23.5

Since T = 23.5, we do not reject the null hypothesis.

16.21.

The hypotheses to test are:

$$H_0: \; \tilde{\mu}_1 - \tilde{\mu}_2 = 0$$
$$H_A: \; \tilde{\mu}_1 - \tilde{\mu}_2 \neq 0$$

Using Appendix N, with n = 7, the decision rule is:

Reject if $T \leq 2$

The following table is found:

Sample 1	Sample 2	d	Rank of d	Rank with smallest sum
1004	1045	-41	-2	2
1245	1145	100	4.5	
1360	1400	-40	-1	1
1150	1000	150	6	
1300	1350	-50	-3	3
1450	1350	100	4.5	
900	1140	-240	-7	7
				T = 13

Since T = 13, we do not reject the null hypothesis.

16.23.

H_0: $\tilde{\mu}_2 = \tilde{\mu}_1$

H_A: $\tilde{\mu}_2 \neq \tilde{\mu}_1$

Sample 1	Sample 2	d	Rank	Ranks with smallest sum
234	245	-11	-5	
221	224	-3	-2	
196	194	2	1	1
245	267	-22	-6	
234	230	4	3	3
204	198	6	4	4
				T = 8

If $T \leq 0$ reject H_0, otherwise do not reject H_0

Since 8 > 0 do not reject H_0 and conclude that the medians are the same.

16.25.

H_0: $\tilde{\mu}_P = \tilde{\mu}_H$

H_A: $\tilde{\mu}_P \neq \tilde{\mu}_H$

U1 = (10)(8) + (10)(10+1)/2 – 92 = 43

U2 = (10)(8) + (8)(8+1)/2 – 79 = 37

Decision Rule:
If $U \leq 13$ reject H_o, otherwise do not reject H_o

Since 37 > 13 do not reject Ho and conclude that the produce would receive the same median ranking from each group

16.27.

H_0: $\tilde{\mu}_S - \tilde{\mu}_J = 0$

H_A: $\tilde{\mu}_S - \tilde{\mu}_J \neq 0$

U1 = (6)(8) + (6)(6+1)/2 – 43 = 26

U2 = (6)(8) + (8)(8+1)/2 – 62 = 22

Utest = 22

The p-value = 0.426 do not reject Ho and conclude that there is no difference in median deductions taken for charitable contributions depending on whether the tax return was filed as a single or joint return.

16.29.

H_0: $\tilde{\mu}_1 = \tilde{\mu}_2$

H_A: $\tilde{\mu}_1 \neq \tilde{\mu}_2$

$\mu = 40(40+1)/4 = 410$

$\sigma = \sqrt{40(40+1)(80+1)/24} = 74.3976$

z = (480 – 410)/74.3976 = 0.94

p-value = (0.5 – 0.3264)2 = (0.1736)(2) = 0.3472 . Therefore do not reject H_o and conclude that the median weight gains are not different

16.31.

a. H_0: $\tilde{\mu}_S \geq \tilde{\mu}_D$

   H_A: $\tilde{\mu}_S < \tilde{\mu}_D$

Day Care	Rank	Stay Home	Rank
18.1	34	12.1	7
17.2	31	12.8	9
13.1	12	12.9	10
12.2	8	11.1	3
14.2	20.5	13	11
17.8	33	14.4	22.5
17.5	32	18.2	35
15.9	28	11.5	5
11.8	6	15.6	26
14.1	19	13.6	16
14.4	22.5	14.2	20.51
13.2	13	11	2
13.7	17	10.3	1
16.4	29	11.3	4
15	25	13.3	14
13.8	18		186
13.4	15		
18.4	36		
17	30		
15.8	27		
14.6	24		
	480		

$U1 = (21)(15) + (21)(21+1)/2 - 480 = 66$

$U2 = (21)(15) + (15)(15+1)/2 - 186 = 249$

$\mu = 21(15)/2 = 157.5$

$\sigma = \sqrt{21(15)(21+15+1)/12} = 31.1649$

$z = (66-157.5)/31.1649 = -2.936$

   critical $z = -1.645$

Since $-2.936 < -1.645$ reject H_0 and conclude the median time for interaction at daycare is higher than the stay-at-home

b.   A Type I error could have been committed

16.33.

a. $H_o: \tilde{\mu}_S = \tilde{\mu}_P$

    $H_a: \tilde{\mu}_S \neq \tilde{\mu}_P$

Physician	Monitor	d	Rank of d	Ranks with smallest sum
112	126	-14	-8	
109	108	1	1	1
139	116	23	13	13
141	123	18	11.5	11.5
120	138	-18	-11.5	
99	123	-24	-14	
128	119	9	7	7
118	122	-4	-5	
120	118	2	2.5	2.5
111	114	-3	-4	
123	108	15	9	9
114	130	-16	-10	
121	123	-2	-2.5	
132	127	5	6	6
			T=	50

One observation was removed because the difference was 0.

If $T \leq 21$ reject H_o, otherwise do not reject H_o

Since $50 > 21$ do not reject H_o and conclude that the medians are the same for the physician tested and Sunbeam monitor.

b. Want to use a paired-t test

 H_0: $\mu_d = 0$

 H_A: $\mu_d \neq 0$

Monitor	Physician	d	$(d\text{-dbar})^2$
126	112	14	181.351
108	109	-1	2.351
116	139	-23	553.818
123	141	-18	343.484
138	120	18	305.084
123	99	24	550.684
119	128	-9	90.884
122	118	4	12.018
116	116	0	0.284
118	120	-2	6.418
114	111	3	6.084
108	123	-15	241.284
130	114	16	239.218
123	121	2	2.151
127	132	-5	30.618
	Average = .533		
	St. Dev. = 13.538		

$$t = (0.533)/(13.538/\sqrt{15}) = 0.1526$$

Since $0.15261 < t$ critical $= 2.1448$ do not reject Ho and conclude that the means are the same.

c. Because you cannot assume a normal distribution the Wilcoxon Matched-Pairs Signed-Ranks Test is the better analysis.

16.35.

a. Want to use a paired-t test

H_0: $\mu_d \geq 0$
H_A: $\mu_d < 0$

Old Material	New Material	d
45.5	47.0	-1.5
50.0	51.0	-1.0
43.0	42.0	1.0
45.5	46.0	-0.5
58.5	58.0	0.5
49.0	50.5	-1.5
29.5	39.0	-9.5
52.0	53.0	-1.0
48.0	48.0	0.0
57.5	61.0	-3.5

Average		-1.7
Std. Dev.		3.011091

$$t = (-1.7)/(3.011091/\sqrt{10}) = -1.785$$

Since $-1.785 > t$ critical $= -2.2622$ do not reject H_0 and conclude that the soles made from the new material do not have a longer mean lifetime than those made from the old material.

b. H_0: $\tilde{\mu}_O \geq \tilde{\mu}_N$
    H_A: $\tilde{\mu}_O < \tilde{\mu}_N$

Old Material	New Material	d	Rank d	Ranks with smallest expected sum
45.5	47.0	-1.5	-6.5	
50.0	51.0	-1.0	-4	
43.0	42.0	1.0	4	4.0
45.5	46.0	-0.5	-1.5	
58.5	58.0	0.5	1.5	1.5
49.0	50.5	-1.5	-6.5	
29.5	39.0	-9.5	-9	
52.0	53.0	-1.0	-4	
57.5	61.0	-3.5	-8	
			T=	5.5

One observation was removed because the difference was 0. Using $\alpha = 0.025$ the decision rule becomes:

If $T \leq 6$ reject H_0, otherwise do not reject H_0

Since $5.5 < 6$ reject H_0 and conclude that the medians are not the same.

c. Because you cannot assume the underlying populations are normal you must use the technique from part b.

16.37.

a. H_0: $\tilde{\mu}_1 = \tilde{\mu}_2 = \tilde{\mu}_3$
   H_A: Not all population medians are equal

b.

Level of Significance	0.05
Group 1	
Sum of Ranks	118.5
Sample Size	8
Group 2	
Sum of Ranks	62
Sample Size	8
Group 3	
Sum of Ranks	119.5
Sample Size	8
Sum of Squared Ranks/Sample Size	4020.813
Sum of Sample Sizes	24
Number of groups	3
H Test Statistic	**5.41625**
Critical Value	**5.991476**
p-Value	0.066662
Do not reject the null hypothesis	

c. H_0: $\mu_1 = \mu_2 = \mu_3$
   H_a: Not all population means are equal

Anova: Single Factor

SUMMARY

Groups	Count	Sum	Average	Variance
Group 1	8	236	29.5	32.57143
Group 2	8	173	21.625	47.125
Group 3	8	237	29.625	66.55357

ANOVA

Source of Variation	SS	df	MS	F	P-value	F crit
Between Groups	336.0833	2	168.0417	3.447009	0.05075	3.466795
Within Groups	1023.75	21	48.75			
Total	1359.833	23				

Since $3.447 < 3.4668$ do not reject H_o and conclude that all population means are equal.

d. Because you cannot assume normal populations you should use the Kruskal-Wallis test.

16.39.

a. H_0: $\tilde{\mu}_1 = \tilde{\mu}_2 = \tilde{\mu}_3 = \tilde{\mu}_4$

   H_A: Not all population medians are equal

b. Using Equation 16-10.

$$H = \frac{12}{N(N+1)} \sum_{i=1}^{k} \frac{R_i^2}{n_i} - 3(N+1) =$$

$$\frac{12}{80(80+1)} \left(\frac{409600}{20} + \frac{608400}{20} + \frac{211600}{20} + \frac{1849600}{20} \right) - 3(81) = 42.11$$

Selecting $\alpha = .05$, $\chi_\alpha^2 = 7.8147$, since H = 42.11, we reject the null hypothesis of equal medians.

16.41.

a. No

b. It is not necessary because the adjustment is only necessary when the null hypothesis is not rejected and the null hypothesis was rejected.

16.43.

H_0: $\tilde{\mu}_1 = \tilde{\mu}_2 = \tilde{\mu}_3$
H_A: Not all population medians are equal

   Using PHStat:

   Kruskal Wallis Rank Test

Level of Significance	0.05
Group 1	
Sum of Ranks	324
Sample Size	14
Group 2	
Sum of Ranks	413
Sample Size	14
Group 3	
Sum of Ranks	166
Sample Size	14
Sum of Squared Ranks/Sample Size	21650.07143
Sum of Sample Sizes	42
Number of groups	3
H Test Statistic	**14.85429521**
Critical Value	**5.991476357**
p-Value	0.000594882
Reject the null hypothesis	

16.45.

H_0: $\tilde{\mu}_1 = \tilde{\mu}_2 = \tilde{\mu}_3$

H_A: Not all population medians are equal

Constructing a table like that shown in Table 16-4, find the following values.

Rank Car 1	Rank Car 2	Rank Car 3
85.5	25.5	120

$H = [12/(21)(21+1)][(85.5^2/8) + (25.5^2/6) + (120^2/7)] - 3(21+1) = 13.9818$

Testing at $\alpha = .05$, $\chi_\alpha^2 = 5.9915$

Since $13.9818 > 5.9915$ reject H_0 and conclude that not all population medians are equal

16.47.

The Kruskal-Wallis one-way analysis of variance is the nonparametric counterpart to the analysis of variance procedure and is used if the decision makers are not willing to assume normally distributed populations. It is applicable any time the variable has a continuous distribution, the data are at least ordinal, the samples are independent, and the samples come from populations whose only possible difference is that at least one may have a different central location than the others. Examples will vary.

16.49.

Student answers will vary depending upon the organization selected.

16.51.

a & b

Possible Sets	Sum of Ranks	Probability
none	-	1/16
1	1	1/16
2	2	1/16
3	3	1/16
4	4	1/16
1,2	3	1/16
1,3	4	1/16
1,4	5	1/16
2,3	5	1/16
2,4	6	1/16
3,4	7	1/16
1,2,3	6	1/16
1,2,4	7	1/16
1,3,4	8	1/16
2,3,4	9	1/16
1,2,3,4	10	1/16

c.

T	0	1	2	3	4	5	6	7	8	9	10
P(T)	1/16	1/16	1/16	2/16	2/16	2/16	2/16	2/16	1/16	1/16	1/16

16.53.

a. H_0: $\widetilde{\mu}_1 - \widetilde{\mu}_2 = 0$

   H_A: $\widetilde{\mu}_1 - \widetilde{\mu}_2 \neq 0$

Company 1	Rank 1	Company 2	Rank 2
246	5	300	8
211	2	305	9
235	3	308	10
270	6	325	14
411	18	340	16
310	11	295	7
450	19	320	13
502	20	330	15
311	12	240	4
200	1	360	17
	97		113

$$U1 = (10)(10) + (10)(10+1)/2 - 97 = 58$$
$$U2 = (10)(10) + (10)(10+1)/2 - 113 = 42$$
$$Utest = 42$$
$$\text{If } \alpha = .10, U_\alpha = 27$$

Since $42 > 27$ do not reject H_0 and conclude that the medians are not different.

b. H_0: $\mu_1 - \mu_2 = 0$
    H_A: $\mu_1 - \mu_2 \neq 0$

	Company 1	Company 2
Mean	314.60	312.30
Std. Dev.	105.2386	32.1906

Testing to see if the variances are equal:

$$F = (105.2386)^2/(32.1906)^2 = 10.6879$$

$$F_{0.05} = 3.179$$

Reject hypothesis of equal variances. Thus, we are required to utilize the t-test for unequal variances. This test requires the calculation of the degrees of freedom as follows:

$$\frac{\left(105.2386^2/10 + 32.1906^2/10\right)^2}{\left(\left(\frac{\left(105.2386^2/10\right)^2}{10-1}\right) + \left(\frac{\left(32.1906^2/10\right)^2}{10-1}\right)\right)} = 10.67 \rightarrow 10 \text{ degrees of freedom}$$

Decision Rule:

If t > 1.8125 or t < -1.8125 reject H_o, otherwise do not reject H_o

$$t = (314.60 - 312.30)/\sqrt{\frac{105.2386^2}{10} + \frac{32.1906^2}{10}} = 0.0661$$

Since 0.0661 < 1.8125 do not reject H_o and conclude that the means are not different.

We must assume normal populations and independence in sampling.

16.55.

a.

H_0: $\tilde{\mu}_1 - \tilde{\mu}_2 = 0$

H_A: $\tilde{\mu}_1 - \tilde{\mu}_2 \neq 0$

Urban	Rank Urban	Rural	Rank Rural
76	12	55	7
90	19	80	14
86	18	94	21
60	9	40	4
43	5	85	17
96	22	92	20
50	6	77	13
20	1	68	10
30	2	35	3
82	15	59	8
75	11		
84	16		
	136		117

$U1 = (12)(10) + (12)(12+1)/2 - 136 = 62$
$U2 = (12)(10) + (10)(10+1)/2 - 117 = 58$
$Utest = 58$

If $\alpha = .02$, $U_\alpha = 24$

Since $58 > 24$ do not reject H_o and conclude that the medians are not different.

b. H_0: $\mu_1 - \mu_2 = 0$
     H_A: $\mu_1 - \mu_2 \neq 0$

	Urban	Rural
Mean	66	68.5
Std. Dev.	24.9909	20.7806

Testing for equal variances:

$$F = 24.9909^2/20.7806^2 \; = 1.4463$$

$$F_\alpha = 5.178 \; \text{at} \; \alpha = .01$$

Accept hypothesis of equal variances.

Decision Rule:

If t > 2.5280 or t < -2.5280 reject H_o, otherwise do not reject H_0

$$S_{pooled} = \sqrt{(12-1)24.9909^2 + (10-1)20.7806^2/(12+10-2)} = 23.1911$$

$$t = (66 - 68.5)/23.1911(\sqrt{(1/12)+(1/10)} = -0.2518$$

Since –0.2518 > -2.5280 do not reject H_o and conclude that the means are not different.

We must assume independence when sampling from normal populations with equal variances.

16.57.

H_0: $\widetilde{\mu}_1 = \widetilde{\mu}_2 = \widetilde{\mu}_3$

H_A: Not all population medians are equal

Method 1	Rank 1	Method 2	Rank 2	Method 3	Rank 3
45	24	39	17.5	26	1
49	32	37	15	31	7
48	31	31	7	32	9
50	33	42	21	40	19
33	10	43	22	44	23
46	26.5	47	29.5	41	20
46	26.5	46	26.5	34	11.5
47	29.5	27	2	28	3
46	26.5	29	4	30	5
39	17.5	31	7	34	11.5
		36	14	35	13
				38	16
	256.5		165.5		139

Number of cases involved in tied rankings:

At 31 rank = 7, number = 3
At 34 rank = 11.5, number = 2
At 39 rank = 17.5, number = 2
At 46 rank = 26.5, number = 4
At 47 rank = 29.5, number 2

$$H = [[12/(33)(33+1)][(256.5^2/10) + (165.5^2/11) + (139^2/12)] - 3(33+1)]/(1-0.0966) = 12.252$$

Chi-square = 5.9915

Since 12.252 > 5.9915 reject H_o and conclude that not all population medians are equal

16.59.

a. The hypotheses being tested are:

$$H_0: \quad \tilde{\mu} = 8.03$$
$$H_A: \quad \tilde{\mu} \neq 8.03$$

b. Using the Wilcoxon Signed Rank test we find W as follows:

Fill	Difference	Absolute Differences	Rank	R+	R-
7.95	-0.08	0.08	14.5		14.5
8.02	-0.01	0.01	2.5		2.5
8.07	0.04	0.04	10.5	10.5	
8.06	0.03	0.03	8.5	8.5	
8.05	0.02	0.02	6	6	
8.04	0.01	0.01	2.5	2.5	
7.97	-0.06	0.06	13		13
8.01	-0.02	0.02	6		6
8.04	0.01	0.01	2.5	2.5	
8.05	0.02	0.02	6	6	
8.08	0.05	0.05	12	12	
8.11	0.08	0.08	14.5	14.5	
7.99	-0.04	0.04	10.5		10.5
8	-0.03	0.03	8.5		8.5
8.02	-0.01	0.01	2.5		2.5
				W = 62.5	W = 57.5

This is a two tailed test with n = 15. Since the significance level is not given, students will have to make a choice. If $\alpha = .05$, using Appendix P, we reject if $W \leq 25$ or $W > 95$. Looking at the two values in the table we see there is not enough evidence to conclude the median is different than 8.03 oz.

16.61.

a. The hypotheses to be tested are:

H_0: $\tilde{\mu}_1 = \tilde{\mu}_2$

H_A: $\tilde{\mu}_1 \neq \tilde{\mu}_2$

Constructing the paired difference table:

Student	Test 1	Test 2	d	Rank	Ranks with smallest sum
1	42	34	8	12.5	
2	36	34	2	3	
3	44	45	-1	-1	1
4	27	30	-3	-6	6
5	40	45	-5	-9.5	9.5
6	34	32	2	3	0
8	50	44	6	11	0
9	29	32	-3	-6	6
10	43	40	3	6	0
11	42	34	8	12.5	0
12	22	32	-10	-14	14
13	26	30	-4	-8	8
14	45	40	5	9.5	0
15	41	39	2	3	0
				T=	44.5

Using Appendix P, with $\alpha = .05$, Reject if $T \leq 21$ or if $T \geq 84$

Since 44.5 > 21 do not reject H_0 and conclude that the medians are the same.

b. A Type II error is the probability of accepting a false null hypothesis. In this case a Type II error would mean we accepted the null hypothesis that the medians of the two tests are the same when, in fact, they are not the same.

16.63.

a. They should use the Wilcoxon Matched-Pairs Signed Rank test since the problem does not say you can assume a normal distribution and because you are using matched pairs.

b   Putting the claim in the alternate hypothesis:

H_0: $\tilde{\mu}_{w/oA} \geq \tilde{\mu}_A$

H_A: $\tilde{\mu}_{w/oA} < \tilde{\mu}_A$.

Automobile	Without Additive	With Additive	d	rank of d	Ranks with smallest expected sum
1	28	28.5	-0.5	-1	
2	25	26	-1	-3	
4	22	21	1	3	3
5	24	26	-2	-6	
6	19	21	-2	-6	
7	26	25	1	3	3
8	27	29	-2	-6	
				T =	6

Using $\alpha = .025$, $T_\alpha = 4$

c. Since $6 > 4$ do not reject H_0 and conclude the additive does not improve the mileage. The claim is not supported.

CD-ROM CHAPTER 17

INTRODUCTION TO QUALITY AND STATISTICAL PROCESS CONTROL

17.1

Both Deming and Juran emphasized that quality was the key component to business competitiveness and that the best way to improve quality came from improving the processes and systems that produce products and deliver services. There are, however, some differences in the philosophies of the two quality pioneers. While Juran focused on quality planning and helping businesses drive down costs by eliminating waste from their processes, Deming advocated a philosophy known as total quality management (TQM), which focused on continuous process improvement directed toward customer satisfaction. In his 14 points, Deming emphasized the importance of leadership if a company is to become a world-class organization. Juran is credited with being one of the first to apply the Pareto Principle to quality improvement activities. This principle is designed to focus management attention on the vital few quality problems that exist in the organization. A primary difference between Deming and Juran is evident in their views regarding goals and targets. While Juran advocated the use of goals and targets in quality improvement activities, Deming argued that goals and targets were detrimental to the constancy of purpose designed to foster a commitment to long-term continuous process improvement activities.

17.3

Student answers will vary. Some students, especially those unfamiliar with the advantage that higher quality can provide a firm, may argue that quality improvement efforts are expensive, since they demand that workers be trained properly and that managers fix quality problems. They may think that these quality improvement costs are never fully recovered by firms in competitive markets. However, others will realize that improving quality can eliminate or reduce rework and scrap. Higher quality may allow a firm to reduce its warranty expense. Also, improved quality translates into greater customer satisfaction and some marketing studies have shown that it is less expensive to keep the customers that you have than it is to try and get new customers. Students who appreciate the strategic importance that high quality can play in an organization will argue that while there are costs to quality, the benefits of having good quality more than make up for any costs incurred in improving the firm's overall product and service quality. Because rework, scrap, and warranty expenses decrease with higher quality, prices for certain high quality goods and services can be competitive.

While student examples will vary, they may cite the experience of electronics manufactures where costs have been declining but quality has increased. Other examples may include automobiles, camping equipment, and personal computers.

17.5.
Student answers will vary depending on the process at their school. A simple example would be

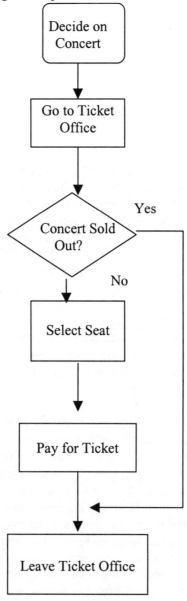

17.7.
Student answers will vary depending upon answers to number 6.

17.9.
Student answers will vary. Some possible causes by category are:

People: Too Few Drivers, High Driver Turnover
Methods: Poor Scheduling, Improper Route Assignments
Equipment: Buses Too Small, Bus Reliability, Too Few Buses
Environment: Weather, Traffic Congestion, Road Construction

*NOTE: Control Chart Limit Values May Differ Slightly Depending on the Software
Used and the Extent of Rounding in the Calculations.*

17.11.

We first find the centerline as follows:

$$\bar{p} = 270/(30*100) = 0.090$$

Assuming that 3-sigma control chart limits are to be established then

$$UCL = 0.090 + 3 * \sqrt{\frac{0.090*(1-0.090)}{100}} = 0.176$$

$$LCL = 0.090 - 3 * \sqrt{\frac{0.090*(1-0.090)}{100}} = 0.004$$

17.13.

Because a process can go out of control rather quickly it is imperative that the control charts be updated as soon as information becomes available. In this way if the process is found to be out of control it can be stopped to determine the assignable cause for the problem.

17.15.

a.

	Panel 1	Panel 2	Panel 3	Panel 4	Panel 5	X-Bar	Range
Hour 41	0.764	0.737	0.724	0.716	0.752	0.7386	0.048
Hour 42	0.766	0.785	0.777	0.79	0.799	0.7834	0.033
Hour 43	0.812	0.774	0.767	0.799	0.821	0.7946	0.054

Notice that the subgroup means and subgroup ranges for Hours 41-43 are within the control limits for the control charts constructed in problem 13. However, the subgroup mean for Hour 43 is close to the upper control limit for the x-bar chart. Also, the subgroup ranges are all below the centerline. While this is not yet a concern a series of nine consecutive values below the centerline (or above the centerline), or six or more consecutive points moving in the same direction would indicate that the process has lost statistical control. At this time, end of Hour 43, there is no evidence that a special cause of variation is present in the process.

b.   Yes. Without the control chart limits it would not be possible for us to see the natural, inherent variation of the process. We need the charts that we developed in problem 13 to determine when evidence of special cause variation is present.

17.17.

a.

Period	Mean	Range
31	5.3325	1.05
32	4.7875	1.25
33	4.975	0.84
34	5.4425	0.91
35	4.8525	1.47
36	5.3025	1.16
37	5.3375	0.65
38	5.38	0.61
39	6.08	2.09
40	6.2525	1.17

Looking at the mean values of these observations it appears that the process has gone out of control since several observations are below the LCL.

b. **Note: The differences in the control chart limits shown here and in problem 17-16 are due only to rounding differences reflected in the type of software used.**

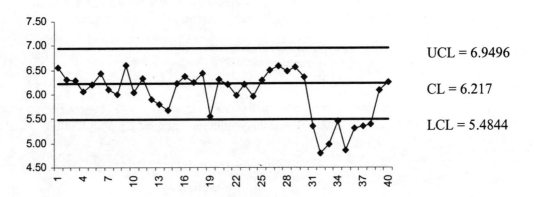

X-bar Chart

UCL = 6.9496

CL = 6.217

LCL = 5.4844

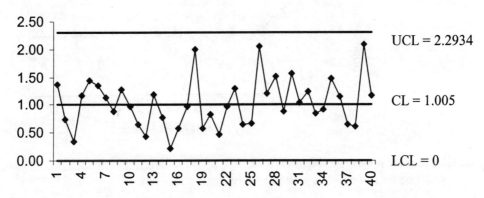

R-chart

UCL = 2.2934

CL = 1.005

LCL = 0

The report will vary with the student, but should certainly comment on the R-chart being in control but the X-bar chart going out of control in periods 31-38. An assignable cause should be found.

17.19.

a.

The appropriate control chart for this situation is a p-chart. The centerline, p-bar, equals the number of account errors/number of accounts sampled. For the sample consisting of 100 account records for each of the last 30 days we find that p-bar equals 238/(30*100) = 0.0793. The estimated standard error is 0.0270 and is calculated as shown below.

$$\sqrt{\frac{0.0793 * (1 - 0.0793)}{100}} = 0.0270$$

The 3-sigma upper control limit is 0.0793 + (3*0.0270) = 0.1603. The 3-sigma lower control limit is 0.0793 - (3*0.0270) = -0.0017 which is then set equal to 0.0000.

The chart is shown below.

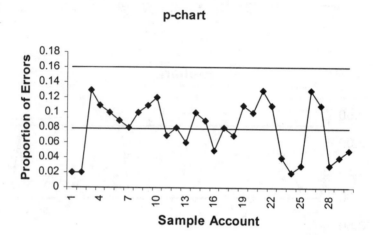

b.   The process appears to be in control. All of the data points are within the upper and lower control limits and there do not appear to be any runs in the data.

c.

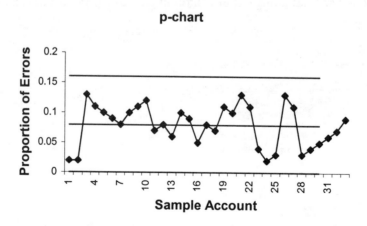

The process still appears to be in statistical control. No sample proportions are outside of the control limits. There is a potential for concern if the next sample proportions continue to trend upward. A sustained upward trend would suggest that an assignable cause was present in the process.

17.21.

a. The x-bar and r-charts are used together to monitor a process where the characteristic of interest is a variable (i.e., a characteristic measured on a continuous scale). Since time is measured, the machine downtime that is being monitored is a variable characteristic and requires that both the x-bar and R-charts be used.

b. The centerline for the x-bar chart is the average of the subgroup means and equals 82.46.

c. The centerline for the R-chart is the average of the subgroup ranges and equals 12.33.

d. UCL = 2.11*12.33 = 26.02   and LCL = 0*12.33 = 0

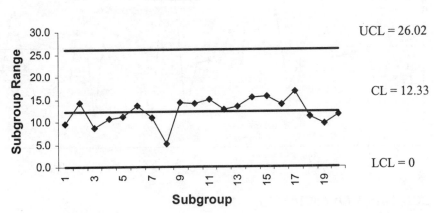

e. UCL = 82.46 + (0.58*12.33) = 89.61.   LCL = 82.46 - (0.58*12.33) = 75.31

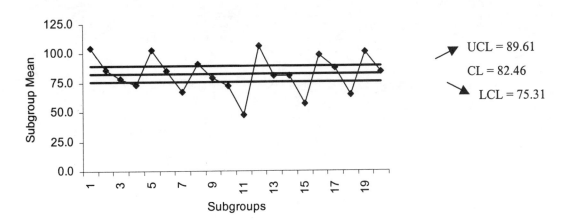

f. While the range chart has no points outside the control chart limits, there is a run of 9 values above the centerline, which indicates a possible loss of statistical control. The x-bar chart exhibits an out of statistical control condition given that there are several subgroup means above the upper control limit and several below the lower control limit. This provides strong evidence that the process was not in statistical control at the time the control chart was developed.

17.23.

a.   UCL = 2.282 * 100.375 = 229.056
CL = 100.375
LCL = 0 * 100.375 = 0

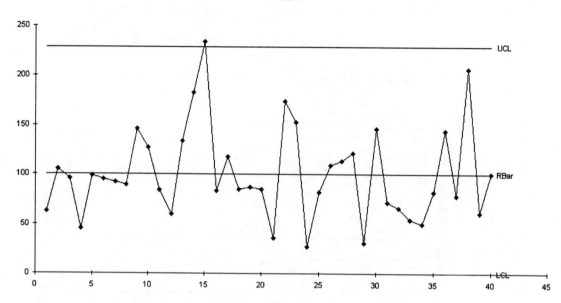

a.   UCL = 415.3 + 0.729(100.375) = 488.473
CL = 415.3
LCL = 415.3 − 0.729(100.375) = 342.127

XBar Chart

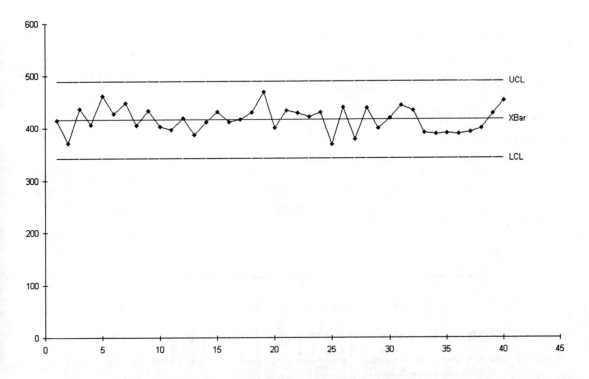

c. The process appears to have lost control with respect to its variability, which is measured by the R-chart. Note that week 15 is above the upper control limit on the R-chart. The range chart measures the dispersion or spread of the process. Ajax should investigate for an assignable cause that could explain the higher variability in week 15. Furthermore, since the range chart shows that the process is out of control, we should question the validity of the x-bar chart. Whenever the range chart reflects an out of control situation, the x-bar chart, which is determined using the average range of the subgroups, is compromised.

17.25.

　a. The appropriate control chart for this data is the p-chart.

　b.　$\bar{p} = 441/(300*50) = 0.0294$

　　　$s = \sqrt{(0.0294)(1 - 0.0294)/50} = 0.0239$

　　　UCL = 0.0294 + 3(0.0239) = 0.1011
　　　LCL = 0.0294 − 3(0.0239) = -0.0423 so set to 0

p-chart

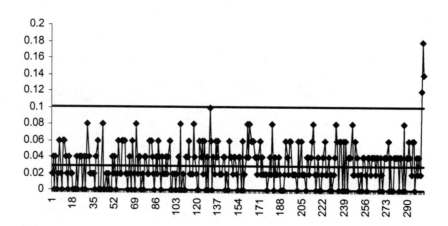

　c.

Sample Number	301	302	303
p-bar	0.12	0.18	0.14

p-chart

All of these points are above the UCL which indicates that the process has gone out of control.

d. The new sample proportion would be 0.28 which is again above the UCL. This suggests that the process is still out of control and getting further out of control.

17.27.

a. $\bar{c} = 29.3333$

   $UCL = 29.3333 + 3(\sqrt{29.3333}) = 45.5814$

   $LCL = 29.3333 - 3(\sqrt{29.3333}) = 13.0852$

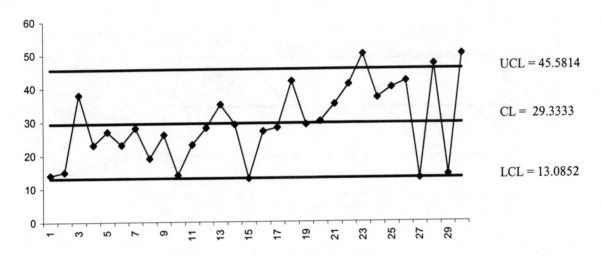

b. The process seems to be out of control since several observations are above the UCL or right at the LCL and there seems to be a run (observation 4 – 12) below the center line and observations 27 – 30 seem to be alternating one above or near the upper UCL and the next below the LCL, etc.

c.   Need to convert the data to bags per passenger by dividing bags by 40 and then developing a u-chart based upon the explanation in CD-Rom optional topics.

$$CL = 29.333/40 = 0.7333$$
$$UCL = 0.7333 + 3*\sqrt{0.7333/40} = 1.1395$$
$$LCL = 0.7333 - 3*\sqrt{0.7333/40} = 0.3271$$

u-chart

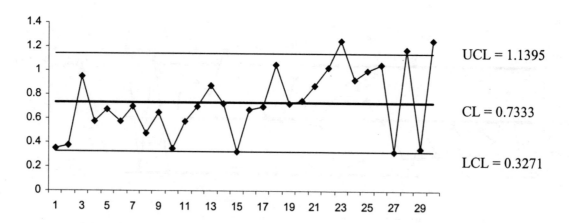

UCL = 1.1395

CL = 0.7333

LCL = 0.3271

17.29.

a.   The Shewart factor for the x-bar chart with a subgroup size of 3 is A2 = 1.02. The Shewart factors for the range chart are D3 = 0.0 and D4 = 2.57 for the lower and upper control limits, respectively.

b.   UCL = 2.57*0.80 = 2.056   LCL = 0*0.80 = 0

c.   UCL = 2.33 + (1.02*0.80) = 3.146   LCL = 2.33 - (1.02*0.80) = 1.514

17.31.

The centerline of the control chart is the average proportion of defective = 720/(20*150) = 0.240. For 3-sigma control chart limits we find

$$UCL = 0.240 + 3*\sqrt{\frac{0.240*(1-0.240)}{150}} = 0.345$$

$$LCL = 0.240 - 3*\sqrt{\frac{0.240*(1-0.240)}{150}} = 0.135$$

17.33.

The appropriate control chart is the p-chart for monitoring the proportion of defectives (in this case we can monitor the proportion of on time shipments). The centerline p-bar is equal to the average of the 21 sample proportions and equals 0.9152. The centerline can also be found by summing the total number of successes (on-time shipments = 1922) and dividing by the total number of samples (21*100 = 2100). The standard error of the subgroup proportions is estimated by the following equation

$$\sqrt{\frac{0.9152*(1-0.9152)}{100}} = 0.0279$$

The 3-sigma control limits are computed as follows:

Lower Control Limit = 0.9152 - 3*0.0279 = 0.8315
Centerline = 0.9152
Upper Control Limit = 0.9152 + 3*0.0279 = 0.9989

The control chart is shown below.

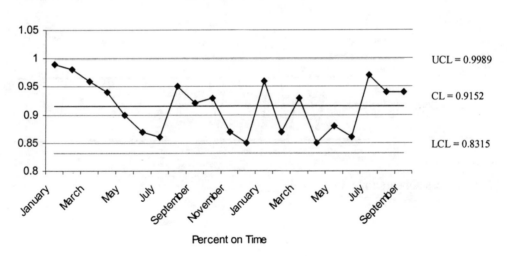

The delivery process appears to be in statistical control. Some concerned might be expressed concerning the first seven sample proportions trending down, which indicates that the proportion of on-time deliveries is falling. There are also some sample proportions close to the lower limit that might be cause for concern and investigation. However, there are no points below the lower control limit.

17.35.

The appropriate chart is the p-chart. $\bar{p} = 0.0524$

$$\sqrt{\frac{0.0524*(1-0.0524)}{100}} = 0.0223$$

The 3-sigma control limits are computed as follows:

Lower Control Limit = 0.0524 - 3*0.0223 = -0.0145 so set to 0
Centerline = 0.0524
Upper Control Limit = 0.0524 + 3*0.0223 = 0.1193

The control chart is shown below.

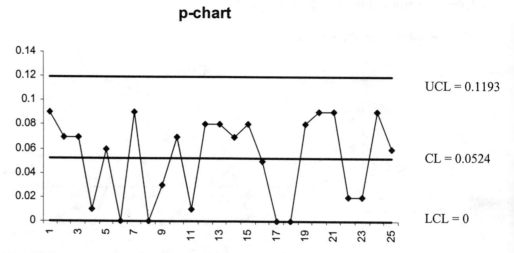

The process appears to be in control.

17.37.

a. x-bar chart: CL = 0.7499
    UCL = 0.7499 + (0.577)(0.0115) = 0.7565
    LCL = 0.7499 – (0.577)(0.0115) = 0.7433

    R-chart: CL = 0.0115
    UCL = (0.0115)(2.114) = 0.0243
    LCL = (0.0115)(0) = 0

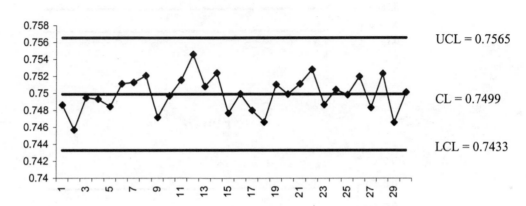

x-bar chart

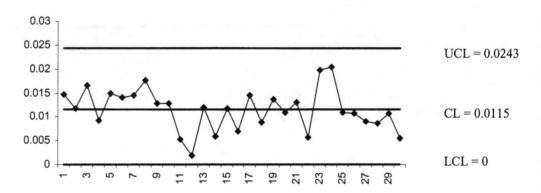

r-chart

The process appears to be in control.

b.

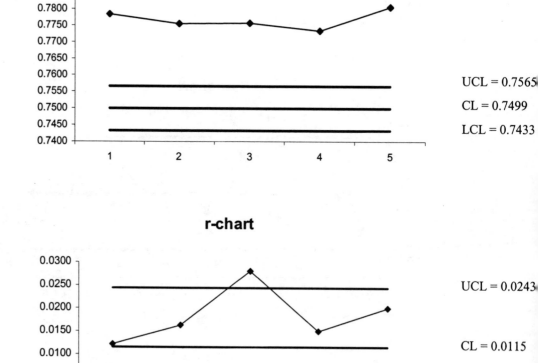

x-bar chart

UCL = 0.7565
CL = 0.7499
LCL = 0.7433

r-chart

UCL = 0.0243
CL = 0.0115
LCL = 0

It now appears that the process is out of control. All of the averages are above the UCL and in the range chart one value is above the UCL.